Advance Praise

"*Two brothers, three uniforms, one bond of service. The Lambrecht brothers give us a compelling look at what it is like to serve during times of peace and war. This book will make you laugh, sit on the edge of your seat, and perhaps even shed a tear. From humble midwestern beginnings, they served as key sentinels in America's defense of freedom. I am grateful that these stories have been captured and are available for everyone to reflect on the core values of commitment and service before self. A must-read!*"

—BRIGADIER GENERAL GREGORY A. FICK, USAF, RETIRED

"*A tremendous yarn of riveting tales from two seasoned combat warriors. These brothers and brothers-in-arms take us on a supersonic journey from the rural Midwest to all corners of the globe, inspiring the reader to turn each page for excitement and knowledge anew. It's difficult to translate to paper what it's really like to be 'up there' in military aviation, but this book does it masterfully!*"

—LIEUTENANT GENERAL WILLIAM H. ETTER, USAF, RETIRED, COMMANDER, FIRST AIR FORCE

"A must-read! Two gifted storytelling military brothers hold the reader while intertwining humor, quotes, and life's lessons learned, giving one cause to reflect along the way. Engaging and enlightening. Journey with them from humble beginnings to military achievement. I have flown with Steve 'Curly' Lambrecht, and he does true justice to the portrayal of military combat flying experiences."

—Brigadier General Richard N. Harris,
USAF, Retired

"The Lambrecht brothers give the reader a behind-the-scenes view of what it takes to be a professional officer in America's modern military. Riveting stories of combat in the air and at sea. Brothers from humble beginnings who accomplished amazing things in the service to their country."

—Brigadier General Henry U. Harder, Jr.,
USAF, Retired

Boundless Brothers

Boundless Brothers

Two Warriors from the Heartland,
One Mission for the Homeland

Commander (Ret) Ronald A. Lambrecht
Brigadier General (Ret) Steven S. Lambrecht

The views expressed in this publication are those of the authors and do not necessarily reflect the official policy or position of the Department of Defense or the US government.

Defense Office of Prepublication and Security Review (DOPSR) clearance for open publication, case number 20-SB-0042, granted March 1, 2021.

 HOUNDSTOOTH PRESS

BOUNDLESS BROTHERS
Two Warriors from the Heartland, One Mission for the Homeland

ISBN   978-1-5445-4017-7   *Hardcover*

       978-1-5445-4018-4   *Paperback*

       978-1-5445-4019-1   *Ebook*

*This book is dedicated to those who have fallen in combat
and to those who remain forever on patrol.
It is you who are the missing persons in our formation,
for whom we pour out a little of our drink onto the ground.*

*In particular, we dedicate this book to Ron's shipmates,
who were lost while on deployment, and to three of
Steve's best friends, who were lost in the line of duty:*

*Lt. Robert "McFly" Forwalder, USN,
26 March 1993, Ionian Sea;*

*Lt. Donald "Stump" Cioffi, USN,
15 March 1996, Atlantic Ocean;*

*Lt. Col. Brett "Boo" Bekken, USMC,
21 April 2004, California desert.*

We have the watch. A nickel on the grass...

Lt. Robert "McFly" Forwalder
(USN)

Lt. Donald "Stump" Cioffi
(USN)

Lt. Col. Brett "Boo" Bekken
(USMC)

Contents

Introduction... xv

A Long Way from Ivanhoe, Minnesota...............................1

PART I: HAYSEEDS AND MASCOTS....................................... 5

Knee-High to a Grasshopper.. 7

Father-Land 13

Watch This... 21

Night School...25

Hopping Freights 29

Milking an Education..35

Oops 39

Maslow's Hierarchy of Needs 43

The Lakeview Supper Club 49

Feeling Blue..53

Setting the Stage...59

Zip to Zap 63

Ice Capades 69

Lake Shaokatan 75

Playing the Odds...79

Bug Juice...83

The Boy Has Rhythm..93

Muscle Memories...97

PART II: FRONTAL LOBE DEVELOPMENT 101

Only Dogs Could Hear Me...103

Rudder Shift 109

Pull Up! Pull UP! PULL UUUUUUPPP!............................115

Formative Experiences..121

Ticket to the Game..129

Canoe U 137

Plebe Ho!...141

Young Dog, Old Tricks...151

Recon 159

The (Almost) Great A-4 Heist 169

Polska Kielbasa Days.. 175

Bulldog...179

The Final Exam 185

Young Dog, New Tricks...191

I Wanted Her. Badly..199

Monkey Business 209

YGBSM 217

Wings 229

Sons and Daughters of Neptune 233

Speed Is Life 239

YGBFSM 247

The Reckoning...255

PART III: BOUNDLESS 259

Attacking the Periscope..261

Bosnia 269

Take Aim 277

Last Training Opportunity to Fail 285

TOPGUN..291

WTI 299

Knowledge Matters 303

Tonto..309

All Hands on Deck...315

Mercenary...325

Fo'c'sle Follies 337

9/11...343

Comrade...349

Thirty Seconds...359

Rapid Response Planning Process 367

Wheelbarrow 373

Operation Restore Hope..381

Mission 92..393

My Finest Hour 403

Twilight 415

Sunset 423

Epilogue...429

Acknowledgments..433

About the Authors..435

Glossary 439

Introduction

Over the years, we have been accused of (or credited with) being storytellers. Admittedly, from growing up in rural America to serving a combined sixty-five-plus years in three branches of the military, we *have* found ourselves with many stories in need of telling.

This book started as an effort by Ron to write about his childhood shenanigans the way Garrison Keillor might. When he began documenting his military career, it occurred to him that, with eighteen years' age difference between them, he and his younger brother, Steve, would have had complementary, yet distinctly different, life experiences. After some discussion, we decided to collaborate.

What came through loud and clear in the telling of our separate stories is our common makeup, resulting from both nature and nurture. We came from humble beginnings, had unimaginable opportunities, and led lives full of adventure and intrigue. As Steve always says, "What we lacked in ability we tried to make up for with brute force."

Our stories are written with an infusion of naval culture and tradition, of which sea stories play a role. A number of the words and phrases herein are part of the vocabulary learned during service in the Navy, Marine Corps, and the United States Air Force. In fact, many of the terms and slang still used today originated from seafaring, ground pounding, and aviating men from days of old (hence the "Nautical Notables" and "Aeronautical Notables" at the beginning of our stories).

While we made every effort to be accurate with our descriptions of events and people, occasionally, names were changed and details were omitted. Usually, this was for security reasons, but sometimes it was to protect the innocent and guilty alike. Where we were unable to verify facts to perfection, we proceeded under the premise that an exhaustive search for the truth should not get in the way of a good yarn.

Now, we invite you to travel with us on the cornfield-flanked railroad tracks of Minnesota, to sail around the world on 100,000-ton aircraft carriers, and to fly supersonic aircraft during times of peace and war.

Ronald A. Lambrecht
Commander (USN) Retired
Federal Service GS-15 Retired

Steven S. Lambrecht
Brigadier General (USAF) Retired
Federal Service GS-14 Retired

A Long Way from Ivanhoe, Minnesota

Ron

December 9, 1992

I stood on the deck of the *USS Tripoli,* surveying the darkened skyline before me. We were anchored two miles from Mogadishu, the former capital of Somalia, and shadows shrouded the city, broken intermittently by distant campfires. One million people lived in this impoverished place, many of them refugees. There was no electricity anywhere in Mogadishu; locals stripped the only power plant and electrical grid of its copper wire and sold it for scrap long ago.

Over the past several hours, I had made multiple trips between the ship's Intelligence Center and the flag bridge, where my boss, "Swede" Peterson, was located. As the Commodore's Intelligence Officer, I was charged with separating fact from fiction in the battle space, and I had been sharing information in support of the impending amphibious landing.

Our entire inventory of helicopters marshaled overhead, waiting for the order to secure the Mogadishu airport, port facility, and the former US Embassy complex. Amphibious Assault Vehicles (AAVs) and Landing Craft, Air Cushion (LCAC) hovercraft assumed a marshaling pattern around the three ships of the amphibious task force: *USS Tripoli, USS Rushmore,* and *USS Juneau.* Our SEAL team deployed earlier in the evening—as well as several nights prior—to survey the landing zones and provide "eyes on target" with reports back to the ship.

All the training, practice, more practice, and planning had come down to these final moments. It is the calm before the storm that gives people pause to consider everything in their history that influenced their destiny, and there, I contemplated the series of events and experiences that led to me standing on the flag bridge of a United States warship. I was about to partake in a mission that, before the action ended, would result in the loss of several American and many Somali lives.

At 0500, the Commodore gave the order. Operation Restore Hope began.

* * *

Steve

2007

I thought my heart would explode right out of my chest. *Be calm,* I told myself. *You've got this. This is what you do.*

It didn't matter. After ninety-one combat missions, sixteen years of training, TOPGUN, the Weapons and Tactics Instructor Course, the Air Combat Tactics Instructor Course, several night carrier landings, and years and years of instructing junior pilots in the art of war, this was it. I was about to be tested in combat.

Adrenaline coursed through my veins. My pulse raced. This wasn't going to be a test, as I had planned. This was going to be a slog through the thick fog of war.

PART I

Hayseeds and Mascots

We moved onto the farm in the winter of 1953, which happened to be the worst winter of the decade. The following summer, the landlord agreed to add onto the barn and to build a silo, all tools essential to creating a dairy farm. The chicken coop is located to the far right. The Allis Chalmers "racing" tractor is parked adjacent to the driveway.

Lincoln County District 29 one-room school (1956). Ron and his classmate occupy the first two desks on the far right, followed by a second and third grader. Fourth and fifth graders are sitting in the middle row, and the row on the left has a sixth, seventh, and eighth grader.

Knee-High
to a Grasshopper

Ron

"If you think you are too small to make a difference, try sleeping with a mosquito."

—THE DALAI LAMA

Nautical Notables:

Nautical: A term that originates from the Greek word *nauti*, meaning sailor.

Helmet Fire: When a pilot becomes so task-saturated in the cockpit that they lose the big picture and situational awareness (SA).

The Leans: A mild case of vertigo. This condition is not always recognized, but it is characterized by your vestibular system telling you that you are at a different attitude from what is displayed on the instruments.

During the late '40s and early '50s, Mom and Dad moved from rented farm to rented farm, agreeing with the landlords to share the proceeds of crops harvested. They started with a tractor, a small assortment of farm machinery, and a few head of livestock.

In 1953, when I turned five, they settled on a farm approximately seven miles from the Minnesota/South Dakota border. Our farm was equidistant from three small towns: Ivanhoe, Lake Benton, and Hendricks. A half mile north of us was Lake Shaokatan, which was a great place to gather in the summer with the neighbor kids after a hard day of farm chores.

Southwest Minnesota defines "rural." Towns are situated approximately ten miles apart and, during my youth, ranged in population from 600 to 800 people. Settled by distinct ethnic groups around the turn of the twentieth century, each local town encapsulates a unique culture, with elders still speaking the native languages of the ancestors who immigrated or migrated there.

Ivanhoe, settled by people of Polish descent, was the closest sign of civilization and boasted a population of 765. Hendricks, to the west, was our Norwegian archrival in basketball. Tyler, to the southeast, was settled by Danes. To the south was our football rival and mostly German neighbors, Lake Benton. You get the idea. Lincoln County, which is composed of Ivanhoe and the surrounding towns, is the only county in Minnesota that to this day does not have a single stoplight!

The first two schools I attended were one-room country schoolhouses, not counting the outhouse. Eight grades were represented, but I had only one classmate in my grade at each school. (Those years remain the only time I found myself in the top two of my class!) Our toilet paper had page numbers, with the catalogs of choice being Montgomery Ward and Sears, Roebuck and Co. (Newspaper-quality index pages were popular, while glossy advertisement pages proved problematic.)

During kindergarten and first grade, Mom walked me to the edge of a field separating the school from our farm and sent me down a corn-row that lined up with the schoolyard. When you are five years old, at the bottom of the food chain for all things that go bump in the night, and are walking blindly through a quarter mile of six-foot-high corn, well...a **helmet fire** could occur.

That quarter mile was the longest of my life. The wind rustled through the cornstalks, strange noises seemed to emanate from everywhere, my short legs stumbled on uneven ground, and corn leaf blades sought to block my vision. Dad had warned me that if I wandered outside the cornrow, he would kick my butt so hard I would have bad breath for a week—and I had firsthand knowledge of what he meant by those nurturing words!

I also learned to really trust my parents. Farm kids grow up early, and to this day, I like to think that I never wore diapers, just short pants. At five, there was no greater feeling than nearing the end of the corn-field, where the sunlight began to permeate the deep dark morass, which eventually gave way to the open schoolyard.

I attended my first *real* school in third grade, when all the country schools closed. Farm kids bussed to one of the neighboring towns, depending on the location of their farmstead, so I attended Ivan-hoe Public School. Admittedly, I experienced a case of **the leans** on my first day when I discovered that I had forty-seven classmates, but what I remember most is learning that the word "wash" doesn't have an "r" in it. The English language would always be a chal-lenge for me because many in our community did not speak proper English.

My closest neighbor across the road attended Hendricks Public School, and the neighbors less than a mile away attended Lake Benton Public School. This meant I had the advantage of getting to know kids from the two other towns through my neighbors, and several of my Ivanhoe classmates got to know kids from the other two towns through me. Greg, a close high school friend of mine, had these relationships to thank for his very life, on a Vietnam battlefield awaiting his eventual arrival.

* * *

Twice a year, my parents made the extended trip (forty miles) to Marshall, a town with a population of approximately 10,000, to shop for school clothes and buy things not available in the smaller towns. During one of these early biannual trips in Dad's '51 Hudson Hornet, I became fixated on a recruiting billboard portraying a young United States Marine Officer in a Dress Blue uniform, sword drawn and at "present arms." It was the most magnificent thing I had seen in my young life, and the size of the billboard added to the impact.

The billboard remained in place for several years (you can't improve on perfection), and every time we made the trip to Marshall, I eagerly awaited the chance to see it. After each sighting, I would think about that Marine Officer for days. He represented something formal and foreign to me. I was awestruck.

However, I was also realistic. Becoming a military Officer seemed beyond my comprehension or possible reality, so I resolved to play the hand reality dealt me. To do otherwise would require years of dedication, contemplation, and development as a problem solver. My daily routine contained few of those opportunities or disciplines.

Or, at least, so I thought.

Ron and sister Sue on the family swing set (1957). The "saintly and quintessential" outhouse can be seen behind Ron.

Photo of three dozen farmers who arrived with their machinery to harvest our crops (1959).

Father-Land

Ron

"Opportunity is missed by most people because it is dressed in overalls and looks like work."

—THOMAS EDISON

Nautical Notables:

Brass Monkey: During the days of sailing ships, cannonballs were stacked in pyramids on brass pallets with divots to hold the cannonballs; these pallets were called brass monkeys. The brass monkey expanded and contracted with the rise and fall of the temperature at a greater rate than the iron cannonballs it supported. If cold enough, the brass monkey contracted sufficiently to cause the cannonballs to pop out of the divots, hence the phrase, "Cold enough to freeze the balls off a brass monkey."

Pea Coat: A heavy topcoat worn in cold, miserable weather by sailors. It was tailored from pilot cloth, a heavy, coarse, stout kind of twilled blue cloth with the nap on one side. The cloth was sometimes called P-cloth for the initial letter of "pilot," and the garment made from it was called a p-jacket and, later, a pea coat. The term has been used since 1723 to denote coats made from that cloth.

Life on the farm was hard and isolated, especially before I was twelve and allowed to drive our pickup to the neighbors' farm to hang out with the other farm kids.

We were a family of five living in a 1,200-square foot two-story farm-house with no running water or indoor plumbing. In other words, our home lacked a bathroom, which definitely proved an inconvenience during **brass monkey** Minnesota winters. Not even a **pea coat** would have been much help while doing our business in the family outhouse. (Dad eventually installed running water, so we no longer had to carry it from an outside well, but it wasn't until long after I left to attend college that he finally built a bathroom.)

Each fall, Dad nailed fiberglass paper over all the windows to protect us from the winter wind. Minnesota winters are rough and long, so living with windows obscured by yellow opaque fiberglass sheeting can lead to cabin fever in short order. Add to that the fact that Dad believed the Six Fat Dutchmen, a German polka band, created the only music fit for human ears, and we had the recipe for sheer insanity.

We are all products of our upbringing, and Dad was no exception. He grew up on a farm in a small German community forty miles west of Minneapolis, near a village called St. Benedict, that lingered one industrial generation behind the national average. As a young boy, I thoroughly enjoyed visits to my grandparents' farm because it was like stepping back in time, even by Ivanhoe's standards.

Farmers in the community still used horses and equipment that performed their functions through mechanisms attached to the wheels. Tractors began to appear on the landscape, but while much of the country harvested hay through baling methods, many people in this small German community still grappled loose hay into their hay lofts the old labor-intensive way. My grandparents rendered their own lard, made their own soap, and cut and sawed their own lumber, among a great many other tasks of self-sufficiency. No wonder Dad's quest for improving creature comforts was uninspired.

A year after Mom and Dad married, they moved from St. Benedict to Ivanhoe and began life as sharecroppers. Mom was raised on a farm near Ivanhoe, so it was a move with connections. Small communities lend themselves to easy integration, and it wasn't long before Dad was active in local community events.

As a member of the Lincoln County Sportsman's Club, Dad became a regular participant in the annual donkey softball tournament. The game required every player to ride a donkey, except for the pitcher, the catcher, and the batter. Once the batter hit the ball, he mounted a donkey and attempted to ride the bases. The outfielders could dismount their donkey to grab the ball, but they had to maintain their grip on the reins. Throwing the ball required first remounting the donkey. Should a player forget to hold the reins or to remount the donkey before throwing the ball, the opposing team would be given a base. Defensive team members had to be on a donkey with the ball in hand before tagging a person out.

This all sounds simple enough, except some donkeys didn't play by the rules. One donkey, for instance, would run, throw its head down, and abruptly stop. Launched into the air, the rider usually landed on his backside while discussing the donkey's father's relationship with its mother.

Some donkeys were trained to go no faster than a walk, while the center field donkey was trained to sit back on its haunches when encouraged by the rider to chase after a ball. For those who knew how to ride, there were donkeys that had been ridden; for those who had never ridden before, there were seemingly donkeys that had never been ridden! I don't know for sure, but I think donkeys can laugh.

Dad knew his way around animals and apparently was a donkey whisperer in a previous life, because he made a donkey run the bases like a stud quarter horse. During one game, after Dad had gone a couple times around the bases, the trainers/owners of the donkeys decided to give him a goat to lead around the diamond instead. Dad was a fast runner, and the goat was no match. Since the goat couldn't keep up, Dad picked it up and carried it around the bases.

The second baseman was waiting for Dad, ready to tag him out, but Dad grabbed one of the goat's teats and sprayed the baseman's donkey. Being sprayed in the face with goat's milk apparently was a new experience for the donkey; the donkey jettisoned his rider and bolted into the outfield. The mayhem inspired other donkeys to follow suit, requiring a time out to round up loose donkeys. Dad, meanwhile, was safe on second.

Later, Dad took his turn at bat and was provided with another goat to accompany him around the bases. This time, the third baseman waited to tag him out. *If it worked the first time, it should work a second time*, Dad figured.

Unfortunately, Dad overlooked the fact that he was given a billy goat. Out at third!

* * *

Dad was thirty-six when he had his first major heart attack. I was in fourth grade.

It took the family doctor only eight minutes to travel the eleven miles from Ivanhoe to our farm, and his rapid response likely saved Dad's life, since Dad was already losing consciousness when the nitroglycerin arrived. That event resulted in a stay in the Sioux Falls, South Dakota, Veteran's hospital for a month.

Once home, Dad, of course, ignored the orders to follow a strict diet and recovery regimen, and his second heart attack came less than a year later. This one was even worse. The only thing that saved him was the nitroglycerin pills he always carried. I don't recall if the family doctor broke his previous speed record, but he was fast, again coming to Dad's aid in time.

It was harvest time in Minnesota. We had a hired hand, but he alone could not do all that was required. It was a concern Dad did not need, especially while recovering from a major heart attack, so within a couple days, the entire community mobilized to help us. Early one morning, three dozen farmers arrived with their machinery to harvest our crops because that was what good neighbors did.

This time, Dad paid attention to the doctor's orders and worked his way back to a point where he was able to live close to a normal life. (Although he did have quadruple and quintuple bypass surgeries and several stents implanted before passing away at the age of seventy-nine.)

Dad stood five feet, five inches tall. Had he grown an inch, he would have been round, but don't let his stature fool you—he was tough as nails. He boxed Golden Gloves in the Army and knew his way around the punching bag he mounted in our hog house feed room. I, on the other hand, was five feet, eight inches and weighed 118 pounds in high school.

Dad required help on the farm, so the last year I was allowed to participate in sports was my sophomore year. Though I lettered in track, I was not God's gift to speed; Dad challenged me to a hundred-yard dash and beat me by seven strides, which did little to support my argument for continued participation in sports.

From that point on, I was destined to be a farm laborer when not attending school. I hung with the neighbor kids as time allowed and was loaned the keys to the car, along with five dollars in my pocket, on Saturday nights, but life was a solid average. I was a realist, and I was learning to cope with my existence.

Ron, Sue, and Pat survey the crop damage after a hailstorm destroyed the corn crops (1964). A field like this one was the scene for the tractor races Ron hosted, unbeknownst to their parents.

Watch This

Ron

"The world is round, so if you do something bad, you had better duck."

—AALIYAH HURLEY

Nautical Notable:

Keelhaul: To be keelhauled today means to be given a severe reprimand for some infraction of the rules. As late as the nineteenth century, however, it was a dire and often fatal torture employed to punish offenders of certain naval laws. An offender was securely bound, both hand and foot, and had heavy weights attached to his body. He was then lowered over the ship's side and slowly dragged along under the ship's hull. If he didn't drown, which was rare, barnacles and crustaceans usually cut him, often causing him to bleed to death.

Summers in Minnesota meant mischievous activity.

For some "unknown reason," the neighbor's watermelon patch never quite produced the crop they expected, and their strawberry harvest was a disappointment as well. (My friends and I might've had something to do with this.) Another neighbor had a school bell displayed in their front yard that begged to be rung late at night. (We might've tied a piece of long twine to the clapper and then pulled it from a safe distance.) Others answered the door to find a burning bag of cow manure, which they would then put out by either stomping on the bag or beating it with a broom. (We might've filled a bag with cow manure, placed it on their doorstep, lit the bag on fire, rang the doorbell, and high-tailed it.)

One time, we decided to conduct tractor races on a track laid out in one of our fields. Farming was and is a dangerous occupation, especially for kids, "boasting" one of the highest rates of accidental death, dismemberment, and debilitating injury of any occupation in the country. In the '50s, though, if a farm implement didn't have an unprotected moving part, auger, or some sort of exposed cutting device, it wasn't worth having. Combine the opportunity for a farm accident with my fearless sense of "WATCH THIS," and it is no wonder that I was the only sibling in the Lambrecht clan upon whom our parents took out a life insurance policy.

In the early fall, with the grain harvested, fields sat barren, with just stubble remaining in the relatively soft soil that had been prepped for spring planting. Perfect for tractor racing. Wednesday meant bowling night for our parents, and we knew they wouldn't arrive home much before midnight.

Dad owned Allis Chalmers tractors, which were slower (with a max speed of roughly fourteen miles per hour) but had a lower center of gravity and cornered on a dime. The neighbors owned various other models. Case and Ford tractors were quite agile, while the

John Deeres and International Harvesters were the fastest but also the most dangerous (due to their high center of gravity and no rear fenders).

Our track was approximately a quarter mile long and included a straight-away on one side and "S" turns on the other. The faster tractors on the straight-away gave us adequate separation going into the "S" turns, but the more agile tractors negotiated the turns at a faster speed, causing the tractors to bunch up after we exited the turns.

By about the fifth or sixth lap, we knew the capabilities of our tractors, and things started to get interesting. It became clear that blocking maneuvers were directly proportional to the amount of testosterone and adrenalin possessed by the driver.

Unfortunately, the trenches our tires made in the field, especially while banking in the turns, left ample evidence of our antics. To this day, I am baffled that no one died, either on the track or when our parents **keelhauled** us after discovering the damage.

* * *

Winter pastimes consisted of hunting; playing King of the Mountain; more hunting; dodgeball, tag, and other macho games staged in barn lofts; and finally, hunting. We were all fairly good shots, even from a moving car.

One winter day, a bunch of us kids tied one end of a fifty-foot rope to the rear bumper of a car and the other end to a refrigerator door. The door, being quite shallow and heavy, cut through the snow drifts around Lake Shaokatan instead of riding on top of them. Hence, I had my stocking cap pulled down over my face.

Traveling at thirty miles per hour while blindfolded made for a zesty ride, but then suddenly, I got the sensation I was traveling in a circle.

The circle seemed to get smaller and smaller until I finally came to a stop. When I lifted my stocking cap, I discovered that the guys doing the towing lost control of the car and spun out; I had wound around the car until both of us came to a stop, which happened to be within five feet of the front bumper.

Again, I was the only Lambrecht child with a life insurance policy because growing up in a risk-filled environment made me fearless. I figured that evolution by natural selection would take care of the weak and less fortunate. *HEY, watch this!*

Night School

Ron

"If you hit the target every time, it's too near or too big."

—Tom Hirshfield

Nautical Notable:

Bamboozle: A Spanish tactic from the seventeenth century of hoisting false flags to deceive (bamboozle) enemies.

Six of us neighbor kids shared numerous exploits, many of them sworn to secrecy to this day. We always seemed to be engaged in some sort of double-dog dare, but on the other hand, it was not uncommon for us to volunteer for certain types of public service.

For instance, when you consider the frantic maneuvers and gyrations the world's drivers will perform in order to avoid running over a skunk crossing a road, it is amazing how many skunks still meet their demise. Must be due to a lack of judgment in time and distance on the part of the driver. It became obvious to the six of us that drivers required training in the art of skunk avoidance; conducting this training was the humane thing to do, and we possessed the ingenuity for the task!

Being the youngest in any juvenile gang is unfortunate; in our gang, that position fell to little Dave. He was easily influenced, probably due to his relative size, and it was a fact not lost on the rest of us. After all, someone had to tie the twine to the dead skunk!

You need three elements to successfully engage in this **bamboozle**: a dead skunk, a dark night, and an escape route. All three are of equal importance.

Dave wasn't picky about where he attached the twine to a dead skunk, as it was probably not a pleasant experience regardless, and we only had to wait for nightfall to get in position for our community service opportunity. Two elements down. Cornfields are plentiful in Minnesota, and they served us well when it came to the third element.

As a car approached, the driver invariably maneuvered to avoid the skunk. Imagine their surprise when the skunk decided to run under the car! Add the ambiance of a hot, sleepy summer evening, along with the frantic response, "SON OF A BITCH" or something to that effect coming from the passenger seat, and we discovered that learning could be both enlightening *and* entertaining.

Since this maneuver usually positioned the skunk off-center on the road, we relocated ourselves in a cornfield on the opposite side of the road and awaited the next training opportunity. When the visual and olfactory stimuli provided to the driver hit their sensory neurons, a helmet fire ensued. Depending on traffic flow, we trained eight to ten drivers in the irrational behavior of a skunk before the immediate area became too foul to continue, thus requiring adjournment of the class.

I learned the art of ingenuity. I learned to be clever, original, inventive, and, when necessary, devious. Above all, I learned to always have an exit strategy!

Hopping Freights

Ron

"The introduction of so powerful an agent as steam to a carriage on wheels will make a great change in the situation of man."

—THOMAS JEFFERSON, 1802

Nautical Notables:

Apple Jack: Twenty-one-day wine made out of Bug Juice (you'll learn what this is in another story), sugar, yeast, and boxed raisins for body. Tastes like an old tennis shoe but packs a powerful wallop.

Apple Jacked (also Applejacked): Extremely intoxicated. A state where a sailor is so shit-housed while on liberty that their shipmates actually notice it.

Wallop: When the French burned the town of Brighton, England, in the 1500s, King Henry VIII sent Admiral Wallop to retaliate and teach the French a lesson. He so thoroughly wrecked the

French coasts that, ever since, a devastating blow is said to be an "awful wallop."

Run the Gauntlet: This phrase comes from the Navy, when a punished crew member was forced to proceed between two lines of men who beat and whipped him.

I was five years old the first time I flew solo behind the wheel of Dad's '54 Ford pickup. Dad walked behind the pickup, stopping every ten feet to remove a steel post from the back and hammer it into the ground with a fence post hammer. Sliding the post hammer (a heavy piece of pipe with a cap welded on one end) over the end of the steel post, he drove the post into the ground.

Dad started the pickup and put it in first gear at idle with me behind the wheel. I couldn't reach the gas or brake pedals, so I made the truck go faster by slightly pulling out the throttle knob on the dash and slowed it down by pushing the knob in. If Dad hit a rock, or something else caused a delay in installing a post, I turned the ignition off to stop the truck.

My driving skills were not unusual. Most farm kids were rudimentary drivers by the time they were ten or eleven.

Although the neighbor kids I hung with were within bicycle range of our farm, riding a bike in the winter in Minnesota was a nonstarter. Because of this, Dad bought me my first car when I was thirteen, a 1953 Pontiac two-door that cost $15.00. We had to replace the transmission for $15.00 and the battery for $15.00, so for $45.00, I owned reliable transportation...and it had a heater!

By the time I was a junior in high school, Dad upgraded me to a 1960 Chevy four-door powered by a six banger with an automatic transmission. That car had absolutely no *cool factor*—it didn't even have enough power to get out of its own way! I thought I was being punished when he brought it home, but in retrospect, I think he was probably trying to keep me from killing myself.

* * *

As a teenager, I felt that proper conduct required by a civilized society was merely a guideline from which to deviate. Drinking and driving was socially acceptable, for instance, even if we were underage. (Unless, of course, we got caught, in which case the judge asked our parents to take away our license for thirty days.) Most cars only came with seat belts as an *option*. Because farm gas was only fourteen to seventeen cents a gallon (three to four less than at the pump), farmers weren't all that concerned about the number of miles we logged on the odometer, so long as we dragged ourselves to the barn by 5:15 a.m. for chores.

As a high school senior with a good understanding of the lay of the land, I knew all the county hot spots, such as The Showboat. A bar and dance hall located nineteen miles from Ivanhoe, The Showboat was the place to be. Every kid within fifty miles (who was not concerned about being kicked off a high school sports team for underage drinking or other shenanigans) was there.

Getting our hands on a case of beer never seemed to be a problem, and once in a while, one of us scored a fifth of **Apple Jack**, which **walloped** us youngsters into tomorrow. Of course, the county and state police also knew about The Showboat, so they positioned themselves to chase us down if we were speeding, driving carelessly, or both. Still, **running the gauntlet** was exciting—unless we got caught.

My luck eventually ran out. After spending a day in court and dealing with my parents, I was out of action for a while; driving responsibilities had to be delegated to others.

While I was in the thirty-day penalty box, the idea of riding the rails came to mind. I had heard of pheasant hunters who let some air out of their tires and positioned their pickups on the railroads; they then rode through the backcountry while hunting from the back of the pickup. It was illegal, of course, but again, laws were merely "a guideline from which to deviate."

One Saturday night after my thirty days were up, my friends and I closed down The Showboat and were heading home when I expressed my interest in the possibility of riding the rails. There wasn't a dissenting voice among them. Besides, what could *possibly* go wrong?

We drove along one of the county roads until we came to a gravel road that had a rail crossing. We positioned the '60 Chevy so that the front and rear wheels aligned with the tracks, then slowly drove the front of the car onto the tracks. Much to our surprise, it stayed.

The wheelbase of the Chevy was such that the rails rode on the inside half of the tire-face. Essentially, the tires slightly folded to the outside of the rails. I was not keen on letting air out of the tires, so we stayed with normal pressure.

Needing to test our newfound mode of transportation, I initially kept my hands on the steering wheel, which led to us falling off the tracks. We backed up and tried again. This time, I kept my hands off the wheel, and sure enough, we stayed on the rails.

A '60 Chevy powered by a six banger with an automatic transmission will, at idle, cruise on the tracks at twelve miles per hour. Up to this point, this was the wildest ride of my life. We rode the rails from Lake Benton to Ivanhoe, crossing roads and highways without incident.

We needed to transit through the small village of Arco, which had a grain elevator. The tracks were preset so that trains passed through the village, but that bit of information remained unknown to us on our maiden voyage. It was a bit unnerving driving through Arco with our lights turned off and no hands on the steering wheel, especially when we experienced several track interchanges where there were additional rails for loading grain onto railroad cars. It was also unnerving going over train trestles and bridges when at the mercy of the rails!

Once the story broke, however—a kid can't keep something that cool to himself—rail transportation became the standard. In the fall of '66, a half-dozen cars would travel home on the rails from The Showboat on a Saturday night, but about two months later, the inevitable showdown with a train occurred.

Being fall, farmers were filling the grain elevators, and additional trains were added to the route to transport the grain. Fortunately, we saw the light from the train engine a couple miles in advance, allowing us time to get to the next intersection and drive off the tracks.

The ability to influence others came naturally to me. As the instigator of semi-illegal activities, I possessed a flair for motivating and teaching my fellow cohorts the finer points of law-breaking—and the art of not getting caught.

Sister Sue and Mom in the milking parlor. The milking stalls were designed and built by Mel and were considered highly innovative for their time (circa 1962).

Milking an Education

Ron

"Here is a test to find whether your mission on Earth is finished: if you're alive, it isn't."

—Richard Bach

Nautical Notables:

He Knows the Ropes: In the very early days, this phrase was written on a seaman's discharge to indicate that he was still a novice; all he knew about being a sailor was the names and uses of the principal ropes (lines). Today, this same phrase means the opposite: that the person fully knows and understands the operation, procedures, or organization.

Reveille: At the beginning of the day, the boatswain pipes, "All Hands," and passes the word, "Reveille, reveille! All hands heave out and trice up! The smoking lamp is lighted in all authorized spaces." In former days, "Heave out and trice up" was a call to the crew to get out of bed (hammocks, whatever) and assemble on the deck to view floggings administered as discipline to crew members.

Swallowing the Anchor: Ceremony of sincere official recognition for a long period of faithful and honorable service.

Life on the farm operated on a tightly structured regimen, and I **knew more than the ropes**.

Milking one hundred cows required six hours in the barn a day. **Reveille** (alarm) was set for 5:00 a.m. To prepare for the 5:30 milking, I arrived dressed by 5:15 a.m., winter and summer, in order to herd the cows from the yard to the holding pens adjacent to the milking parlor.

During the school year, I helped with the milking until 7:20 a.m. That left thirty minutes to get to the house, wa'r'sh, get dressed, eat breakfast, and be at the end of the driveway to catch the school bus, which arrived at 7:50 a.m. In the afternoon, the bus dropped us off at 4:20 p.m., giving me twenty minutes to walk up the driveway, change clothes, and be in the barn for evening chores. Twenty minutes later (5:00 p.m.), we ate dinner (supper) for thirty minutes. We milked from 5:30 p.m. until around 8:00 p.m.

This constituted our milking schedule seven days a week, eleven months a year. (We stopped milking one month before the cows were due to give birth, at which time the entire cycle started over.) Milking cows developed my endurance, fortitude, and perseverance, but it also provided me with a matchless drive to find something else to do with my life.

One spring morning during my senior year of high school (1967), Dad asked what I had planned after graduation. Dad had a seventh-grade education; Mom graduated from high school but went no further. No one on either side of the family had attended college, with the exception of one aunt (mom's oldest sister), who, by joining the Army, created a career path that eventually led to a teaching degree.

Options seemed limited, but I knew one thing: I would not be farming. It wasn't for me.

Although we were in the middle of the Vietnam War, the military appeared to be my only option for getting off the farm. Education was not a high priority in our family, so imagine my surprise when Dad suggested I check into going to college. As I reflect back on that morning, it is obvious Dad was trying to figure out a way to keep me out of the war.

Fortunately for me, the only requirement to get into college in those days was a high school diploma and money. My diploma was imminent, but I did not yet know where to get the money.

That same spring, my brother, Steve, was born. We didn't know it at the time, but Mom had given birth to two career military men, eighteen years apart. Steve and I lived under the same roof for six months, but then it was time for my non-ceremonial **swallow the anchor**, and I headed for uncharted seas.

Steve on Ron's lap during a summer visit home from college (1968).

Mel and Clarice Lambrecht in the dining room of The Lakeview Supper Club (1971). The kitchen, to the left and not pictured, is where Pam and Steve slept on a rollaway bed. Notice the glulam beams overhead.

Oops

Steve

"If you fall, I'll always be there."

Aeronautical Notable:

Situational awareness (SA): Knowing what your airplane is doing relative to its envelope, where your adversary is, where the ground is, the status of enemy threats on the ground, and hundreds of other variables.

My experience growing up differed markedly from that of my brother.

The youngest of five children, eighteen years separate me from my eldest sibling, my only brother, Ron. Three sisters fill the gap in between, and my next closest sibling, Pam, is four years my senior.

My siblings refer to me as the "oops." I'm not sure of the exact circumstances of my conception, as I was not there at the time, but I'm quite certain my siblings weren't either. I conclude that they are speculating. I'm told that Ron, destined to one day become a Naval Intelligence Officer, had information suggesting the act was quite deliberate.

I grew up on the same farm as my elder siblings until the age of eight, although my family quit farming the land in 1968, when I was one. Ron graduated high school and moved on a few short months after my birth, having made clear a couple years prior that he was unwilling to become a farmer. After one year of going it with only himself, three young girls, and hired help, Dad knew he was unable to sustain the farm under those circumstances. He decided to hang up his plow and set his sights on owning a small bar across the lake from the farm.

O'Dell's was a small (very small) store, where, in 1967, fishermen stopped by for bait, snacks, camping supplies, and some camaraderie with neighbors and adventuring anglers seeking to land "the big one." Measuring about fifteen by thirty feet, the joint offered little but had no competition for eight miles in any direction. It had cabins for rent, complete with a propane stove, a refrigerator, and beds. Additional space was available for tent campers. For the privilege of your visit, you were free to enjoy the relaxation of the outhouse when nature called.

After selling the farm, Dad purchased O'Dell's for an undisclosed sum. He then set about doing what he always did best: working his ass off. After one year operating as Mel's, he added a kitchen and dining room, a lobby and coat room, and as a technological leap, indoor men's and women's restrooms. Mel's became The Lakeview Supper Club, nearly tripling its size. For the first eight years of my life, The Club (as we called it), was my second home.

Dad did a superb job building the addition, even creating laminated beams to support the roof. These beams were probably the first example of glulam construction used anywhere in the area, and Dad later boasted how a representative from a regional building company came to see them firsthand, having heard about them secondhand. The representative's company had apparently never spanned an area of that size with such beams before. He was duly impressed. The endeavors of adding the additions to The Club, then to our farmhouse, inspired Dad to pursue a career in construction later in life.

Old and poorly insulated, our farmhouse held three small bedrooms upstairs and a small living room and kitchen on the main floor. There was no indoor bathroom. The house also featured a spider-filled and spooky basement, complete with a dirt cellar, a must-have for storing food in those days.

A couple strategically placed oil burning stoves heated the house. Common in those days, there were several registers in the first-floor ceiling. Registers were holes in the ceiling that allowed air to circulate throughout the house, warming the second floor. Decorative iron grills adorned the registers, with one fastened to the ceiling below the hole and the other inserted into and resting over the hole in the floor above. They collected dust and occasionally needed cleaning. Mom loved to clean, so our registers got more attention than any in the county.

On one such occasion, when I was no older than three, Mom and my sister removed the top covers and set about moving from room-to-room with the vacuum, cleaning them. Meanwhile, I marched about upstairs, impersonating a soldier, staring straight ahead with my broom-handle rifle fixed smartly to my shoulder. General Patton would have been proud.

The booby trap was set! Patton's soldier marched impressively about, with little to no **SA**, and then disappeared in a puff of yet-to-be-vacuumed dust. My mother watched in horror.

I have no recollection of what happened when I stepped into the hole, but seconds later, my mother and sister, having set a new land-speed record racing downstairs to rescue me, discovered that I had already scrambled from the floor to the nearby couch. On the way down, my weight ripped the bottom half of the register off the ceiling below. Apparently, I grasped the light fixture fastened next to the register and ripped it off the ceiling as well.

Aside from being scared silent, I somehow emerged unscathed! It was my first official flight, and while I was neither aerodynamic nor graceful, my number of takeoffs equaled my number of landings. I later discovered this to be a crucial statistic in the field of aviation.

Maslow's Hierarchy
of Needs

Ron

"If you're in control, you're not going fast enough."

—PARNELLI JONES

Aeronautical Notables:

Mayday: A distress call by voice radio for vessels and people in serious trouble, in the air or at sea. An anglicization of the French *m'aidez* (help me), the term was made official by an international telecommunications conference in 1948.

Aileron Roll: An aerobatic maneuver in which the aircraft does a full 360° revolution about its longitudinal axis. When executed perfectly, there is no change in altitude, and the aircraft exits the maneuver on the same heading as it entered.

Barrel Roll: An aerial maneuver in which an airplane makes a complete rotation on both its longitudinal and lateral axes while following a helical path, finishing on its original heading.

The summer after I graduated, my classmate Wayne and I entered a joint venture as stock car drivers extraordinaire. After purchasing a '54 Ford, we raced every Saturday night, as well as during special events at the Canby Race Way, eighteen miles north of Ivanhoe. We had great fun and ended up placing in the top two in every race we ran.

A lot of dismantling goes into creating a stock car; if a car part does not serve the purpose of getting you around the track faster than the competition, it is removed. What remains after all the modifications is a steel container with wheels, one seat, an engine, and a miniature gas tank, which was strapped in behind the driver's seat.

Farm boys aren't typically safety conscious, but Wayne and I were fairly religious about removing the gas tank when welding was required. Without upholstery, the entire car was metal-on-metal, and we did not want to end up with a spark that could cause a gas tank explosion. That is, we were religious about removing the gas tank except that one time!

We had raced the previous Saturday evening, when a scrape between our car and another on the track caused our front bumper to break loose. The Fourth of July races were just around the corner, so we had to get the bumper back on quickly. We decided to chance the weld. After all, the bumper was in the front, and the gas tank was in the back. What could *possibly* go wrong?

Wayne was the welder; I was the positive thinker and primary driver. Rightfully paranoid about welding with the tank still in the car,

Wayne eventually assumed a squatting position next to the bumper and struck an arc. He welded a few seconds, stopped and inspected the gas tank (not sure what good that did), and then resumed welding for a few more seconds. Convinced the car and garage were not going to explode around him, he settled into welding the bumper.

With the Fourth of July approaching, firecrackers were abundant. I was packing a cherry bomb, which can easily remove a digit or two if it goes off in your hand. As Wayne worked, I lit the bomb and lobbed it decisively behind him. It seemed like something a good friend ought to do.

From outside, a cherry bomb explosion sounds like cannon fire. Inside, in close quarters—well, think battleship *USS New Jersey.* KA-BOOOOM.

In that instant, I witnessed all that I later learned in college psychology class about Maslow's hierarchy of needs. In 1.5 seconds, Wayne levitated, removed his welding gear, rotated ninety degrees, and cleared the building. He traveled a good twenty feet, took inventory of his extremities, determined he was still alive (first row of Maslow's hierarchy), and moved onto the second tier. *SCROTUM TO BRAIN, SCROTUM TO BRAIN, IT'S MY TURN!* **MAYDAY, MAYDAY,** *THIS IS NOT A DRILL.*

Apparently, the concussion associated with a cherry bomb exploding inches from your testicles results in "not inconsiderable discomfort." Wayne grabbed his boys with both hands and performed a maneuver I discovered later in my Navy career to be a combined **aileron/barrel roll**, inspired by the added influence of gravity.

Gravity eventually proved the greater force, causing Wayne to crash land, but he was planning to hit the ground anyway in order to pray to the Pain God. When he tired of that position, he jumped to his feet, further expressing his discomfort through "left full rudder, no new course given" interpretive dance.

Wayne was no longer in the mood to run. I was faster than him anyway, but my head was on a swivel for a few days until he finally understood my only motive was to educate him on the importance of safety. That's my story, and I'm sticking to it.

I learned to be an innovative self-starter. I collected facts, analyzed them, then made decisions quickly and confidently. Sometimes, my decisions scared the shit out of people!

Steve and next older sibling Pam during a loosely supervised excursion in Lake Shaokatan.

Steve getting an early start on honing his drumming skills at The Club. Live music was a huge draw on Friday and Saturday nights (circa 1969).

The Lakeview Supper Club

Steve

"I refuse to join any club that would have me as a member."

—Groucho Marx

Nautical Notable:

Pipe Down: A boatswain's call, denoting the completion of an all-hands evolution (stating that you can go below). It was the last signal from the Bosun's pipe each day, which meant "lights out" and "silence."

In addition to the normal fare of worms, minnows, chubs, and bad beer, The Lakeview Supper Club now offered full dining, with meals served by one of the best cooks I've ever known: my mother. As an added benefit, customers enjoyed the hard work and occasionally enthusiastic customer service provided, free of charge, by my two eldest sisters, Sue and Pat. It was indeed a family affair.

We owned The Club for eight years, leasing it to new owners when I was eight. I have many vivid memories of those years. The nights were long and the days full of adventure. The bar portion of The Club opened at 1:00 p.m., while the dining room opened at 5:00 p.m. In addition to the dining area, Dad included a dance floor and an alcove for a band. On the weekends, locals danced to live music until the wee hours. While the band played, I watched the drummer. Whenever the band took a break from playing, I snuck in, sat behind the drum set, picked up the sticks and fiddled around with the many and differing drums and cymbals. I can remember Dad counting money at 4:00 a.m. It was never quite enough, but then again, he was never very good with it either.

* * *

My youngest sister Pam and I usually roamed about the premises until we ran out of energy, then **piped down** to our nightly digs: a roll-away mattress in the utility room flanked by the furnace, hot water heater, chest freezer, and things that go bump in the night. Although ungodly hot, I eventually surrendered my consciousness to the smell of cooking grease, heat from the appliances, the noise of a busy kitchen, happy customers, and live music. (The smells and sounds are still vivid, even fifty years later. It works that way with memories.) I also remember being scared out of my wits by the startling sound of wrapped frozen meat, retrieved from the freezer next to my sleeping head and dropped on the floor to separate the portions for serving. Like I said: things that go bump in the night.

While my parents and older siblings became fully immersed in the day-to-day needs of the business (cleaning, cooking, serving customers, ordering supplies, etc.), I was looked after by siblings with white space on their schedule, as well as customers and friends. When everyone lost track of me, I was free to roam the territory and make my own contributions to this entrepreneurial endeavor.

One summer evening, during a wedding event in the dining room, no one paid particular attention to the young and usually obnoxious mascot (me). I crawled under the expansive length of the head table, *mostly* clandestinely, drawing only the occasional snicker from an amused guest as I brushed by their legs. I subsequently emerged from the end of the table hoisting the purses of every lady present!

Another memorable event occurred when I was three. During the height of the dinner hour, I appeared outside the expansive lakeside windows, which gave The Lakeview Supper Club its name. In addition to fine dining, ambiance, and superb sunset views of Lake Shaokatan, customers were treated to a view of me relieving myself against those very windows! Since we couldn't afford one of those fancy statues of a boy peeing, I figured I would fill in...free of charge. Like I said, it was a family affair.

Feeling Blue

Ron

"Possession isn't nine-tenths of the law. It's nine-tenths of the problem."

—JOHN LENNON

Nautical Notables:

Forging Ahead: Going ahead slowly.

Devil to Pay: Today the expression is used primarily to describe having an unpleasant result from some action that has been taken; for instance, someone has done something they shouldn't have, and as a result, "There will be the devil to pay." Originally, this expression described one of the unpleasant tasks aboard a wooden ship. The "devil" was the wooden ship's longest seam in the hull. Caulking was done with "pay" or pitch (a kind of tar). The task of "paying the devil" (caulking the longest seam) by squatting in the bilges was despised by every seaman.

I may not be the sharpest tack in the box, but I am astute at recognizing life-changing opportunities when they occur, and college obviously provided one. Though I barely graduated from high school in the spring of '67, I concluded that if a grade of seventy wasn't good enough, it wouldn't be passing.

In the fall, I headed north to Moorhead State University in Moorhead, Minnesota. Moving off the farm and into a dorm room was a step up, not least of which was 24/7 access to an indoor bathroom, and there, I hoped to become an industrial arts teacher. Moorhead State had an excellent industrial arts program, and at the time, it was the only field I had a snowball's chance in hell of successfully completing.

College provided an education, some of which was even academic, but with no **forging ahead** for me, I pledged a fraternity and took a crash course in *Animal House* fundamentals. Weekends seemed to be made for partying, and I quickly made a name for myself.

My college roommate, Doug, hailed from a small town named Barrett, not unlike Ivanhoe, Minnesota. The youngest of three boys, Doug learned to fend for himself at an early age. Only a year or two separated him from the second oldest, so as a young boy, Doug received all kinds of hostile activity instigated by this older brother. This conduct continued unabated until Doug discovered his brother's deathly fear: chickens.

Unfortunately for Doug's brother, livestock, including chickens, were often raised to feed a farmer's family. One day, while exploring the deep dark secrets of his farmyard, young Doug happened onto a dried-up head of a chicken that had met its demise some weeks prior. From that point on, Doug carried the chicken head in his pocket and presented it to his brother whenever he got within a threatening range.

It was this level of creative ingenuity that Doug brought to college, and between the two of us, there were few problems we couldn't solve. Of course, in order to hone our skills, ensure mutual respect, and establish the dormitory male hierarchy, we practiced our abilities on one another from time to time. They say turnabout is fair play, and the cherry bomb prank on Wayne, my former racing partner, was about to be avenged.

One Friday evening, Doug and I stopped by the dorm room of a fellow fraternity brother, Mike, to strategize the evening's events. His dad was a pharmacist, and Mike had a bottle of every "vitamin pill" known to man lined up on top of the cabinet above his desk.

I need to declare my innocence at this point. Yes, it was 1967, and in many parts of the country, colleges were in the midst of a full-blown drug culture revolution. In my small circle of friends, however, the strongest medicine we had was aspirin. Oh yeah, and what I was about to discover: methylene blue pills.

Being the ever inquisitive one, I asked the purpose of all the pills. Mike stated that he always took a handful of "vitamins" before heading to a party in order to soften the ensuing hangover. Fraternity parties have a well-earned reputation for devilishness, after all. Mike's logic made sense to me, so I asked him to load me up, and off we headed.

About an hour into the evening, I needed to relieve myself. Imagine my surprise when I peed the brightest neon blue created by pharmacology! Of course, I was the only one at the party up to that point who did not know of the prank, and there was no hiding the evidence because I left a neon blue ring in the toilet.

Methylene blue has many uses, one of which is to act as a dye to make the liver show up on an X-ray. The side effect is that you pee neon blue for four to five days. After I stopped marking my territory, I convinced Mike to give me a pill and allowed the fact to get out. Soon, there would be the **Devil to pay**; neon-blue-hysteria reigned on campus until spring break.

The last night of the winter quarter, Doug and I pulled an all-nighter studying for a chemistry final exam. At about 3:00 a.m., running on auxiliary power, I walked down to the lobby and bought a Mars Bar and a can of Coke. I cut the Mars Bar in half, hollowed out a cavity, and loaded the pill. I poured the Coke into two cups and offered the Coke and half of the Mars Bar to my roommate, who gladly accepted it.

Mars Bars used to come with a couple of almonds on top of the candy bar, so biting into something hard did not raise suspicion...initially. But when it comes to survival, Maslow was on to something.

As Doug began to chew on the hard pill, his wheels began to turn. *MOUTH TO BRAIN, MOUTH TO BRAIN—METHYLENE BLUE PILL.*

It was a timely chemistry experiment: a mixture of chocolate and methylene blue makes neon blue. A mixture of toothpaste and methylene blue makes neon blue. The best you can hope for when brushing is to partially whiten the face of your teeth, but each tooth remains highlighted in neon blue, along with your tongue, lips, and tonsils. Doug also discovered that you don't have to swallow much to gain the additional benefit of marking your territory.

That event led to an hour-long distraction from our studies, but we finally got refocused, albeit with one of us doing the giggle, giggle, tee-hee routine for the remainder of the night.

After our final exams, four of us loaded into a car and took the three-hour trip to Minneapolis to catch the opening game of the Minnesota Twins. Not having the funds to buy a seat in the grandstand, we settled on the grassy knoll section, where we stood and viewed the game from over the fence. Insufficient funds for a seat did not mean insufficient funds for adult beverages, and with no metal detectors in those days, bringing in cans of beer under our coats was not difficult.

About an hour into the game, Doug needed to relieve himself. Unfortunately for him, the urinal consisted of a trough that ran the full length of the men's room. There were a lot of inquisitive minds downstream, and Doug's blue lips and teeth added to the conversation. Like I said, there would be the Devil to pay, and I possessed the passion to ensure it was paid in full.

I could never prove it, but after that day, I suspected Doug started to carry a chicken head again.

Setting the Stage

Steve

"Necessity is the mother of taking chances."

—MARK TWAIN

Nautical Notables:

Bought the Farm: Pilot killed. Originated from the practice of the government reimbursing farmers for crops destroyed due to aviation accidents on their fields. Farmers inflated the value of lost crops to the point that, in effect, the pilot bought the farm.

Footloose: The bottom portion of a sail is called the foot. If not secured, it dances randomly in the wind and is referred to as footloose.

In addition to the many curiosities inherent to life on a lake (boats, water skiers, fish, and more fish), The Club offered other adventures. There was also pool and foosball!

Conveniently, the average height of a pool table is not much less than the top of a three-year-old boy's head. As such, I dragged a chair around the pool table and stood on it while I refined my aim and skills. In the evenings, I watched the adults play, and then I spent my mornings practicing while my family finished cleaning and preparing for the opening of the bar. Soon, I was challenging the afternoon arrivals to a match.

My first question was "Do you want to play pool?"

My second question was "Do you have a quarter?"

Initially, they accepted the challenge as a way to be gracious and kind to a child. Hundreds of hours became thousands as I dragged my chair around the table, lined the chair up with the shot, climbed up, and made the balls disappear. Soon, I was beating the adults consistently.

Eventually, Dad showed me how to rest the pool cue on my shoulder, using both hands on the front of the cue as a guide. By the time I turned seven or eight, the chair was no longer required, and my adult antagonists were less anxious to become the next victim of a young child turned pool shark!

Similarly, I studied adults playing foosball. I climbed my chair, practiced during my downtime, and then challenged my older sisters' high school and college friends. The results were identical. Being eye-level with the playing field, coupled with countless hours of practice, resulted in a level of expertise that I am convinced formed a fractional basis of my skills as a fighter pilot. Lining up pool balls with the holes, and quickly reacting to an opponent's foosball moves, one day proved to be valuable skills when landing on carrier decks and engaging in aerial combat.

When not refining my bar-game skills, I wandered around the property and beyond, exploring everything there was to offer. Starting at about the age of six, I was more or less free to wander the premises, with someone generally keeping an eye on me. How I never **bought the farm** by falling off the dock and drowning when no one was looking, I will never know, but I somehow passed the Darwinian tests of Lake Shaokatan.

Once, while **footloose**, I wandered over to the neighbor's property (a seasonal trailer) and decided to use their outhouse. I locked the door, which consisted of a standard metal hook and eye, but because the door was warped, I was unable to unlatch the hook. I couldn't get out.

After yelling for help for what seemed like a couple hours, I tried throwing a small rock against the window some four feet above my head in hopes of breaking the glass. After nearly falling into the hole of despair, I gave up and fell asleep.

Eventually, someone noticed the mascot was missing, and a search party formed. I awoke to the sound of my name being called. When they found me, my cousin leaned against the door as I unlatched the hook with my roughly six-year-old hands. I was rescued!

* * *

An indoor bathroom may not seem like a big deal to some, but to the Melvin Lambrecht residence, it was a significant milestone. The Club had indoor bathrooms before we had one in our own home!

Mom was reportedly *so* upset by this order of events that she hung up on Dad during a telephone conversation. Her understandable discontent resulted in the first indoor bathroom the Melvin Lambrecht family home had ever bolstered, but by the time it was completed, Ron had been out of the nest for a few years, and Sue, the next in line, had finished high school and moved on to vocational school. That left me, at age five, Pam, and our middle sibling, Pat, in the house to enjoy all the modern conveniences.

With our time split between The Club and our farm, major explorations took place at both locales. There was a barn, a massive chicken coop, a silo, and an assortment of other out-buildings, not counting the outhouse. Woods surrounded the entire premises, full of abandoned cars, junk piles, and other mysterious areas too scary for a six-year-old and his ten-year-old sister to brave.

The barn was simply too massive and the heights too intimidating for a child my age to spend much time negotiating, not that I didn't give it a go from time to time. The silo was similarly daunting, but the sheds and the chicken coop were a different story. Once, finding some cans of old paint in one of the sheds, I set off to create some of the finest wall and floor art ever mastered by a boy of my tender age. Rembrandt, however, would have likely agreed with my parents, who were neither impressed nor amused.

The long-abandoned chicken coop sported dozens of windows, each with multiple divided panes of glass. After extensive searching, I found a rock sizable enough to make it through a pane of glass without bouncing off. As I found only one such rock, I set about the laborious task of throwing it through one pane, walking all the way to the end of and into the chicken coop, finding the rock, then hurling it back out through another. The process was repeated until either I ran out of steam or lost interest.

I don't remember my parents' reaction when they saw what I had done. Perhaps I have simply blocked it out. It is probably better that way.

In the years that followed, I learned to hunt, fish, fend for myself, and be the man of the house in Dad's absence, as he was on the road working construction. I learned the value of hard physical labor and, unbeknownst to me, the endless pursuit of perfection that results from being the son of a father for whom nothing was ever good enough.

Zip to Zap

Ron

"Don't criticize what you can't understand."

—Bob Dylan

Nautical Notable:

No Quarter Given: Giving an opponent no opportunity to surrender. This phrase stems from the old custom of officers ransoming themselves by paying one quarter of a year's pay.

In the spring of 1969, I was finishing my second year at Moorhead State. Though the university was located far from the centers of the hippie movement on the coasts of the United States, we were aware of the actions of our peers at schools elsewhere in the country. Across the United States, college campuses had devolved into chaos, with students protesting the actions of the US in the Vietnam War. Local and national media portrayed the protests as a cultural, racial, and generational civil war.

Arguably, 1969 proved to be the worst year in American history for civil disorders. The National Guard had been called to intervene in over 200 incidents relating to the war and racial tensions, but it did not occur to me that an event of that magnitude could take place in the Midwest. It certainly wasn't on my mind as three of my fraternity brothers and I headed to Zap, North Dakota, during spring break.

"Zip to Zap" originated in the mind of Chuck Stroup, a student at North Dakota State University, located in Fargo, Moorhead's sister city.[1] Realizing most of us Midwest small-town college students could not afford to attend the more traditional spring break festivities held in Fort Lauderdale, Florida, Chuck developed the idea: "Zip to Zap, a Grand Festival of Light and Love." With a knack for marketing, Stroup generated excitement across the campuses of the Midwest through cryptic ads and articles posted in various college newspapers. Eventually, newspapers throughout the nation started covering the event, furthering student interest from as far away as Texas and Florida.

Located in a valley of the Knife River about 280 miles west of Fargo/ Moorhead, Zap's population of 250 was quick to embrace the idea. They saw an opportunity for publicity...and a way to make some money. The two local bars stockpiled a supply of beer, and local diners began marketing Zapburgers in anticipation of the event. "We thought, well, we'll put ourselves on the map here," remembered Norman Fuchs, the mayor of Zap in 1969.

Publicity surrounding the event evolved from impressive to titanic. The Wham-O toy company used the event to launch a toy called the Zip-Zap, consisting of a sponge-coated weight guided on a flexible bungee line. Held between the knees of two opponents positioned ten feet apart, the objective was to strike the opponent in any part of the body by hitting the projectile with a paddle, which then was guided

---

1   Merry Helm, "Zip to Zap Was a Prank That Turned into a Riot Where the National Guard Was Called In," *Williston Herald,* May 10, 2021, https://www.willistonherald.com/ community/zip-to-zap-was-a-prank-that-turned-into-a-riot-where-the-national-guard/ article_629b9e04-ad06-11eb-8a65-4fd88aef6e26.html.

wildly along the bungee toward the opponent. The game was not a big seller, but Mayor Fuchs was even photographed playing with the toy.[2]

The organizers of Zip to Zap, as well as the local government and residents of Zap, were caught up in a whirlwind of publicity but gave little regard to dealing with thousands of college-aged kids out for a good time. On May 9, 1969, between 2,000 and 3,000 young folks descended upon the small town of Zap. It was "pandelirium!" Bathroom facilities were nonexistent, local eateries ran out of food almost immediately, and the two local bars set the stage for resentment by selling their inventory of beer at three to four times the standard rate.

As the small country town's resources were depleted, the amiable mood turned ugly, and Zap's residents asked the visitors to leave. Some complied, but many others stayed behind.

The bitter cold of the evening added to the misery. At about 3:00 a.m., in order to keep from freezing in our sleeping bags, my three fraternity brothers and I headed up one of the hills surrounding the town, hoping the temperature would be a few degrees warmer. Meanwhile, the temperature dropped below freezing in the valley, and lacking adequate shelter, visitors began dismantling a condemned and dilapidated building to start a bonfire in the middle of the town. From that point, the event spread out of control.

At around 6:00 a.m., I awoke to a military cadence sounded by 500 National Guardsmen, who had been called in to disperse the crowd. They were positioned at each end of the downtown area, bayonets fixed, and it became obvious to the most casual observer that **no quarter would be given.**

A Guardsman was positioned with his back against one of the buildings facing the street. The next Guardsman moved into position with his back against the first Guardsman's chest, and the process

---

2 "Zip to Zap Was a Prank That Turned into a Riot Where the National Guard Was Called In."

continued until a solid line of soldiers blocked off all of downtown Zap. The process took about fifteen minutes, allowing the folks causing the problems to vacate the area, which they did with vigor.

The Zip to Zap event went down in history as the only official riot in the history of North Dakota put down by the National Guard. As my frat brothers and I left the morning of May 10, we observed an endless line of cars full of college-aged kids still heading toward Zap. Had the event been properly organized, I estimate attendance could have exceeded 6,000–7,000. Unfortunately, Zip to Zap made the *CBS Evening News with Walter Cronkite, Pravda* (the news outlet for the Communist Party of the Soviet Union), and the *Stars and Stripes* of the United States Armed Forces: the reviews were not good and served as propaganda in the Soviet Union, a future adversary of mine.

The riot caused more than $25,000 in damage, and ultimately the student governments of North Dakota State University and the University of North Dakota paid the bills.[3] Interestingly, Zip to Zap occurred three months before Woodstock and was the closest I got to the rebelliousness unleashing in America at the time.

What I remember most, though, is how cold I felt and how comfortable the well-equipped Guardsmen looked in their warm winter uniforms. The revelation was not lost on me.

---

3 "Zip to Zap."

Dad and Ron in Dad's freshly restored 1956 pickup in the 2003 Polska Kielbasa Days parade. The spotlight used for all sorts of shenanigans is mounted on the cowl to the left of the driver. This photo was taken one week prior to Dad's passing as a result of a failed quadruple bypass surgery. The truck is now owned by Steve and is affectionately named "Mater."

Ice Capades

Ron

"I do hunt, and I do fish, and I don't apologize to anybody for hunting and fishing."

—General Norman Schwarzkopf

Nautical Notables:

Abreast: Meaning alongside the beam of a ship (or aircraft). Now a common expression, "keeping abreast of a situation" means staying in touch with or keeping up with something.

Gadgets: This widely used word was originally the nautical name for hooks.

In the winter, a small village of fish houses appeared on Lake Shaokatan. Shacks of every design were dragged or towed onto the lake and placed over holes cut in the ice for the purpose of fishing. Some shacks were quite elaborate, possessing a heater, a television with an antenna affixed to the roof, a stove, bunk beds, and a toilet of some sort; most were just six-by-six-foot wooden insulated boxes consisting of chairs, a beer cooler, and a heater.

Fishermen normally used a fishing rod with small, brightly colored lures or hooks with bait, such as worms or shiner minnows. Sitting beside a hole in the ice for hours waiting for a fish to swim by is not unlike watching grass grow, hence the beer cooler. But across North America, many cars, trucks, SUVs, snowmobiles, and fish houses had fallen through the ice, and over the years, Lake Shaokatan claimed a few of her own.

One winter day, Dad and I were visiting various fishermen to keep **abreast** of the latest community gossip (and share a beer or two). While driving the Hudson Hornet, now relegated to hunting duties rather than trips to Marshall, we happened to drive between a small island and an adjacent peninsula of land. Unbeknownst to us, beavers kept a channel open under the ice so that they could swim from the island to the mainland—and with a sudden thud, we found the channel.

Fortunately, the entire car did not fit through the narrow channel and only dropped to the bottom of the doors. A couple tractor pulls later, the car was back up on the ice, but the event took some of the fun out of the day, as we knew neither of us was a strong swimmer.

* * *

Later, Dad became a frequent and expected visitor during the winter ice fishing months. One year, he took note of the fish house locations and their inhabitants in order to determine who was likely to be fishing unlawfully. This bit of data can result in conniving activity of the highest order!

The law was simple: one fisherman, one license, one fishing pole, and one hook. Game wardens found it difficult to enforce the law, however, due to the long commute between the shore and the fish houses, plus the communal smoke signals (horns, car lights, barking dogs, and fishermen closest to the shore moving with a level of vigor) that alerted others to their presence.

I was home for a visit one winter and, after closing The Club, Dad invited me to participate in a (very) late check on the fish house inhabitants. We jumped into his '56 Ford pickup and headed out onto the lake. Dad had bought a portable police beacon at one of the many farm auctions that occurred each fall after the crops were harvested, and he attached it to the roof of the pickup. (At that time, small farm owners were beginning to disappear, and farm sales were a common occurrence. How the previous owner was able to acquire the beacon is anyone's guess.)

The truck also sported a spotlight (for illegal night hunting, of course), and we blasted out onto the lake, intent upon mischief. Dad did everything he could to draw attention to his presence, including turning his headlights on and off, continuously blasting the horn, and sweeping the spotlight across the fish houses. We pulled up to the first fish house with smoke coming out of the stove pipe, jumped out of the truck, and yanked the door open.

Only somewhat protected from the inhospitable Minnesota winter by a layer of boards fashioned together to serve as a fish house, the inhabitant, Agata Remerouski, was wearing multiple layers of insulation, making him look like an astronaut donning a space suit. Agata's startled, icy flail resulted in first one, then multiple embedded hooks. He wrapped himself in three fishing lines, with three or more **gadgets** per line. A quick "Gotcha," and we were off to the next fish house.

Fishing was good that night. We found Jerzy Popowski flopping on the floor like a beached fish, and if memory serves, we caught three "walleye-skis," two big mouth "bass-skis," and a "Norwegian jumping carp." The fun continued as we visited others who were now "in compliance" but found it difficult to explain the wet lines and live bait on the fishing poles now stored in their racks.

Ludwik Stanasheski lost his best fishing tackle by dumping it into the hole in the ice. He didn't see the humor in the event, at least not as much as we did, but after a couple cans of beer and an explanation of the importance of preparedness, all was forgiven.

Dad was the leader in this particular escapade, but he inspired me to undertake many similar feats of my own.

Steve on his Honda minibike. Lake Shaokatan and one rental cabin appear in the background (circa 1975).

Lake Shaokatan

Steve

"You have to do your own growing no matter how tall your grandfather was."

—ABRAHAM LINCOLN

Aeronautical Notable:

Sierra Hotel: Means "shit hot." The pilot's favorite and all-purpose expression of approval or high praise.

I didn't realize it at the time, but growing up in the environment I did filled my toolbox with many tools. Those tools later served me in ways I couldn't possibly have imagined.

During their final year of nightclub ownership, my parents purchased a manufactured home, dug/poured a basement next to The Club, and placed the house on top of it. Ron helped with the project, including building the garage, but being too young to be of any use, I occupied my time playing in the mountains of dirt.

Using my Tonka trucks to create all manner of structures and thoroughfares, I waged massive battles with my extensive collection of plastic army men and vehicles. Clumps of dirt became projectiles, and firecrackers reigned supreme as the battle for Lake Shaokatan raged on for weeks.

When the house was complete, we moved in. That house became my home for the remainder of my school-age years, and to Mom's delight, it boasted *two* bathrooms!

The new house gave me additional opportunities to explore the surrounding countryside. For instance, shortly after moving in, Dad purchased a BB gun for my sister and me. We learned to shoot with accuracy and consistency, and I learned to stalk prey; the groundwork was laid for a life of hunting.

Dad was enamored with wildlife, yet one wouldn't know it by the way he treated animals. I learned to shoot not just by aiming at targets and aluminum cans retrieved from the open-pit dump behind our house, but also by shooting sparrows illuminated by a flashlight under the eaves of the rental cabins after dark. Later in life, I quipped about how Dad took it upon himself to single-handedly balance nature.

While I remain an avid hunter to this day, proper respect for the animal kingdom came only with the enlightenment of my formative years. I no longer hunt for sport, and I adhere to a strict policy of "you kill it, you eat it."

* * *

After eight years of slogging it out in the nightclub business, and the graduation and departure of my middle sister, Pat, Dad once again saw the writing on the wall. With only himself, Mom, and hired help—as

Pam and I were too young to contribute in any meaningful way—Dad chose to lease The Club to entrepreneurs and seek a new living in construction.

As he became increasingly successful, Dad went to work for a large construction company based in Minneapolis, ascending to the position of construction superintendent. He traveled the country building Radio Shacks, Hallmark Card stores, and Perkins restaurants, to name just a few, and he was gone a lot, usually three to six weeks at a time. During his absences, I inherited increasing levels of work and responsibility at home.

Agriculture ran deep in Dad's DNA. When he was gone, my responsibilities included mowing our three-acre property, tending to the extensive gardens, and watering/weeding the countless flower beds. Each time he was away, I waited in fear for his return to see if my labors proved adequate. Adequate resulted in silence; inadequate resulted in unpleasant sounds of disapproval.

On one occasion, I apparently did a particularly good job of keeping up with the place, and Mom told me that Dad said the place looked nice. He never said it directly to me, but I took Mom's comment as a genuine **sierra hotel**.

* * *

When Dad came home, we worked...hard. We cut firewood for the winter, put up fencing, and did many and varied construction projects. No day passed without work of some kind, and we joked about how Dad was "strong, like bull...smart, like tractor."

Many people commented that Dad was the hardest working man they knew, and to this day, I have to agree. But Dad didn't just work. While moving around on the job site, he walked at a pace fast enough to have both feet off the ground simultaneously. Some might call this running, but it didn't quite seem to fit the standard definition. None of us kids could beat him in a sprint—not even me, some eighteen years after Ron was humiliated by his own attempt. Dad was simply too fast for us.

As mentioned previously, Dad boxed during his time in the Army and owned two sets of boxing gloves and a speed bag. He taught me to use both. Nobody messed with Dad, but he took it easy on me, usually fighting on his knees and only using one hand.

Another source of amusement was a Honda 50 minibike Ron purchased from a drummer he played with. The motorcycle was designed for on- and off-road terrain, and with a top speed of thirty-five miles per hour, it provided me with many thrilling and near-death experiences. I created jumps, riding courses, and rode that thing literally to death.

Once, while riding on a back road connecting our property to the neighbor's, I screamed along at a good clip when I found myself abruptly on the ground, having been cleaned off the Honda by a single, barely visible, black rubber-coated copper wire! I forgot Dad had strung a single-wire fence across the road to discourage some of our vandalizing neighbors from crossing our property on their way to The Lakeview Supper Club, now under new ownership. Luckily, it hit me at chest/shoulder height and not a few inches higher, or else I may have become "The Headless Honda 50-Horse Man."

As I grew older, Dad bought me my first .22 caliber rifle, a Remington Speedmaster semi-automatic with a fifteen-round tube-style magazine. I graduated from sparrows to cottontail rabbits and squirrels, all of which we ate. We also hunted jackrabbits, which we fed to the German Shephard dogs we bred and sold. During summers and winters alike, when I wasn't working, I roamed the countryside hunting rabbits and squirrels, and I became an expert shot. Moving targets proved little match.

It was a skill that would serve me well in combat, in a desert half a world away, thirty years into a future I had not yet contemplated.

Playing the Odds

Ron

"Success is always somebody else's opinion of you; but it doesn't amount to a damn compared to your own opinion of yourself."

—Jack Lemmon

Nautical Notable:

Listless: When powered by the wind, a sailing vessel lists to either port or starboard; this term originally referred to when a ship rode on an even keel due to a lack of wind. Today, it means to be lazy or without energy.

I was 90 percent focused on college the first quarter, 70 percent focused the second quarter, and 60 percent focused the third quarter. The percentage varied after that, with the trend definitely heading downward.

Vietnam was on everyone's mind during this period, and the war was a motivator for most male college students to maintain a minimum passing GPA. Unfortunately, I was not one of those motivated males. I thought 4.0 had something to do with blood alcohol content.

Still, the war was personal, as we all knew someone who had been either wounded or killed. Ivanhoe was no exception; one of our local boys, Sgt. (USA) Ronald Ray Wallace, was killed within the first thirty days of arriving in Vietnam. I also had several high school classmates who were either drafted or volunteered to serve.

Shortly after arriving in Vietnam, my close friend Greg, a participant in many of the aforementioned exploits by me and my neighbors from the surrounding schools, was hit by a mortar, resulting in significant trauma to the left side of his skull, arm, and leg. With several soldiers wounded that day, Greg was staged in triage with a low probability of survival.

As fate would have it, Dave, my neighbor who attended Hendricks High, had been drafted into the Army as a medical specialist. Dave was prioritizing the wounded for surgery based on the severity of wounds and probability of survival, but recognizing Greg from our shared high school frivolities, Dave prioritized him. He saved Greg's life in a Vietnam field hospital 10,000 miles from Southwest Minnesota.

* * *

By the fall of my junior year (1969), I had fallen behind in the number of credits required to retain my draft deferment status, and sure enough, I received my reclassification to 1-A (draft eligible). I fully expected to receive a draft notice, but the local draft board held off on sending notices until after the draft lottery, which took place in December 1969. Lottery night was **listless** for many young men, as they went to bed with a sinking feeling in their gut, knowing that their future included draft notices and Vietnam.

In December, the draft assigned a number to each birthdate. September 14 was drawn first, meaning that if your birthdate was September 14, you should start saying your goodbyes. My stars were aligned that day; my birthday was the 349th drawn out of 366 (February 29, leap day, was included), a number so high that orphans and grandmas would be drafted before me. One hundred ninety-five dates (birthdays) were eventually called up for service that year to meet the military manpower quota.

Though I avoided the draft, I was not mature enough to be a schoolteacher at the age of twenty-two, and college became a low priority. Shortly after, I quit school and started working full time for anyone who hired me. This is when I discovered that if you have fifty cents to live on for a week, it will cost you fifty cents that week to live.

I had ambition but little sense of purpose. I sold cookware, toted pails of hot tar for roofers, cleaned lice-infested chicken coups, drove a cab, worked on a road survey crew, worked for an aluminum door manufacturing company, and learned the hard way not to touch the ceiling of my pup tent in the middle of a hailstorm (yes, I was occasionally homeless). My compass always steered me toward pleasure and away from career goals.

Oh yeah, and I became a musician.

Bug Juice

Steve

"The two most common elements in the universe are hydrogen and stupidity."

—Harlan Ellison

Aeronautical Notables:

Flying by the Seat of Your Pants: This expression was first recorded in 1938 and comes from the days of early aircraft, which were very basic and had little instrumentation. A pilot, sitting in the cockpit, could literally feel the least change in engine note, vibration, and movement of the aircraft and interpreted this input to help control the plane to the best of their ability. Today, this expression means to act without proper direction or contemplation.

Bug Juice: Name given to various colored drinks served from dispensers in the ship's galley. The ingredients of said drinks remain a mystery to scientific communities the world over, but it is rumored that three-parts bug juice and two parts soft serve ice cream are the ingredients for polyester.

Pucker Factor: When you get nervous and your whole body tenses up from top to sphincter. Pucker factor increases as a function of increasing stress, akin to the Richter Scale.

Trips to town during the summer were rare. Just as well, given the amount of trouble I managed to find.

When we did make the venture, my parents released my sister and me into the wild with a few bucks in our pocket. They bellied up to the bar at the Ivanhoe Liquor Store or another of the local establishments, and it was up to us kids to find/make friends and choose our activities.

In its heyday, Ivanhoe boasted a municipal liquor store, two bars, three cafes, two grocery stores, a hardware store, a bowling alley, a teen center, a senior citizen's center, a VFW, three gas stations, various other businesses, and of course, a farm implement dealership. Some of the town folk hung a sheet on the back of the neighborhood drug store and projected movies every Saturday night, free for kids. It was a great way to pass the time.

When I couldn't find anything small-town proper to do, I sought excitement, unburdened by rules and unencumbered by legal constraints. Over the course of the next few years, I sometimes ran with a questionable crowd and increasingly became a child-at-risk, more and more often finding myself on the wrong side of school officials, townspeople, and the law. I did too much **flying by the seat of my pants**, and I learned some lessons the hard way.

On one hot summer afternoon, at the tender age of twelve, I tracked down Floyd, one of my miscreant friends, and we set out into the booming metropolis in search of something to do. We decided to wander down to the town ball diamond, where softball was frequently played. With neither people nor activity to be found, we invented our own form of recreation.

The ball diamond abutted the town grain elevator, and there, we found an old red Volkswagen Bug. Being a small town, everyone in Ivanhoe knew everyone else and what they drove. There were only a couple Beetles around, so we knew the red one belonged to Mr. Ragnar, one of our teachers; the other belonged to Floyd's mother. Therefore, as fate would have it, Floyd had a rudimentary understanding of the Beetle and its basic operating parameters.

We decided to get in. I was nervous as hell, but there I was, sitting in the passenger seat of my teacher's car. What could *possibly* go wrong?

There were no keys in the ignition, and one can't listen to the radio without the keys, so naturally, we searched for them. We discovered the keys cleverly hidden in the door pocket, and Floyd put them into the ignition. As anyone who has operated a vehicle knows, the radio can't produce music simply by putting the key into the ignition; the key must be rotated to supply electricity to the radio. How far does one rotate the key? At our young age, we had no idea.

Floyd rotated the key, and the Beetle promptly surged ahead! Not only had he rotated the key *past* the necessary point, but he had also engaged the starter. It is standard practice to leave a manual transmission vehicle in gear once parked, to prevent the vehicle from rolling, so by engaging the starter, he had also engaged the transmission, causing it to surge forward.

After looking around, frightened at the prospect of having given away our presence, we realized tiny Ivanhoe had somehow missed this epic event, and we burst out in a round of laughter.

Floyd immediately knew what he had done wrong. With the car in gear, the fix was to simply engage the clutch, eliminating any possibility of the Beetle lunging forward, particularly into the grain wagon parked directly in front of us. So, engage the clutch he did.

As if in slow motion, we waited to see what happened next. Once again, Floyd turned the key *past* the position required to supply electricity to the radio, and the starter engaged. Unencumbered by the transmission, the tiny four-cylinder engine roared to life!

"HOLY SHIT!" Floyd exclaimed as our eyes flung wide open.

So startled was Floyd that his foot came off the clutch, and the Beetle hurdled forward into the aforementioned grain wagon. The engine died.

Oh man, we were screwed! We jumped out of the Beetle and surveyed the damage, but unbelievably, there was none. Or, at least, nothing discernable from the other blemishes left by the old girl's years of living.

Who knew you could crash a car into a grain wagon and not cause any damage? We had discovered utopia! Utilizing the infinitesimal sum of our collective sound judgment, we reasoned that if we could accomplish such a feat without consequence once, certainly it was repeatable.

This time it was my turn. I repeated the endeavor from behind the wheel no less than three times. We laughed profusely.

After exiting the vehicle one last time to ensure there was no damage, we discovered, much to our dismay, repeated impacts *could*, in fact, cause a dent in old rusty metal. We needed a plan to avoid certain downfall. Floyd was back behind the wheel as we attempted to plan our escape and formulate our cover story.

Yes. There's more.

It naturally followed that if we may already be in serious trouble, we might as well take full advantage of the situation and enjoy a short ride in the old girl. Being seasoned drivers now, we knew how to effectively operate the vehicle's controls, and Floyd proceeded to maneuver the Beetle along the gravel road encircling the ball diamond's parking area. As we approached the end of the tiny complex and Main Street, I sensed an increased likelihood of being discovered and urged Floyd to cut through the grass and back toward our parking spot, which he did.

There was just one, very large, old-growth problem. Well, several of them, actually. They were tall, gray with green trim, and moved from side to side across our windshield as we undulated with indecision.

There wasn't much time to think. With approximately three minutes of experience behind us, our driving ability proved no match for twentieth century mechanical engineering. Before us lay oak, elm, and ash trees that were far enough apart to accommodate *multiple* borrowed Beetles. However, we had clearly overestimated our ability to negotiate a path between them.

After we spared the first couple trees the displeasure of our embrace, there loomed a particularly stubborn adversary who seemed to move in concert with our indecision. Floyd veered right; I coached him to the left. Floyd complied, despite his better and correct judgment, and veered left.

"NO! RIGHT!" I exclaimed, realizing his original choice was superior to my correction.

Floyd complied.

Oh, if only Floyd had not listened to me on either occasion!

The sturdy oak sentinel greeted us on the driver's side front fender, and we came to an abrupt halt. The engine died with the impact of the fifty-year-old hardwood. While the decision to take a joyride had required some minuscule measure of contemplation, the realization that we were fucked did not.

We got out and, as was the case with the grain wagon, surveyed the damage. While the grain wagon's bumper had only put a visible crease in the hood of the Beetle, the oak had no such sense of humor. The entire left fender was smashed in against the front wheel—so much so that it was in firm contact with the tire. Thankfully, the impact had not caused a release of **bug juice** from the radiator, as there isn't one in a rear-engine Beetle.

Once again, we called upon the infinitesimal sum of our collective sound judgment and reasoned that if we returned the vehicle to its original location, it would somehow seem as if it had never happened. Together, we grasped the front fender and pulled. Our adrenaline-supplemented save-my-ass motivations willed the fender away from the tire sufficiently for the vehicle to roll.

We climbed back in, and Floyd nursed the Beetle back to her original location. We fled the scene like two young boys who had just stolen a car and crashed it into a tree.

Certain we'd gotten away with it, we were almost successful in pushing it from our minds. Months passed, and at our age, months seemed like years. We figured everyone must have given up trying to solve the case.

Officer Myles Sleek, the town constable, had a different opinion on the matter.

One evening in late fall, it was very quiet and somber around the house, almost as if someone had driven a vehicle into a tree, and everyone had recently found out that I was the guilty party! Ron happened to be home for a visit, and he summoned me, saying, "We have to go to town."

DATE *Jan 10, 1980* PLACE *Sheriff's office* TIME STARTED *8:24 P.M.* M.

I, the undersigned, *Steven Scott Rambrecht* am *12* years of age, having been born

on *March 31, 1967* at *Tyler*

I now live at *Hendricks*

I have been duly warned and advised by, _____ a person who has identified himself as

Police officer that I do not have to make any statement at all, nor answer any questions or do anything that might tend to go against me or incriminate me in any manner, and that any statement I make may be used against me on the trial or trials for the offense or offenses concerning which the following statement is herein made. I was also warned and advised of my right to the advice and presence of a lawyer of my own choice before or at any time during any questioning or statement I make, and if I am not able to hire a lawyer I may request and have a lawyer appointed for me, by the proper authority, without cost or charge to me.

I do not want to talk to a lawyer, and I hereby knowingly and purposely waive my right to the advice and presence of a lawyer before and during any questioning or at any time before or while I voluntarily make the following statement to the aforesaid person, knowing that anything I say can and will be used against me in a court or courts of law.

I declare that the following voluntary statement is made to the aforesaid person of my own free will without promise of hope or reward, without fear or threat of physical harm, without coercion, favor or offer of favor, without leniency or offer of leniency, by any person or persons whomsoever.

On a summer day, me and _____ were walking around town and we went down to the baseball park to use the bathroom. We saw Mr. _____ car parked by the grain elevator and _____ said Let's get in and the first reason was he wanted to show me that his car was sort of like his Moms car. We got in and sat for a little while, and he started to look for the keys in a door pouch and told me too look to, I did. He found the keys on his side, and turned the car on. He put it in gear and went ahead and hit a wagon by mistake. He hit it for 2 more times and told me to try it. I did for 2 times and then he drove around a road on the North side. I said not to go any further and so he cut through the grass to get back and hit a tree. He backed up and drove back to park it and we got out and looked at the damage and left.

I have read this statement consisting of ___ page(s), and I certify that the facts contained therein are true and correct. I further certify that I made no request for the advice or presence of a lawyer before or during any part of this statement, nor at any time before it was finished did I request that this statement be stopped. I also declare that I was not told or prompted what to say in this statement.

This statement was completed at *8:36* M. on the *10* day of *January* 19 *0*

WITNESS: *Mel Lambrecht*

WITNESS: _____

Signature of person giving voluntary statement *Steve Lambrecht*

I have received a copy of this statement *Steve Lambrecht*

Ron and I had been typical brothers, engaged in jovial banter, practical jokes, and shenanigans. But that night, and his words, made it clear that the next phase of my human development was about to unfold.

It was a supremely quiet eight-mile ride to Ivanhoe. As we drove near the place where I had shot a beaver only a month before, I thought about how I'd planned to use the money from the pelt to purchase a new scope for my rifle. Ron and I had identical Remington

Speedmaster .22 caliber rifles, but while his sported a scope, mine did not. I could match him shot for shot with my iron sights, but as with other things in life, I wanted to have a scope, and to be more like him.

We passed the location where the beaver sacrificed its life for my aspirations, and Ron and Dad commented that the money from the pelt would be spent elsewhere. I sensed a reckoning awaited me in Ivanhoe.

Slowly, I realized the journey would almost certainly end at Mr. Ragnar's home, where I would hand over the money, along with my dignity, and formally begin my journey of atonement. However, as we entered Ivanhoe, instead of continuing straight ahead where Mr. Ragnar's home awaited us, we turned left. I was surprised but guessed we were heading to the school instead; Mr. Ragnar was probably there and likely preferred to address the crime in a formal setting rather than in his home.

What surprised and simultaneously terrified me was that we stopped short of the school and parked outside the sheriff's office. **Pucker factor**: a perfect 10.0!

About a year prior, my elementary class had taken a field trip to the police station, where we toured the facilities, the interrogation room, and the cells where prisoners were kept. The intent, undoubtedly, was to instill a measure of fear in us youths, who would eventually become adults and, therefore, potential criminals. In my case, the warning was clearly to no avail.

We were ushered into an office and shown our seats. The police officer sat behind the desk; I sat in a modest but sturdy chair, apparently able to withstand physical tremors measuring 8.9 on the Sphincter Scale; and Dad sat behind me somewhere out of my line of sight, which was just fine with me. Ron was far enough away to be invisible in the dim light, yet close enough to allow the LASER beam of his disapproving gaze to scorch the back of my goose-bump-embellished neck.

I was read my rights, I crapped my pants, and I folded like a taco. When I wrote my statement, it was factual and contrite. We paid for the repairs.

Later in life, I realized this had been somewhat scripted ahead of time with the intent of delivering a specific message and instilling the proper measure of fear, contrition, and respect into two miscreants. (Mission accomplished.) The police had offered a $25 reward for any information leading to the finding of said criminals, and I assume a rat—to whom Floyd had apparently entrusted the details—spent the money wisely.

I also later found out that disparities existed in the versions Floyd and I gave of that hot summer day: our accounts differed on who was driving when we met our demise. It matters not. We were in it together.

Fortunately, nothing was entered into my official record. This was a negotiated and benevolent agreement designed to leave the door to prosperity open, should I choose to pass through it.

After the joyride in the VW Bug, however, I engaged in multiple other nefarious activities absent from my official record and was rightfully characterized as a troubled child. In the sixth grade, there was talk of moving me up to the seventh grade (part of the problem, it was postulated, was that the classwork at my grade level was too easy for me, so I used the extra time to screw around and cause trouble), but after consideration and discussion with the members of the class ahead of me, it was accurately determined that I lacked the maturity to advance ahead of my grade. I stayed where I was.

Clashing with the law, persistently in trouble with teachers, and otherwise building a reputation as a degenerate, I was a rudderless ship adrift in a storm of my own making.

The Boy Has Rhythm

Ron

"Life is what happens while you are busy making other plans."

—JOHN LENNON

Nautical Notable:

Holy Mackerel: Because mackerel is a fish that spoils quickly, merchants were allowed to sell it on Sundays, contradicting the Blue Laws in seventeenth-century England that restricted or banned some or all Sunday activities. The phrase "holy mackerel!" is still used today as an expression of surprise and/or astonishment.

Probably not much different from any other young man of the time, I envied the life of rock 'n' roll stars. Back on the farm, I *really* wanted to learn how to play a guitar, but there was little opportunity or encouragement to do so.

Considering the time and commitment required to be a proficient player, I started late in life for such a venture, but I decided to try anyway. My logic was simple: if learning how to play six strings is hard, then learning to play four strings is probably a third less hard. So, with guarded confidence, I bought a bass.

At the time, one of the guys I lived with played a six-string and another roommate played drums. I now owned a bass, with nowhere to go but up. We had a band.

The lead guitarist taught me how to recognize his finger configurations for all the chords. He then showed me on the bass the corresponding note locations. He played a "G" chord, and I plucked the "G" note. Since most of the early rock 'n' roll and country rock songs were three chord progressions, I only had to learn three notes per song.

Boom, boom, boom (A-A-A), boom, boom (D-D), boom, boom (G-G), boom, boom (D-D), boom (G), boom, boom, boom (A-A-A). "Hey, let's put words to it." *Louie, Louie, oh no, me got to go.* "Wait, wait. I have another." *G-l-o-r-i-a, Gloria, G-l-o-r-i-a, Gloria.* **"Holy mackerel!"**

My theatrical gyrations (resembling someone with an inner ear infection), combined with my facial expressions (which could humble a mime), were something to behold, but we actually started to get bookings in the Fargo/Moorhead area. Soon, we earned just about enough money to pay the bills.

Once acquainted with the location of the primary notes, I began to work on scales and note relationships. In my case, the best part about evolving as a bass player was that I could do it while performing in the background because the focal point of most garage bands is the lead guitarist and singer. The bassist only stands out if they are good.

I played in several bands from that point on: "Fur" (we played fuzzy guitars), "Higher You Fly, The Much," "Clown," "Boogey Man," "Hard

Road," etc. Some good, some not so good, but over time, I became a proficient bass player. Eventually, our territory expanded to include North and South Dakota, Minnesota, Iowa, and Manitoba, Canada. Be careful what you ask for! I eventually played five, six, and sometimes seven nights a week in nightclubs, dance halls, VFWs, homecomings, proms, etc.

The luster of being a musician/entertainer began to wear off. I started to think about going back to school, but I also began thinking about doing a stint in the military. If I joined the military, I could move out of the North Country (God bless those of you who stayed) and have the rest of my degree paid for through the GI Bill. I finally decided to make the fateful plunge and join the Navy on a one-year delayed enlistment program, giving me just enough time to get into the right state of mind while still doing what I enjoyed.

Since I no longer pursued a career in music, I was not motivated to hook up with a band long term. I simply listed my name with the local musicians' union and filled in for bands needing a bass player.

During one of these last-minute gigs, I met three guys who were starting up a country rock band called "The Midnight Cowboys" or, as I called the group, "The Midnight Ca-boys." The lead guitar player had a PhD in mathematics and was head of the math department at Moorhead State. The rhythm player and lead singer was an English teacher, and the drummer, a high school student, was the son of the lead guitarist (one of the better drummers I ever played with, by the way).

We played together for one evening in a small honky-tonk, and a week later, they called me to fill in again. After the second engagement, they sat me down and showed me contracts extending through the entire next year and asked if I was interested in becoming a permanent member. I decided job security was worth it, so I joined the group.

Had I decided to stay in the music business, it probably would have provided a lifelong career, but fortunately, I had a couple new band members as examples of what kind of life two careers could provide. Confident, I decided to spend four years in the Navy, finish my degree, get out, and become a teacher who played in a band on the weekends.

A year later, I left the band. I never looked back.

Muscle Memories

Steve

"Education is what remains after one has forgotten what one has learned in school."

—Albert Einstein

Nautical Notables:

Under the Weather: The top deck of the ship is referred to as the weather deck. If a sailor became ill, he was sent below the weather deck; thus, an ill sailor was said to be "under the weather." Alternatively, watch standers on the windward side of the bow of a ship were exposed to wind, weather, and waves. When exposed, they were said to be "under the weather." They were often soaked and became ill and even died.

Tide Over: In the absence of wind, sailing ships could move with the tide. Such a maneuver would "tide the ship over" until the wind returned. Today, it means to acquire a small bit of something (often money, as in borrowing some money to tide you over till payday).

Around the time I turned twelve, Dad began taking me with him on some of his construction jobs, where I earned extra money as a general laborer, sweeping floors and picking up the construction debris. It was real money, good money—and it also constituted quality time with Dad. I became privy to adult conversations and practical jokes, making this boy feel more like a man.

Eventually, the union reps clued in, and my tenure ended. I didn't appreciate it at the time, but I understand it now. Grown-ups need to make a living, and I was taking someone else's job.

In addition to working with Dad on jobs both at home and away, I spent my summers walking beans, picking rocks, and baling hay. Walking beans is pretty much what it sounds like: we walked through rows of soybeans, in seemingly endless fields, pulling weeds as we went. Often, the farmer stood on top of a hill or in some other location where he could observe the entire field; if we missed one, he pointed it out.

Once, while riding down the road in a car, I was gazing at bean fields. Out of habit, I noticed some milkweeds growing in a field and pointed it out to my brother-in-law, who was driving. He asked if I wanted him to stop, and we laughed profusely. What I didn't realize was how my ability to find a milkweed in a soybean field from a moving car speeding down a highway would serve me in a combat zone nearly three decades later.

Picking rocks was by far my least favorite endeavor. It involved walking through plowed fields with five-gallon buckets and filling them with rocks the size of a fist or larger, which could damage a combine if ingested. Once the buckets were full, we lugged them to a flatbed hay wagon and dumped them. We repeated the process until the fields were cleared. Next, we rode the wagon to a central dumping location, usually along a fence line, and manually unloaded the rocks one at a time. The entire process proved about as intellectually stimulating as counting sand, but it helped build fortitude and grit, while simultaneously lining my pockets.

My favorite job was baling hay. There is something about the smell of alfalfa, as well as the fact that the job requires not just brute force, but also a minimal level of skill. Although the days were long and hot, the endeavor was somewhat enjoyable.

I remember one day being in the loft of a barn stacking bales as they came off the elevator, with a nearly constant stream of sweat running off my nose. On another occasion, I suffered heat stroke, though neither I nor the farmer knew what was happening or what to do about it. I recovered and went on working, albeit feeling a bit **under the weather**. We had no idea such a condition could be life-threatening.

I built a reputation for being a hard worker and one of the best hay bale throwers around. It was a good situation; I was never short of work.

Walking beans paid $1 per hour, and during all of those summer endeavors, I don't recall ever being paid more than $2 per hour. For a young man with a paycheck for the first time, however, it seemed like a fortune. It served quite well to **tide me over**.

Part II

Frontal Lobe Development

Ron's graduation from Navy boot camp at the Naval Recruit Training Center (NRTC) San Diego (1975).

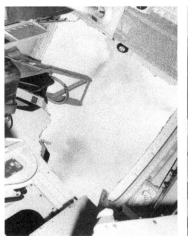

A basket slap and subsequent explosive jettison of Ron's canopy while conducting in-flight refueling off the coast of San Diego (June 1977).

Only Dogs Could Hear Me

Anti-Submarine Warfare Operator Second Class (AW2) Ron Lambrecht

"If you're faced with a forced landing, fly the thing as far into the crash as possible."

—BOB HOOVER

Nautical Notables:

Boot Camp: During the Spanish-American War, Sailors wore leggings called boots, which came to mean a Navy (or Marine) recruit. These recruits trained in boot camps.

Windfall: A rush of wind from the high land; a stroke of good luck.

Before the Mast: Literally, the position of the crew whose living quarters on board were in the forecastle (the section of a ship forward of the foremast). The term is also used more generally to compare seamen with Officers, in phrases such as "he sailed before the mast."

Hunky-Dory: This term, meaning everything is okay, was named after a street called "Honki-Dori" in Yokohama, Japan. Since the inhabitants of this street catered to the pleasures of Sailors, it is easy to understand why the street's name became synonymous for anything that is enjoyable or at least satisfactory. The logical follow-on is "Okey-dokey."

Being enlisted in **boot camp** at the age of twenty six and a half was a challenge, not physically but mentally. The average age of my fellow booters was eighteen, and for most of them, it was their first time away from home. Let's just say I couldn't relate.

Those of us who played an instrument or sang—or were members of a Crack Rifle Team or a Drummer Brigade in our prior lives—were directed to identify ourselves on the first day of boot camp. As a result, I ended up in the Blue Jacket Choir, a recruit choir that performed at various events around San Diego and on graduation days. This choir proved to be a **windfall** because I was then assigned to a Special Company, where life was *much* easier (relatively speaking). From this point, my life began to come into focus; my days on the farm were germane to this life of structure and discipline.

I was quite successful while in the enlisted ranks, receiving an accelerated promotion to Third Class Petty Officer out of "A" school (school to train Sailors in their selected career fields). As a result, I received eighteen months' credit toward time-in-service. Since there was a two-year service requirement between pay grades, this made me eligible to take the Second-Class test six months after the day I made Third. I passed the test, so fifteen months after entering boot camp as a recruit E-1, I became a Second Class (E-5) Petty Officer.

Although my permanent residence was located **before the mast**, I was now off of the business end of a mop! I became an Anti-Submarine Warfare Operator (AW) and was assigned to fly as a crewman in the Lockheed Martin S-3A Viking.

The S-3 is configured for four crewmen (pilot, co-pilot, Tactical Coordinator (TACCO), and an AW), but the AW is the only enlisted member of the crew; the other three crewmen are Officers. I worked closely with the Officers since we depended on each other during emergencies. Though it was somewhat dangerous, flying off of aircraft carriers was in keeping with my sense of adventure.

Everyone in the plane was at the mercy of the pilot's good judgment, and I discovered on multiple occasions that pilots are humans too. For instance, to remain qualified for in-flight refueling, pilots were required to perform the maneuver a minimum of seven times in a six-month period. Since the S-3 had large internal fuel tanks and was a subsonic aircraft, the plane could stay airborne in excess of three hours without the need to refuel. Consequently, pilots grew rusty between deployments, as opportunities to refuel were almost nonexistent.

When pilots reached five months and twenty-nine days without an opportunity to practice refueling, the squadron's Operations Department scheduled a flight with a training tanker to requalify the pilots. The pilots executed the maneuver, connecting the plane's refueling probe to the fueling basket in seven quick successions, requalifying them for another five months and twenty-nine days. They may have been certified, but they were not necessarily proficient.

One afternoon, we conducted this very exercise twenty miles off the coast of San Diego at 20,000 feet altitude in an oval pattern. You may have seen planes refueling in movies, gracefully flying in formation, but I assure you that depiction is deceiving. The refueling probe on an S-3 extends from a hatch directly above the windscreen (front canopy). Because the nose of an S-3 is blunt, with a windscreen that is somewhat vertical, the pilot must use an aggressive closure rate, or the basket rides up on air flowing over the top of the plane, causing a miss in the connection. The second plane is flying through the jet wash from the first plane, so the ride is bumpy—very bumpy.

We successfully connected with the basket three times when the tanker began to make its turn to head in the opposite direction. The pilot decided to go for a connection while in the turn. After all, what could *possibly* go wrong?

We hit the side of the basket, missing the connection. Due to the aggressive closure rate, we continued to close until we were directly under the tanker with approximately fifteen to twenty vertical feet separating the two aircraft. A long length of refueling hose loosely dangled between us, and we still did not have a connection with the basket.

Things can happen quickly at 250 miles per hour! The basket slipped off of the probe, hit the engine on the left side (my side) of the plane, oscillated up, and came down in a "crack the whip" fashion, hitting the wing. It then re-oscillated and came down on my canopy, causing it to explode.

The pitch of my voice was so high only dogs could hear me! There are only two ways the canopy can be functionally separated from the aircraft in flight: if the AW pulls the ejection handle or if a pilot/co-pilot pulls the ejection handle. Well, I didn't pull the handle, so that only left one other option in my mind's eye.

I fully expected my carcass to be implanted in the belly of the tanker flying above us. Alternatively, if luck was on my side, I'd be hanging in my parachute on my way back to Earth. I realized I prefer to be in control of my own destiny, like I was while racing stock cars and tractors, but neither of my expected outcomes occurred.

Things weren't **hunky-dory** at this point, but I got to see all kinds of interesting things. First, the cockpit is pressurized to within 5,000 feet of actual altitude, causing everything that wasn't tied down to make a run for the exit, which happened to be above my head. Second, the pilot made a quick inverted roll in order to expedite separation from the tanker and transit to a low-level altitude, which gave me an unencumbered, panoramic front-row view of the surrounding environment and the ocean below.

The remainder of the flight back to base was uneventful, with the exception of the wind causing my lips to beat my ears to death. I suspect the pilot rehearsed his description of events for what would be a humbling moment of accountability in front of the Skipper.

I thought I was living on the edge in high school, riding the railroad tracks in my '60 Chevy, but I definitely graduated to the big leagues of excitement on this particular day. Through this experience, I learned a thing or two about how to communicate under pressure: voice inflection is important but must be governed in order to be effective.

Steve and Dad (Mel) perched on the bow of the USS Kitty Hawk. Photo credit: Ron Lambrecht (1981).

Rudder Shift

Steve

"[Mistakes] are like knives, that either serve us or cut us, as we grasp them by the blade or the handle."

—James Russell Lowell

Nautical Notables:

Mother: Term of endearment used by Sailors in reference to the aircraft carrier.

Head on a Swivel: Keeping your eyes peeled in all directions for threats, such as an enemy aircraft or other dangers inherent to flying.

Vulture's Row: A catwalk on an aircraft carrier's superstructure (island), which doubles as a viewing gallery for the observation of flight deck operations. Name intended to invoke an image of the macabre.

Shift Your Rudder: A command given to the helmsman (person steering a ship) to immediately move the rudder from the current position to an equal position in the opposite direction. For example, from ten degrees right to ten degrees left.

Aeronautical Notable:

Rudder Hardover: A situation where an aircraft's rudder has been deflected significantly enough to cause the aircraft to lose control in flight.

Two pivotal things happened when I was fourteen years old that changed my trajectory forever.

First, Ron invited Dad and me on a Tiger Cruise. Only men served on ships in those days, and male family members of the ship's company could sail for six days on the *USS Kitty Hawk*, an aircraft carrier, from Hawaii to San Diego. We went.

As part of the journey, we got to travel to Hawaii, and for the first time in my life, I flew in an airplane. I burned a whole roll of 35mm film taking pictures of clouds. *What a new, interesting, and unique perspective!*

Then there was Hawaii. Exotic. Sunny. The ocean. Beaches. We were there for one day and one night while we awaited the arrival of the *USS Kitty Hawk.*

The Tiger Cruise itself was unimaginable. I don't remember many details of when the ship arrived, or even the initial boarding, but I have a clear memory of so many other things about the experience. The ship was vast. *Huge.* It had a labyrinth of corridors, ladders (stairs), and knee-knockers (structural supports throughout the ship, which require the traveler to step over or risk knocking shins and knees into solid steel).

Like the smell of the furnace room in The Club where I slept as a young child, the smell of aircraft carriers sticks with me, even today. It is hard to describe, but it seems to be a combination of steam, lubricants, and greasy cheeseburgers. The steam smell is the product of the catapults, which launch aircraft off the carrier, and also the boilers, which are part of the propulsion system. The lubricants consist of innumerable variations of oil and grease used for all the many mechanical purposes on board a floating city of war. Finally, the greasy burger smell emanates from the galleys, where chow is prepared virtually 24/7 to accommodate the ship's crew, who likewise work 24/7. Like New York City, a ship at sea never sleeps.

Those smells—or more correctly, that combination of smells—are like no others in the world. On this occasion, and many that followed, that smell became familiar and oddly comforting. To the inhaler, it represents the relative safety of being aboard **Mother**.

As we got underway, the sense of anticipation overwhelmed me; being on the behemoth *Kitty Hawk* as she set sail was awe-inspiring. The open ocean stretched in front of us, while the land behind us shrank first into insignificance, then finally into nonexistence. I felt fearful, excited, and safe, all at the same time.

The open ocean reflected a beautiful vibrant blue by day. At night, the ship's propellers churned up the aquatic sea life, invoking a green glow of bioluminescence. Dolphins chased the bow waves, and flying fish scattered before us. The carrier battle group, consisting of around a dozen ships and submarines, surrounded us in a blanket of protection and deterrence that no other nation has mustered to date.

Despite the relative security of the battle group, with all of the activities taking place, there were still a hundred ways to die. Keeping one's **head on a swivel** was a must.

Excitement filled our days. The other ships in the battle group performed a firepower demonstration; each took its turn coming alongside, firing its guns, and steaming away with music blasting over its loudspeakers. An underway replenishment (UNREP) demonstration followed. Resupply ships came alongside, cast lines and fuel hoses over to the carrier, and transferred supplies and fuel to us. Simultaneously, helicopters transported material by air from the surrounding tenders (supply ships) to our decks—all of this while steaming ahead through the waters!

The Marines on the fantail (the aft end of the flight deck, where I fired an M-16 rifle for the first time) provided another demonstration of firepower. In addition, a boxing smoker allowed members of the crew to gear up and challenge each other to boxing matches. These experiences resonated with this young country boy, who fought the Battle of Lake Shaokatan, who grew up hunting, and whose dad taught him to box.

But the most spectacular event of all was flight operations. Every aircraft in the United States Navy's carrier inventory launched from the *Kitty Hawk's* deck: E-2 Skyhawk early warning RADAR aircraft, F-8 Crusader fighters, A-7 Corsair II and A-3 Skywarrior attack aircraft, S-3 Viking anti-submarine sub hunters, F-14 Tomcats (later made famous by the movie *Top Gun*), SH-3 Sea King helicopters, and finally, F/A-18 Hornets, the newest addition to the arsenal. We watched the launches and recoveries from **Vulture's Row** on the large superstructure that protrudes above the flight deck. We also observed from the catwalks surrounding the ship, which gave us an eye-level view of the catapult launches.

Being mere feet away from fighter aircraft catapulting off the ship while in full afterburner astounded me. The engineering, daring, and prowess were beyond description. I no longer had any question about what I wanted to do with my life—I would be a Naval Aviator—a Navy Fighter Pilot, to be exact—and nothing was going to stop me!

* * *

The second pivotal moment that changed the trajectory of my life happened when I walked back into shop class after the summer break.

One year prior, upon entering his classroom for the first time, the teacher immediately pointed to me and yelled, "You! Front of the classroom! Sit up here where I can keep an eye on you." My reputation had preceded me.

At the start of my freshman year, however, having returned from my life-changing experience on the *USS Kitty Hawk*, things took a different tone. Mr. Colman had served in Vietnam and was now in the Navy Reserves, and having heard about my experience, he asked me, "Do you want to go to the Naval Academy?"

I had no earthly idea what the Naval Academy was. None. But the mere sound of it resonated nicely in my ears. I immediately replied, "Yes!"

Heretofore, I had been flying with my **rudder hardover**, on a collision course with disaster, but over the next three-and-a-half years, Ron, my teachers, my guidance counselor, and several others shaped, groomed, coached, and helped me become something altogether different from what my first fourteen years foretold. It was time to **shift my rudder**, find a new course, and sail for uncharted seas.

Ron is pictured seated in the S-3A SENSO seat, in his full flight equipment prior to flight.

Outstanding performance in the AW "A" school, Millington, Tennessee, led to accelerated advancement to Third Class Petty Officer (E-4). Six months later, Ron took and passed the Second-Class exam, becoming a Second Class Petty Officer fifteen months from the time he entered boot camp (December 1976).

Pull Up! Pull UP! PULL UUUUUUPPP!

AW2 Ron Lambrecht

S-3A SENSO

"Fight on and fly on to the last drop of blood and the last drop of fuel, to the last beat of the heart."

—Manfred von Richthofen (The Red Baron)

Nautical Notables:

Bat-turn: A tight, high-G change of heading. A reference to the rapid 180-degree Batmobile maneuver in the original *Batman* television series.

Guns, Guns: Adversary pilot has taken up a tail position where they can simulate a shot using the gun.

Bandit: Airborne adversary positively identified as a bad guy.

Goes Away: What happens to an enemy aircraft when it is shot down.

Naval Air Station (NAS) Fallon, Nevada is the home to the Navy Fighter Weapon School (TOPGUN) and is the United States Navy's premier air-to-air and air-to-ground training facility. Located southeast of the city of Fallon in western Nevada, it consists of 84,000 acres of bombing and electronic warfare ranges.

NAS Fallon is also home to the Naval Strike and Air Warfare Center (NSAWC) and is a facility used to train the entire carrier air wing in combat strike tactics. Each carrier air wing spends a week prior to deployment at NSAWC in order to receive training in strike planning and execution. These missions are conducted on the bombing range, and to add an additional level of excitement, an aggressor squadron is tasked to defend the range.

The S-3A was an anti-submarine warfare aircraft designed to fly low and slow over the ocean in pursuit of submarines. The S-3 was *so* slow, in fact, that it was once quipped that an S-3 encountered a rear-of-the-aircraft bird strike, meaning a bird impacted it from behind because the bird was flying faster than its lumbering man-made counterpart.

Although not designed to fight in air-to-air combat, S-3 pilots were unconvinced. A potential secondary, perhaps tertiary, mission of the S-3 was to perform long-range bombing missions, so we found ourselves in the middle of a strike force, alongside F-14 Tomcats, A-6 Intruders, A-7 Corsairs, and A-5 Vigilante reconnaissance aircraft. The fighter guys loved us because we were easy prey, as the aggressor aircraft focused on us while the attack aircraft performed their primary strike mission.

I have to hand it to the S-3 pilots: they didn't go down without a fight. The S-3 can turn on a dime, much tighter than the A-4 Skyhawk flown at the time by the aggressor squadron. Assuming the S-3 pilot saw the A-4 in time, he could perform extremely tight **bat-turns**, preventing the Skyhawk from taking up a tail **guns**, **guns** position resulting in **goes away**. This tactic required flying a second S-3 along a mountain ridge independent of the strike formation to act as a bird-dog to watch for **Bandits**. Should a Skyhawk be spotted, the co-pilot in the bird-dog aircraft called out compass headings and recommended evasive actions.

On one mission, I was a member of the crew in the primary strike aircraft. We were flying low, very low, and as fast as the S-3 could muster. (A rule of thumb when flying low: if your shadow and aircraft are the same size, you are *too* low!) We were eventually spotted by an aggressor, which rolled in on us to take the simulated shot. Seeing this, the co-pilot in the bird-dog aircraft yelled out over the net: "Pull up! Pull UP! PULL UUUUUUUPPP!"

Apparently, his own pilot thought he was screaming at him! Pulling a few Gs without prior notification causes an interesting inflection in someone's speech pattern. It also creates a lot of giggling and harassing by others on the net, so you have to re-establish your credibility by buying multiple rounds at the Tailhook Bar when you return to base.

Although we trained as a four-man crew in the S-3 training pipeline, I became a free agent when my pilot chose to resign his commission prior to deployment. Without a crew, I was the first alternate when another AW was either outside his crew rest schedule, sick in quarters, or wasn't able to fly for a multitude of other reasons.

During the two years after I had qualified in the aircraft and earned my aircrew wings, I accumulated 400 flight hours and fifty catapults and arrested landings, which was an impressive tally for an S-3 qualified AW. Spending that amount of time working with Officers and gaining their respect, I began to realize that a commission as a Naval Officer was not beyond my grasp. So, I decided to go back to school in pursuit of the all-elusive degree.

The age limit to become a pilot was twenty-seven, so that was not an option. The age limit for getting a commission as a Naval Flight Officer (NFO) or Intelligence Officer, however, was thirty and a half *if* the candidate had prior service, which I did. That gave me approximately two years to finish my degree, apply for Aviation Officer Candidate School (AOCS), be accepted, and then successfully complete the twenty weeks of training in Pensacola, Florida.

One hundred percent focused on the target, I took classes in the evenings and on weekends, testing out of courses where possible. During a six-month Western Pacific deployment on the *USS Enterprise,* I also took courses offered on the carrier. Thanks to the support and recommendations from the Officers I served with at the time, the degree and acceptance into AOCS happened in parallel.

In January 1979, I loaded all of my worldly possessions into my van and headed east to Pensacola, Florida. It is difficult to describe the excitement and apprehension I experienced during the four days on the road from San Diego to Pensacola. The failure rate at AOCS was close to 50 percent, and since I was enlisted, I would go back to the enlisted ranks if I failed.

I mustered every bit of inner confidence and intestinal fortitude I possessed. Focus is a trait I learned when utilizing an outhouse in the Minnesota winters, where paying attention to what matters is paramount. Failure was not an option.

Steve's graduation from Navy boot camp at the Naval Recruit Training Center (NRTC), Great Lakes, Illinois (1984).

Steve and best friend Ben Nielsen saying their goodbyes at the Sioux Falls, South Dakota, regional airport on July 1, 1985.

Formative Experiences

Seaman Recruit Steve Lambrecht

"I'm not afraid of storms, for I'm learning to sail my ship."

—AESCHYLUS

Nautical Notables:

Long Shot: The accuracy of any weapon decreases with increasing range. On old Navy warships, cannon accuracy also varied due to inconsistent gunpowder quality. The odds for success were always greater at short range, thus the desire for ships to close the distance with an enemy before firing their cannons. Taking a long shot has since become synonymous with trying something with a low probability of success.

Three Sheets to the Wind: A sheet is a rope that controls the tension on the downwind side of a square sail. On a three-masted fully rigged ship, if the sheets of the three lowest sails are loose, they are said to be "to the wind." The sails will flap and flutter, and a ship in this condition will flounder and wander aimlessly downwind.

Aeronautical Notable:

Dot: Refers to how a distant aircraft looks on the horizon. "I'm a dot" means "I'm out of here."

After the Tiger Cruise, attending a military service academy seemed like a bit of a **long shot** but, at the same time, achievable. To build a competitive résumé for admission, I needed to participate in as many extracurricular activities and sports as possible.

Watching live music at The Club as a kid, along with listening to the seldom-silent jukebox, got me interested in playing an instrument. All of my elder siblings played some sort of instrument, but it wasn't until the sixth grade that I had the opportunity to learn one. I joined the school band, choosing to learn the drums, and I took to it immediately. My band instructors recognized the knack germinating in a young boy who had spent too many late nights watching professional drummers display their skills in a lakeside bar. Now, with my sights set upon a service academy, I already had one item on my résumé.

However, that was it. Due to the farming and night-club labor requirements levied upon them by my parents, my elder siblings were severely limited with respect to extracurricular activities, and I wasn't faring much better. Ron, well on his way to a successful Navy career at this point, provided the necessary persuasion to my parents.

"If you don't let him participate in these activities, he won't be competitive enough to get into an academy," he said.

They listened. They weren't always happy about it, but they listened.

Dad worked distant construction jobs, and Mom was not a good winter driver. Driving me back and forth to activities put her in danger, as several locals had frozen to death over the years after ending up in ditches during snowstorms. Because the risk was too high, during almost every winter week of the school year, I stayed with my grandmother who lived in Ivanhoe. This allowed me to participate in afterschool activities, such as football, basketball, track, band, and chorus.

During the heart of winter, my grandmother visited my aunt in California, and I was left to stay at my grandmother's house alone, Monday through Friday. I walked to school, which, in Minnesota, made for many face-freezing experiences. My diet consisted of only the finest cuisine an adolescent was capable of creating, namely cream of mushroom and cream of chicken soup, along with grilled cheese sandwiches. With a little money left over from working in the summers, and a bit of extra money from my parents, I added sodas and candy from the local convenience store as necessary dietary staples. In the evenings, I did my homework at the kitchen table and sometimes hung out with my best friend for life, Ben Nielsen. I spent the better part of two winters like this and learned a level of independence and self-sufficiency uncommon among other fourteen- and fifteen-year-olds.

In addition, with farm work at a lull during the winter, the local taverns hosted monthly pool tournaments. Locals congregated to test their skills at shooting stick, and Dad and I were frequent participants. The skills I honed while growing up in a nightclub gave me the ability to provide myself a modest income during the nonagricultural time of year. I didn't win all the tournaments by a long shot, but I did well for myself.

* * *

During my junior year of high school, Mr. Colman suggested I consider enlisting in the Navy Reserves. The Navy offered a program back then called the Sea/Air Mariner program, which was modeled as a split-training program. With parental consent, participants were allowed to enlist at age seventeen. Boot camp occurred during the summer break between a participant's junior and senior year of high school, and the newly trained Sailors drilled as reservists during their senior year. They could then go on to training in a chosen specialty upon graduation.

On April 30, 1984, at the ripe age of seventeen years and one month, I enlisted in the United States Navy. I attended boot camp at Recruit Training Command (RTC) Great Lakes in Illinois and returned to finish high school while attending monthly drills in Sioux Falls, South Dakota. (Sioux Falls is, of course, well known for its enormous naval armada, consisting of small fishing boats trailered in driveways, garages, and barns, since there isn't a significant body of water for many hundreds of miles in any direction.)

So, as a newly minted seventeen-year-old, I traveled to RTC Great Lakes, just north of Chicago, Illinois. Navy boot camp epitomized the classic combination of harassment, fitness, team building, and attention-to-detail-inspiring essentials one should expect in such an experience. There, I received a self-identity-eliminating head shave, the first of three I ultimately experienced.

Screaming Navy Drill Instructors (DIs) greeted me at RTC Great Lakes. I found that marching came easily to me. I learned to march early as part of the high school marching band—and if you recall, the marching experience leading to my disappearance, at age three, through a heat register in our farmhouse.

The rest of the Navy experience was a *simple* matter of memorization, attention to detail, and keeping my nose clean. We learned to fold our clothes without a single crease or dimple in them. We made our beds tight as a drum. We did push-ups and sit-ups until our DIs grew tired of the endeavor. We polished brass for the sake of polishing brass. In front of the barracks stood torpedoes with giant brass nose cones, and we polished them to a perfect shine, until a Chief casually poured a cup of coffee on them, causing the chore to be repeated...daily.

We trained continuously in drill, memorization, and inspections. At the galley (chow hall), those in the back half of the line needed to eat whatever we managed to swallow between the end of the serving line and the beginning of the tray turn-in area, having no time to sit down in between. As time went on, the weakest recruits were weeded out, and we were given more time to eat. At this point, the training shifted to more important items, like standing watch and battling emergencies onboard ships.

The entire gauntlet was time-tested and proven, ensuring only those capable of military life emerged as a Sailor. Individual identity became subordinate to being a member of a team and to serving the country. Details mattered, we were taught, because on a ship, *every* detail matters: leave a hatch open, and the ship can sink. Misplaced tools meant the ship might not be fixed, and we depended on the ship for our lives.

After graduation from boot camp, several of us pooled our money, rented a limo, toured some museums in downtown Chicago, and drank away a good portion of our paychecks in the spirit of "the last check you write should be to the undertaker, and it should bounce." We were **three sheets to the wind**, making the most of our newly obtained freedom.

I returned to Ivanhoe a couple of weeks before the start of the football season and the start of my senior year of high school. During my senior year, I participated in varsity football, basketball, and track. I was also a member of the band, jazz band, choir, and swing choir. I became class president, and I lettered in all my activities.

That year, I had more fun than was probably good for me. I stayed out late with both genders (for different reasons), spending countless hours laughing with friends while consuming adult beverages, which were all too plentiful and readily available in those days. We won the conference championship in football, and I made the All-Conference team as an outside linebacker.

All that hard work on the farms, along with Navy boot camp, paid off. I enjoyed success in musical endeavors, scoring top ratings at the state competition and won positions in All State Band and Chorus. Those endless hours watching musicians at The Club had also paid off.

* * *

I seriously contemplated attending the Air Force Academy (USAFA) instead of the Naval Academy at Annapolis (USNA). The Air Force's F-16 looked like an awesome fighter, and I figured my odds of flying would increase if I went to USAFA instead of USNA. I applied to both, along with the Military Academy at West Point (USMA) in order to keep all my options open.

The process to get into a service academy is thorough, competitive, rigorous, and daunting. Coming from a supremely small town had advantages and disadvantages: I had the opportunity to build a strong résumé of sports, extracurriculars, and student-government activities, but I lacked exposure to calculus and certain activities offered only in larger schools.

The first step toward getting into a service academy was to receive a nomination from either a senator or congressional representative. Nominations were available from other sources as well (such as the President or Vice President, or by being the descendent of a Medal of Honor recipient), but I was about as likely to get one of those as I was to get drafted by the NBA. I also needed letters of recommendation, which, thanks to my aforementioned rudder shift, were forthcoming.

In addition, the admissions process included filling out an extensive application, passing a physical fitness test, and doing well on either the ACT or SAT exams. I was strong in math and science, but the written and spoken word were a different matter. In order to get my verbal score into the competitive range, I took the ACT three times.

In the spring of my senior year of high school, I was accepted to all three academies and was offered a Navy scholarship to MIT. I chose to stick with the Navy because I wanted to sail the world and experience adventure. One thing I knew for certain: I was not going to be a Marine. Marines lived hard, my brother told me, and endured a harsher lifestyle, stationed in more austere environments.

Being the last Lambrecht child to leave the nest, it was a difficult time for my mom, who wept. Dad, meanwhile, wasn't one to show emotion and didn't make an exception on this occasion.

Saying goodbye to my best friend Ben was a different matter. Countless hours of shenanigans, laughter, and bonding made my departure a tearful, solemn affair.

And so, on July 1, 1985, armed with a solid work ethic, a decent education, extracurricular skills, fourteen months of credit toward a military retirement, and a somewhat adjusted attitude, this midwestern country boy was a **dot**.

Ron received a commission as an Ensign in the United States Navy on June 8, 1979, from Aviation Officers Candidate School, Pensacola, Florida.

The Dilbert Dunker begins in the elevated position and, when released, accelerates down the rails, impacts the water, and rolls inverted. In order to pass the test, aspiring pilots must release their straps, exit the device, and reach the surface of the water unassisted. Photo courtesy of DVIDS.

Ticket to the Game

Aviation Officer
Candidate Ron Lambrecht

"A diamond is merely a lump of coal that did well under pressure."

—UNKNOWN

Nautical Notables:

Dogsbodys: The Royal Navy used dried peas and eggs boiled in a bag as one of their staple foods circa the early nineteenth century. Sailors nicknamed this item "dog's body." In the early twentieth century, Junior Officers and Midshipmen who performed jobs that more senior Officers did not want to do began to be called "dogsbodys."

Voluntold: When a subordinate is volunteered into a collateral duty by his superior. "I need a volunteer. You, over there!"

Dismantle: To unrig a vessel and discharge all stores.

Dilbert Dunker: A device for training aviators on how to correctly escape a submerged plane. Though it was invented by Ensign Wilfred Kaneb, an aviation engineer at NAS Pensacola, in 1943-1944, the device has been known since its earliest days as the "Dilbert Dunker" in reference to Dilbert Groundloop, a World War II-era cartoon character.

Naval Intelligence Officer: US Naval Intelligence Officers are responsible for supervising the collection, analysis, and dissemination of information related to an adversary's strengths, weaknesses, capabilities, and intentions. They lead Sailors, oversee the work of Intelligence Specialists, and carry out specific intelligence duties crucial to their command's mission. Sharing this information with high-level military and political decision makers with assessments and recommendations is one of the many high-stress job requirements of the Naval Intelligence Officer.

Made famous by the movie *An Officer and a Gentleman*, Aviation Officer Candidate School, Pensacola, Florida, was not a fun place to be. Though Officer Candidates have the luxury of dropping on request (DOR) at any time during the training pipeline, I entered training with the attitude that my Marine Drill Instructor could kick my butt until he needed new shoes. I wasn't going anywhere without a commission.

As in boot camp, we were canvassed to determine who played a musical instrument. I acknowledged that I played bass guitar, confident that I would never end up in a marching band, but I was assigned to drums! I was not happy. While undertaking twenty weeks of **dogsbodys** fundamentals, I did not need the additional burden of losing precious study time to practice in the band, but I soon discovered my personal concerns were irrelevant when it came to being **voluntold**.

The DI's primary objective was to **dismantle** our civilian concept of what life is like and replace it with military structure and discipline—and they excelled at it. (I am fairly certain Drill Instructor school includes a prerequisite assignment in the dungeons under the Tower of London.) I started with a class of forty-six Officer Candidates, but only twenty-three received commissions. Through ingenuity and creative activities, the DIs motivated the other twenty-three of my fellow candidates to DOR. Performing as a pilot or NFO in a multimillion-dollar plane requires a level of focus, motivation, and aptitude the possession of which training (and weeding out) ensures.

In 1979, all Aviation Intelligence Officers received the same commissioning training as aviators. The purpose was to give us credibility and to earn the aviator's trust; it was important that aviators understood we all had the same level of structure and discipline in earning our commissions. Although we would not be in the plane when they went into combat, we were instrumental in the planning of the mission.

All Officer Candidates arrived with a college degree and a higher level of maturity than what I experienced in enlisted boot camp. Hence, there was an expectation among the DIs and Officers assigned over us that we possessed an above-average standard of ambition, academic performance, and practical understanding of life until, of course, we proved otherwise.

We did so on multiple occasions, but we learned from our mistakes.

* * *

Although I grew up in Minnesota, land of 10,000 lakes, and spent summer evenings with my neighbor friends at the local swimming hole, I was not a strong swimmer. For Naval Aviators flying over vast expanses of ocean and beyond the range of land, an ability to swim was an absolute survival essential.

We all had to prove our prowess in the water, and I failed. Magnificently. My training was put on hold, and I was given two weeks to become a proficient swimmer. If I didn't, it was game over.

X-Company was a holding pen for Officer Candidates experiencing medical problems, academic deficiencies, administrative issues (such as obtaining a security clearance), or for some of us, enrollment in "stupid swim." Finding myself in yet another crash course where failure was not an option, I spent six to eight hours a day in the pool.

Requirements included swimming a mile in a flight suit; drownproofing (floating face down in the water, lying motionless except to lift your head for a breath of air) for thirty minutes; and swimming the length of an Olympic size pool underwater (coming up for air only twice, simulating clearing water that had burning oil floating on the surface). We were also taught to tread water for thirty minutes, first with our hands out of the water, then using all our limbs.

One of the more challenging tests included a ride strapped to an ejection seat (**Dilbert Dunker**), which free fell down a rail into the water and then flipped over. We were required to stay strapped to the Dunker until an underwater swimmer signaled for us to release ourselves. Then we swam to the surface.

My SEAL friends will laugh at this part of the story, but this was serious stuff for me to master in two weeks. Thanks to the level of endurance I learned as a youth in the milking parlor, I did.

* * *

Once back in a regular company, the fun really began. Drill Instructors are superhuman: physical fitness events (such as cross-country runs, stints through the obstacle courses, double-time marching, etc.) were usually performed alongside us, except they ran backwards.

Our Drill Instructor had just returned from thirty days of probation after a confrontation he had with an Officer Candidate in his previous company. Drill Instructors are not allowed to strike an Officer Candidate, but apparently, he came close (or did). The incident was reviewed and eventually dismissed, but the story got our attention!

As training progressed, I discovered marching band might save me after all. If the drum hung around my neck, the DI couldn't mess with me.

Every other Friday was commissioning day for a class of Officers, so the Thursday before the ceremony, all of the companies of Officer Candidates spent two hours on the parade field practicing close-order drill (marching). It was two hours of sheer hell, as the DIs used this period as an opportunity to test the mettle of their respective Officer Candidates. I had the pleasure of observing the chaos from a safe distance, holding my drum while concealing a smile.

A Candidate in my company, Bogenov, grew up in San Diego as a surfer boy and possessed all the charisma and self-confidence required to be a jet-jock. The problem was Bogenov couldn't march to save his soul—or the souls of those around him. Jumping jacks, push-ups, burpees, and lengthy runs around the parade field with his 9.6-pound M1 rifle held above his head didn't seem to help improve his marching skills, although the DI was sure it would.

One fine Thursday morning late in our training regimen, I noticed the DI observing Bogenov still marching out of step from the rest of the company. This went on for about two minutes, and then the DI threw his hat on the ground. In perfect DI-speak, he yelled, "BOGENOV!"

This was followed by an immediate, "YES SIR!"

"SEE THAT PIGEON?" A pigeon was walking across the parade field.

Bogenov replied, "YES SIR!"

The Drill Instructor said, "BRING IT HERE!"

Bogenov fell out of formation and started running after the pigeon, which immediately flew away. That did not matter. The order was to bring the pigeon to the DI, so unless Bogenov could come up with a set of wings of his own, he was about to set out on an interesting mission.

Approximately fifteen minutes passed before our DI noticed a hole in the ranks of his company. "FILL THAT HOLE, CANDIDATE. WHAT IS THE HOLE THERE FOR?"

Someone mentioned Bogenov's name.

"Oh *shit*, where's Bogenov?"

We finally saw him disappearing over the horizon, presumably heading for a local grocery store to buy a Cornish hen.

* * *

Our own commissioning day was a proud day, indeed. Just as our company did throughout training, all of the underclassmen participated in the ceremony. We marched, including Bogenov, onto the Pensacola parade field with our single gold stripe on our shoulder boards, each of us hoping to serve as an inspiration to the Officer Candidates behind us still engaged in the rigors of training. Moms, dads, wives, family members, and girlfriends were in the bleachers sharing in our excitement.

A lot of emotion was experienced that day, both in the bleachers and on the parade field, but though I felt the significance of the day, I had no sense of the gravity it had for others. I was not raised to think that way. It never occurred to me to invite my parents to the commissioning ceremony because it was a challenge I took on independently. Should I succeed or fail, it was my burden alone.

After the formal ceremony, each of us newly commissioned Ensigns walked in turn along a narrow path, where our Drill Instructor stood at attention. In a very humbling ritual, he became the first enlisted man to salute us. In that moment, I could not help but reflect back on my days as a young farm boy observing the Marine Officer looking down on me from the billboard as our family made biannual trips to Marshall. I wondered if that Marine somehow provided me with the subliminal drive leading to this day.

With the ceremony completed, I headed to Minnesota. Having just finished a Western Pacific deployment prior to AOCS, I had some leave (vacation time) on the books. My class convening date for intelligence school in Colorado was in thirty days, so I decided to spend the downtime with my parents.

After three days on the road, I arrived late one evening, tired but glad to be home. The homecoming I experienced was totally unexpected; I never saw Dad so proud. In my thirty years, he never once patted me on the back, but he did so no less than six times that evening.

Dad was drafted near the end of WWII and became an Army E-4 Corporal during his two-year enlistment. His experience in the Army was typical of an enlisted man drafted during time of war: it was ingrained in him to obey, without question, the orders of the Officers assigned over him. They were authority figures whose orders were never to be questioned.

As I write this, it occurs to me that Dad—and those like him, with little or no formal education or military training other than boot camp and basic infantry—was totally dependent on the decisions made by their

Officers. So, there I was, his son and the oldest in the family, achieving a level of import never previously experienced within the Lambrecht heritage. It set the stage for more to come.

* * *

The Air Force's and Navy's intelligence schools in 1979 were co-located in Aurora, Colorado. When class convened, the school day started at 0600 and usually began with a quiz. In order to study for the quiz, we had to be at the classified library by 0500, so our day usually began with a 0400 wake-up call.

Classroom instruction ended at 1200 (noon), and we then had the rest of the day and evening until 2200 (10:00 p.m.) to do our research and studying in the classified library. We were required to memorize laundry lists of Soviet weapon systems, including ranges, flight profiles, associated RADARs, etc. We were required to recognize all of the Soviet aircraft, ships, and submarines. We needed to have a good understanding of geography as it applied to military operations, and we needed to be proficient briefers of the information.

Needless to say, the school kept us out of the bars, certainly during the week. I learned to make promises to myself, think positively, and then create the conditions that led to favorable outcomes. Twenty-three weeks later, after being fed through a firehose, I was a **Naval Intelligence Officer**.

Canoe U

Midshipman Fourth Class Steve Lambrecht

"I refuse to answer that question on the grounds that I don't know the answer."

—Douglas Adams

Nautical Notables:

Canoe U: Pet name given to USNA by Midshipmen. It is short for "Canoe University."

The Yard: The entire grounds of USNA.

USNA: Acronym pronounced "OOOS-nay." The official title is "The United States Naval Academy," but the acronym is always used alone, without "The" as a preface.

The first time I saw the Naval Academy in person was from the back-seat of Captain (Retired) Bill Morrow's car, the day before Induction Day. Induction Day (or "I Day," for short), is the first day of a Naval Academy freshman's adventure. It was July 1, 1985.

Bill and his gem of a wife, Nancy, picked me up at BWI Airport and took me directly to see the Academy before proceeding to their home in Annapolis. As we crested the hill on Route 450 heading south-bound, the **Yard** sprang suddenly into view. I was in awe. The ornate and expansive granite buildings, adorned with green copper roofs, exuded a level of importance I had never before beheld.

The place looked simultaneously inspiring and intimidating. Butter-flies danced in my stomach as I contemplated the enormity and magnificence of it, along with the daunting prospect of what I had gotten myself into.

Bill, Ron's father-in-law, retired as a Captain after serving thirty years in the Navy, having graduated from **USNA** in 1941. Bill's class was supposed to graduate in 1942, but their graduation was moved up to December of 1941 due to the bombing of Pearl Harbor. Raised in the Navy while WWII was raging, Bill also served during the Korean War and the Cold War era. Throughout his career, he commanded the *USS Meredith (DD-890)*, *USS Frontier (AD-25)*, Destroyer Division 153 (the Navy's first guided missile division), and Destroyer Squadron 22. He had a distinguished odyssey, to be certain.

Bill was old-school, coming from a time when the Captain was God and ruled with an iron fist. He had a soft, pleasant inside, but one would never know it while he toured me around the Yard. Driving through the streets, he named hall after hall, providing the history of the distinguished Officer or noteworthy person for whom it was named. Names such as Nimitz, Halsey, Rickover, Mahan, Dewey, and others rolled off his tongue like one would expect from a professor of naval history.

I was astounded at how he knew so much about each building and monument, even though he had graduated so long ago. After he told me about Rickover Hall, the details of which had escaped me, I asked Bill, "Who was that one named after again?"

He gruffly and aptly responded, "You'll know it soon enough." Such knowledge, I soon learned, would become ingrained into my own brain for all of eternity. The Naval Academy required memorization and regurgitation, ad nauseam.

Plebe Ho!

Midshipman Fourth Class
Steve Lambrecht

"Father Time has no sense of humor."

—STEVE LAMBRECHT

Nautical Notables:

Plebe: A freshman at the Naval Academy. Short for "plebeian." A plebeian was an uneducated or uncultured member of the lower class of Roman citizens.

Come-Around: The term used to describe an oral quiz session visited on a Plebe by an upper-class member. The Plebe reports to the upper-class member for the occasion, thus the term "come-around."

Wash Out: To be removed from any military training program due to poor performance.

Plebe Ho: A command, shouted by an upper-class member, ordering all Plebes assigned as subordinates to chop smartly out of their rooms and assume the position of attention against the bulkhead.

Chop: To run while at the position of attention, staring straight ahead and raising the knees high enough that the thigh becomes parallel with the deck.

Bulkhead: The nautical term for a wall.

Deck: Floor or ground.

Filled with excitement and trepidation, I barely slept at Bill and Nancy's house the night before I reported to the Naval Academy. The next day, Bill delivered me to Halsey Field House for induction into the Brigade of Midshipmen, where I joined my 1,374 classmates.

We spent our morning being ushered from place to place, being issued uniforms and physical fitness gear, and changing our clothes into the same. Ask anyone who has ever served in the military if they remember any smells from their first day, and they will likely tell you they remember the smell of the new uniforms they were issued; it is a unique and memorable smell.

We were issued two types of uniforms on day one: our physical fitness uniforms and our White Works. White Works is a white uniform designed to look like the traditional Cracker Jack uniform worn by enlisted Sailors. It is topped off with a white Dixie Cup hat, encircled with a blue ring, making the wearer readily identifiable as a Midshipman. After receiving our uniforms, we moved on to the barber shop for, you guessed it, a self-identity-eliminating head-shave, the second of my military career.

The whirlwind day, full of events too numerous to recall—and augmented by plenty of yelling and stress-inducing activities—culminated in the famous "Swearing In." The entire class formed up in uniform, for the first time, to take the Oath of Office. Parents, who saw their child off at Halsey Field House, beheld them again several hours later, groomed, in uniform and in formation, with their right hands in the air.

We swore allegiance to the Constitution and to support and defend our nation against all enemies, foreign and domestic. Parents wept. Mine could not afford to make the journey from Minnesota.

* * *

Time management, stress management, and attention to detail: these are the three overarching lessons learned during **Plebe** Summer. Each one feeds on the other; each is crucial to success, whether managing the day at USNA or while under fire from the enemy in a battle yet to be waged. I was grateful for having experienced boot camp prior to the trials of Plebe Summer.

During any whisper of time not otherwise dedicated (be it standing in line for a haircut, shots, or chow), a Plebe is expected to have their *Reef Points* in front of their face and held smartly at eye level. *Reef Points* is the Plebe's book of knowledge and, when not in use, is hung over the front of the White Works trousers. It contains every meaningful piece of naval history, particularly as it applies to the Yard. Building names and monuments, military platforms employed by the United States, history, tradition, rank structures...all have to be committed to memory by every Plebe. Also inside the book's timeless pages are *The Laws of the Navy*: twenty-seven four-line stanzas of important lessons, woven into poetry, written by retired Royal Navy Admiral R.A. Hopwood in 1896.

Collectively, these mandatory memory items are referred to as "rates." Every Plebe has to know their rates.

Oral interrogations by taskmasters (First Class Midshipmen) occur at mealtimes, **come-arounds**, and various other times of opportunity. Knowledge and ability to perform under pressure are continuously tested and evaluated, but this is not intended as harassment for harassment's sake. It serves a very important purpose.

During one's entire time at the Academy, and during much of one's time in the service, the total number of tasks assigned almost always exceeds the time available to accomplish them. By heaping mountains of tasks upon us, we learned to prioritize and to accomplish each one as efficiently as humanly possible. Lack of ability to meet the minimum level of accomplishment results in failure and being **washed out**.

A typical day of Plebe Summer begins with a wake up at 0530, followed by a trip to the athletic fields for the Physical Education Program from 0600 to 0730. After a quick shower and room cleanup, morning meal formation occurs at 0810, followed by breakfast, during which oral interrogations are continuous. After morning meal, the rest of the day is filled with a dizzying array of activities, including classes on sailing, swimming, obstacle courses, weapons qualification, naval history, seamanship and navigation, character development, uniform fittings, formation, marching, haircuts, medical examinations, etiquette, and dozens of other requirements. These activities are only interrupted by noon and evening meal formations—and the corresponding meals/ interrogations. The evenings are filled with drill, lectures, inspections, and more interrogations.

Because too much is never enough, additional stress is heaped on in the form of stern condemnation and even being written up (or "fried") for a conduct offense. The result is demerits and the marching of tours.

Marching tours involves mustering for a uniform inspection, followed by marching back and forth across a terrace with a rifle. Each tour lasts thirty minutes, which gives you even less time to memorize rates, digging you even further into a hole.

More stress is added in the form of uniform races. Uniform races consist of upperclassmen demanding Plebes change into one of multiple regulation uniforms within a strict time limit. First the time is set at two minutes. Then one minute. Then thirty seconds. Each uniform change ends with a uniform inspection and a room inspection to ensure proper uniform compliance and the proper stowing of all clothing in designated locations. All of this serves to increase efficiency and prepare Plebes for performance under pressure. It also instills an attention to detail inherent in the process.

Our Platoon Commander was Midshipman First Class Greg Glaros. Midshipman First Class Glaros stood approximately 5' 11" and was a lean, wiry 165 or so pounds, with jet black hair and olive skin. He embodied a creature best described as a combination of Tasmanian devil, honey badger, and vampire bat. His eyes, the gaze from which could melt a candle from twenty paces, were dark enough to absorb both light and hope. His uniform appeared to be painted directly onto his skin. Never a wrinkle, speck of dust, nor atom of tarnished brass was tolerated on him or any of his Plebes. Despite the hard tile floors in the rooms and hallways, and the hard-soled uniform shoes we all wore, he had the uncanny ability to appear, undetected, inches behind an unsuspecting Plebe, at will.

The mere thought of him terrified us. A military machine, Glaros excelled at creating other military machines. He haunted our days and was the Academy Award–winning star of our nightmares.

"PLEBE HO! Plebe ho, plebe ho, plebe ho, plebe ho, PLEBE HO!" Glaros yelled.

As rapidly as possible, yet somehow never quickly enough, we scrambled to the hallways outside our rooms. We first **chopped** to the center of the hallway, then squared the corner and returned to our designated place of interrogation, the **bulkhead**. We stood at the position of attention. It was time for the reckoning.

Randomly, Glaros called upon individuals of our thirty-something member platoon of Plebes, and the grilling began. "Look at your classmate! Who is this? Where is she from?" Each Plebe is expected to know the name and hometown of every Plebe in the platoon, to build classmate loyalty. Plebes are expected to pull their own weight as individuals, but also to work as a team. Teamwork was required if we were to survive the Glaros Armageddon.

Each Plebe is also required to memorize the menu for the upcoming two meals ("chow"). A Plebe assigned to Chow Call appears on a square metallic tile at the position of attention, ready to make their Chow Call by the time the second hand reaches the assigned time. The metallic tiles are built into the floors at the intersection of every hallway. Chow Calls are an additional opportunity to, at best, break even.

Invariably, a member of the First Class Plebe Detail awaits. Show up too early, and you provide the upperclassman extra time to evaluate appearance and to ask additional questions. Show up too late, and you face the consequences.

At precisely ten minutes before and again five minutes before each meal formation, the Plebe shouts the Chow Call:

> Sir, you now have ten minutes until (morning meal/noon meal/evening meal) formation. Noon meal formation goes outside. The uniform for noon meal formation is Working Uniform Blue Alpha. Stripers carry swords. The menu for noon meal is tuna salad sandwich kit, sweet pickle chips, cheese doodles, mayonnaise, sliced tomato, lettuce and onion, white bread, Lady Baltimore layer cake, iced tea with lemon wedges and milk. The Officers of the Watch

are: the Officer of the Watch is Lt. John Doe, First Company Officer; the Midshipman Officer of the Watch is Midshipmen Lt. John Smith, Brigade Assistant Operations Officer. The professional topic of the week is naval aviation. The major events in the Yard today are: 0800 blood drive on **Deck** 4-0; 1600 men's water polo vs Army, Lejeune Hall; 1900 Company Officer's time. You now have ten minutes, sir!

All the while, the upperclassman (sometimes more than one) yells too, poking at uniform discrepancies and trying to make the Plebe screw up. Focus and calm under fire are the unspoken lessons.

Such is the battle rhythm of Plebe Summer. Up at 0530, nonstop movement, action, and torment until the nightly gathering of Plebes in the hallway at 2145 for the singing of The Navy Blue and Gold, the traditional Navy fight song heard at the end of every Army–Navy football game. Lights out at 2200.

I became so mentally disciplined that I was able to force myself to sleep within ten seconds of my head hitting the pillow. *Today was a hard day, but the sun will come up tomorrow,* I told myself as I drifted off to sleep. If only I were so efficient today.

* * *

Designed for many purposes, Plebe Summer indoctrinates Plebes into military service, educates in all things Navy and Naval Academy, increases physical fitness, and creates a mastery of time management and stress control. It is also designed to weed out those unable or unfit to be future combat leaders. We began Plebe Summer with 1,374 classmates. We finished with about one hundred fewer.

Despite having performed well during Plebe Summer, as the academic year approached, I couldn't help feeling I was out of my league. Classmate after classmate told me how they had graduated high school with a 4.0 GPA or greater.

"Valedictorian out of a class of 400."

"Valedictorian out of 150."

Their résumés impressed and intimidated. I, on the other hand, graduated number five of thirty. Furthermore, wanting to be a fighter pilot, I chose aerospace engineering as a major. It seemed like a logical fit for my intended career path. Aerospace, I came to find out later, had a washout rate of 50 percent!

As Plebe Summer wound down, we all lived in fear of the return of the Brigade, which included all the upperclassmen. This was a big deal for a couple reasons. First, Plebe Summer was run by seniors (First Class Midshipmen, or Firsties); the returning juniors (Second Class Midshipmen) would be placed in charge of our development going forward, and they were notoriously grumpy. Their academic load was the highest and hardest of any year, and they had the added burden of holding the Plebes to task with regard to our professional knowledge and development. Second, our platoon was run by four Firsties during Plebe Summer; the ratio was four Firsties to thirty-six Plebes. Beginning with the return of the Brigade, we Plebes were outnumbered three to one!

I was certain of only one thing: I would NOT wash out of Annapolis of my own accord. I may not have been "the sharpest marble in the bag," but what I lacked in intelligence or ability, I intended to make up for with brute force and determination. These were the tools in the Lambrecht toolkit, borne from countless hours of manual labor, study, practice, and a life of not measuring up to Dad's expectations.

If none of that was good enough, then *I* simply wasn't good enough.

An aerial starboard bow view of the guided missile destroyer USS Henry B. Wilson (DDG-7). (Photo Credit: Wiki Commons open source)

Young Dog, Old Tricks

Midshipman Third and Second Class
Steve Lambrecht

"I have principles. If you don't like those, I have others!"

—GROUCHO MARX

Aeronautical Notables:

To Push the Envelope (or to push the edge of the envelope): To come near to, or extend, the boundaries of what's possible. In aviation parlance, an envelope (or a flight envelope) refers to the limits set by the laws of physics and aerodynamics, depicted by an energy versus maneuverability diagram first conceived by Col. John Boyd. To push this metaphorical envelope is to test or go beyond such limits, a necessary practice in aeronautical research.

Behind the Power Curve: In aviation, being at an energy state where increasing power alone will not result in increased airspeed; lowering the nose is required to add energy. In military terms, it means not keeping up with expectations.

Nautical Notables:

Sea Legs: The ability to walk steadily on the deck of a boat or ship under all conditions. The phrase is used as a metaphor for adjusting to living/traveling at sea. Sea legs may also refer to the illusion of motion felt on dry land after spending time at sea.

PROTRAMID: Professional Training of Midshipmen. A six-week summer program when Mids participate in the major areas of warfighting specialties: aviation, Marine Corps, and submarine warfare. Surface warfare is introduced separately during other summer cruises.

Mids: Short for Midshipmen, or Naval Academy students.

Happy Hour (also known as happy hours): This term originated in 1914 aboard the *USS Arizona*. Sailors held a weekly event to break up the boredom of sea service, and activities included boxing, wrestling, music, motion pictures, etc. The term began its affiliation with alcohol during the prohibition era, when people gathered at speakeasies to consume alcohol, illegally, before going out to dinner. The transition to modern meaning occurred during the 1950s and '60s.

Coming from rural Minnesota, I was no stranger to alcohol. It nearly cost me my career.

After completing Plebe year, each class is "scrambled," meaning dispersed to one of thirty-five other companies in the Brigade. The intent is to give everyone a fresh start and to have the opportunity to build a renewed reputation, if required. Assigned to 15th Company, I was to report in the fall of 1986.

During the summer prior to my sophomore (Youngster) year, I was sent out to the fleet for what was called "Youngster Cruise." A Youngster cruise typically lasted about three weeks, during which we were assigned to live and work with the enlisted Sailors. I was assigned to the *USS Henry B. Wilson (DDG-7)*, a guided-missile destroyer stationed in San Diego, California. As fate would have it, another 15th Company Midshipman was assigned to the *Wilson* for his senior (First Class) cruise, where he lived and sailed with the Officers. He was to become the 15th Company Commander upon his return to USNA in the fall.

The cruise was a superb experience. I was able to spend time with my siblings Ron and Pam, as both were living in San Diego. I went to sea on the *Wilson*, cruising up the West Coast of the US. We entered port in Vancouver, British Columbia, a beautiful city with no shortage of sights to explore and ways for a young Sailor to experience life.

I spent my working hours, in port and at sea, accomplishing an assigned list of tasks intended to educate and expand my eager mind. I learned about steam-boiler propulsion and helped perform maintenance on the five-inch .54 caliber guns, which we fired. Despite being assigned as an enlisted Sailor, I spent time on the bridge and experienced firsthand the duties of a Surface Warfare Officer. The whole experience was new and profound, including the part where I became seasick and donated my lunch to King Neptune. (It took me a while to develop my **sea legs**—and to lose them again once reestablished on dry land.)

Youngster Cruise went exceptionally well for me, and my evaluation reflected the same. Upon return to USNA and 15th Company in the fall, the Company Commander with whom I had sailed asked me to serve as the Youngster Company Commander. I anxiously accepted.

I began my journey toward an aerospace engineering degree and discovered the academics were every bit the challenge expected at an institution like Annapolis. Doubly so for this midwestern country boy with no previous exposure to calculus! Nonetheless, it was nice to be finished with the Plebe year gauntlet. I enjoyed my new freedoms immensely.

In 1987, with my Plebe and Youngster years successfully behind me, things were looking up. I had but one blemish on my record: an alcohol-related conduct offense, trumped up, in my opinion, due to having consumed alcohol in the presence of Plebes. I had been fried for consuming alcohol underage, a 3000 series offense, and also for fraternization, a 5000 series offense. The highest offenses possible were 6000 series, which usually resulted in expulsion.

It's true, when it was time to play, I was apt to **push the edge of the envelope**, but when it came to military traditions, knowledge, and decorum, I was a stickler. It seemed unjustified to be fried for fraternization.

During the summer between Youngster and Second-Class years, all Midshipmen underwent **PROTRAMID**, designed to expose **Mids** to all possible career paths available upon graduation. It was a dizzying array of fun and wonderment. With the Marines in Quantico, Virginia, we fired M-16 rifles, M-9 pistols, various machine guns, and then rode in helicopters. We dove underwater in fast attack submarines in the Caribbean and flew in T-34C Mentor turboprop trainers in Pensacola, Florida.

In Pensacola, I had my next, and final, run-in with the conduct system. We were given permission to consume alcohol in the Officers' Club after completion of the training day, which many of us did to excess. We were there in time for **Happy Hour**. The Officers' Club was a new environment to us, full of aviation memorabilia, song, and celebration.

The following morning, I stood in formation in the hot, humid Florida sun, feeling less than spectacular. As the sweat began to trickle down my back, I began to feel nauseous. It was clear what was about to happen, so I excused myself from formation and proceeded to the bushes in the rear. I hoped they might conceal what was coming.

I regurgitated the previous night's libations, an act that did not go unnoticed. Pushing the envelope can sometimes end badly.

Later in the day, I was summoned to the Officer in Charge of the PROTRAMID detachment, a Company Officer from USNA. I received my second 5000 series alcohol-related conduct offense, this time for "Conduct Unbecoming a Midshipman." Punishment would be levied upon returning to USNA.

For 5000 series offenses, the Battalion Commander awarded punishment. Ours was a Marine, and this was the second time my name had come across his desk.

Lieutenant Colonel Kunkle was not a man we saw much of, and that was just fine with us. A lean, harsh-looking man, Kunkle's gaze inspired the recipient to immediately rethink their entire existence. I did not look forward to the meeting.

My Company Officer went in first. They spoke for fifteen to twenty minutes, while I remained outside at the position of parade rest. At parade rest, the individual has their hands overlapped smartly behind their back, feet shoulder-width apart, and stares straight ahead, silently.

When summoned, I entered the room and reported. "Sir, Midshipman Second Class Lambrecht reports as ordered, sir!"

"At ease, Midshipman Lambrecht," Kunkle said, in a surprisingly fatherly tone.

We had a talk about my decision-making processes and how I had put myself **behind the power curve**. I reflected upon how the plentiful and accessible alcohol I so readily consumed in high school had come close to costing me my career.

It was clear that my Company Officer, Lieutenant Thomas J. Moore, who went on to become an Admiral, had put in a good word for me. They both thought I might prosper from the benefit of sage counsel. At the end of the conversation, Kunkle's self-reflection-inspiring gaze returned as he proffered me his final words of wisdom: "One more alcohol-related offense, and you will be part of naval history. Understand?"

Message received.

Steve (second from the left, next to the ninja) and nine of his cohorts with the cannonball appropriated for the scavenger hunt.

Recon

Midshipman Second Class
Steve Lambrecht

"Damn the torpedoes. Full speed ahead!"

—Admiral David Glasgow Farragut

Nautical Notables:

Head: Navy term for bathroom, originating from the location on ships where sailors went to relieve themselves. The front of the ship was almost always down-wind, as ships could only sail with the wind. Located at the front (head), facilities were cleaned by the wash of water and sea spray as the bow cut through the waves.

Recon Raid: A surveillance operation conducted outside friendly territory. In USNA parlance, it refers to an act of mischief, usually conducted under cover of darkness, designed to blow off steam, show spirit, or both.

Gouge: Informal information channel, the grapevine, the straight scoop, the skinny, inside information. Gouge is passed on via the gouge train. Live by the gouge, die by the gouge.

All Hands: An entire ship's company, or all members of any team.

The Naval Academy boasts a robust system of regulations and accountability. With curfew at 2300 (11:00 p.m.), accountability is taken to ensure all Midshipmen are in their company spaces, where they are required to remain until reveille the following morning.

Each room has its own sink and shower but not a toilet, so the only acceptable place for Plebes after 2300 was in the rack (bed) or in the **head**. Upperclassmen, however, can be anywhere inside company spaces, which consists of a specific section of Bancroft Hall. To ensure compliance, an Officer of the Watch (OOW) remains on duty, prowling the halls and looking for miscreants. (An OOW is sort of like a resident advisor at a college, only with rank, a sword, an attitude, and a fist full of demerits ready to deliver to any wayward Midshipman in need of a rudder shift.)

Underneath the Academy, there exists a complex system of tunnels housing the electrical, communications, water, and heating infrastructure for the entire Yard. This network of tunnels is affectionately known as the Ho Chi Minh Trail, after a system of roads, trails, and tunnels used by the Viet Kong during the Vietnam Conflict. For us, it was a way to traverse the Academy grounds at night, after hours, undetected during our **Recon Raids**.

Recon Raids or Recon Missions ("Recons," for short) were a way for Mids to blow off the steam accumulated as a result of endless days of study, effort, and stress. The objective of Recons could be anything from hanging up a "Beat Army" banner to acquiring artifacts from around the Yard to fulfill a scavenger hunt checklist, or any number of other shenanigans.

One night in the dead of winter, we used the Ho Chi Minh Trail to get to the crew rowing facility, where we did a "Penguin Plunge." A Penguin Plunge involves jumping into the water, in this case College Creek, when outside air temperatures are below freezing.

On another occasion, several of us reconned our way to Hospital Point, home to the Naval Academy cemetery. There, we engaged in a paintball gun battle with our recently purchased toys.

Bancroft Hall is the largest dormitory in the United States, boasting 1,700 rooms, 4.8 miles of corridors, and 33 acres of floor space. It is home to the entire Brigade of Midshipmen. Just as there is a system of tunnels under the Yard, Bancroft contains vast attic space under its roof, affectionately known as "the Catacombs" in honor of the subterranean burial grounds of Paris.

Access to the Catacombs can be gained through various doors in the central rotunda area, but also at various places above the suspended ceiling on the top floor of dorm rooms. Over the decades, Midshipmen cut holes through the ceiling structure, hidden above the ceiling tiles, giving access to the Catacombs. One can, upon ascending into them, traverse the attic structure until finding another room where a similar access hole has been cut.

From there, the shenanigans ranged from simple eavesdropping to dramatic and unexpected entrances, usually directly into the top bunk in someone else's room.

* * *

At the Naval Academy, we lived by an honor code. The code was simple and profoundly impactful: "We will not lie, cheat, or steal." That's it.

It was a highly effective code with no gray area. More importantly, anyone encountering a potential honor violation has an obligation to either turn in the offender, counsel them and then turn them in, or counsel them and drop the case altogether. Inaction is not acceptable; the matter always has to be resolved, and responsibility is placed on the individual Midshipman to act.

However, the honor code of "We will not lie, cheat, or steal" should not be confused with the lesser well-known and whimsically invoked, "We *will* exaggerate, get the **gouge**, and appropriate (borrow)."

The mother of all appropriation endeavors was a challenge put out to the entire Brigade as part of the Color Company competition. Each year, all thirty-six companies in the Brigade competed for points to determine which company was to be dubbed the Color Company. The competition is comprised of a myriad of criteria, including grades, fitness scores, parade competition, and "spirit points." Spirit points were earned in various ways, such as showing extra enthusiasm and support at sporting events, especially the Army–Navy football game. In this case, a scavenger hunt was added. It was an event seemingly created just for me.

For those who do not know, a scavenger hunt is a game of clues. Participants are expected to collect certain artifacts or pieces of information in order to get points. This particular scavenger hunt required all participants to deliver their information to a member of the spirit committee; artifacts were to be delivered to one specific member.

One artifact on the list was a cannonball. There were plenty of cannonballs around the Yard, few of them accessible and all of them heavy. *Well, it's not going to appropriate itself,* me thunk. Being among the highest point-value items on the list, it practically begged to be mine.

Going to and from class, I scouted the Yard for an achievable target. The seemingly simplest one was at the end of Stribling Walk, right in front of Mahan Hall. There were several there, stacked neatly as if staged in a brass monkey, but I had no idea if they were welded together or simply free-standing. There was only one way to find out.

A short trip down the Ho Chi Minh Trail later, ten of us emerged near Mahan Hall. We set about the task.

At night, the Yard is eerily silent. USNA is insulated from the surrounding town of Annapolis, an otherwise sleepy little fishing village with quaint homes and cobblestone streets. At 2:00 a.m., the only sounds in the Yard are those caused by wind and weather, and inside the rotunda, it is doubly so. A cockroach walking across the marble floors makes a sound akin to an army of Stormtroopers.

To wrestle one of the cannonballs up Stribling Walk to the scorekeeper's room, we had to roll it about 300 meters across the Yard, roll it an additional fifty meters to a ground-level entrance into Bancroft Hall, roll it into an elevator, and then ascend to the fourth floor. A roll down the hall to the scorekeeper's room, followed by presentation for credit, would complete the mission. We would have to pass uncomfortably close to the office where the OOW and their staff were on duty. It was an additional opportunity for disaster. What could possibly go wrong?

Cloaked in our customary black clothing and camouflage makeup, we set about the task. Upon reaching the cannonball, however, we were immediately stricken by how large it was. We had never really contemplated the actual size of the thing; there were so many around the Yard that we had no cause to take particular notice.

I tried to move it with all my might, but it barely budged. I solicited the aid of my accomplices, and together we released it from its purchase. It began to roll.

It was massive. And heavy. My estimate: 400 pounds! As my Dad always said, "It doesn't take many of those to make a dozen." We giggled at the prospect of what we were attempting.

164 | BOUNDLESS BROTHERS

We may have been miscreants, but we weren't dumb miscreants. We knew if we didn't keep it closely in check, the cannonball would make up its own mind, and at roughly 400 pounds, we would be helpless to alter its momentum. Left to do as it pleased, it might damage a monument in the Yard or perhaps even hurt one of us. With the best interest of our toes in mind, we proceeded.

Rolling the cannonball up the constant incline of Stribling Walk, we were **all hands** keeping it in check. We crossed Tecumseh Court (T-Court) and proceeded toward the door at the ground-level entrance to Bancroft Hall. As we approached, one member of the team went ahead to open the south door. IT WAS LOCKED!

We paused to contemplate a plan B, which would have been a fine thing to have done before beginning the endeavor. We then sent a scout to check the doors on the opposite side of T-Court. One was open, so we proceeded to roll the cannonball across T-Court and into the northern ground-level entrance to Mother B (Bancroft Hall).

We wrestled our prize into the elevator, then proceeded to the fourth floor. Upon reaching the fourth floor, we poked our heads out of the elevator. The coast was clear. We rolled the behemoth down the hallway and around the corner, only to discover there was no way to cross the rotunda on the fourth floor. (Only floors one through three crossed the rotunda.) Back down the hallway, onto the elevator, and down to floor three.

As we rounded the corner and proceeded down the hallway, the rotunda loomed in the distance. The rotunda is a beautiful and humbling place inside the entrance to Bancroft Hall, showcasing granite structures, ornate marble floors, and a ceiling that vaults precisely fifty-one feet, nine and fifteen-sixteenths inches above the floor. It is adorned with intricate brass railings at each balcony of the three internal stories, and paintings of famous naval battles. In the rear of the rotunda is a solemn staircase ascending to Memorial Hall, where all Naval Academy graduates who have fallen in the line of duty are honored. As an awe-inspiring spectacle, there are few finer. As an echo chamber, it is unsurpassed.

We would have to traverse the balcony overlooking the rotunda, while proceeding to the opposite side of Bancroft Hall. We commenced.

We were met with the immediate, deafening roar consistent with 400 pounds of iron rumbling across a marble floor inside a giant echo chamber. It was unavoidable, but still, we hadn't anticipated it. We stopped, gasped, and giggled. Realizing we had no choice but to continue, we pushed, and the thunderous roll commenced once more, drowning out the sound of our giggles.

We pushed the button to the elevator and waited, expecting the OOW to come bounding around the corner from the office below and across the rotunda from our position. *Ding.* The elevator arrived, and we rolled the 400-pound beast aboard.

Our lookout bounded up the steps and awaited our arrival on the fourth floor. We ascended in the elevator, expecting the doors to open to our lookout held at sword-point by the OOW, but when we arrived, it was all clear.

The hallway ahead was floored with tiles over concrete and was much quieter than the rotunda—or so it seemed to us. We proceeded to the scorekeeper's room, taunted by a guarded feeling of impending victory.

Upon arrival, we quietly knocked on the door, posing proudly with our 400-pound prey. No answer. We knocked again. Still no answer. We knocked loudly. Nothing. We pushed slightly on the door. It was locked.

Women were allowed to lock their doors at night, but we had not come all this way to be ignored! We pounded on the door. Nothing. Out of ideas and patience, we decided to let the cannonball do the knocking.

We rolled the ball away from the door, then pushed it firmly, yet not too briskly, toward the door. It impacted the heavy wooden door, causing it to give at the base by about an inch. The deadbolt held firmly, and the ball was pushed gently back in our direction. Giggles ensued. We repeated the process, this time with more vigor. More give, similar results, more giggles. Again, we repeated the process, this time with greater determination.

The door gave in at the base by about four inches. We heard wood fibers cracking, yet the cannonball returned in our direction. "Holy shit!" we giggled, knowing we had reached the maximum capacity of the door and further attempts would likely end in permanent damage.

We considered taking the cannonball back to one of our rooms and attempting a delivery the next day, but doing so would entail moving it to the opposite end of Bancroft Hall, roughly three-fourths of a mile away, and traversing the rotunda yet again. After further contemplation, we decided to leave the cannonball outside her room and slid a note under the door stating which company had delivered the goods. We then retired for the evening.

The next day, one of us contacted the scorekeeper to ensure we received credit for our delivery. She reported there was no cannonball to be found outside her room!

After the competition was over, we discovered another company had gotten credit for a cannonball. To this day, we are unsure of the fate of our 400-pound prize, but we are pretty sure someone else made good on our efforts. Well played, strangers. Well played.

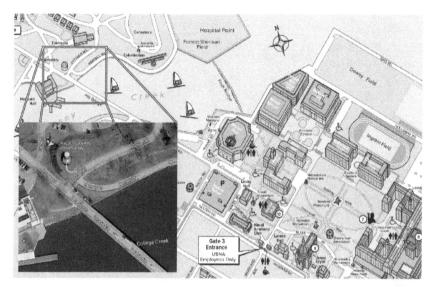

Visitor's diagram of a portion of the Yard at USNA. The Ho Chi Minh Trail resides below the portion of the Yard in the bottom right third of the photo. The center showcase of the Yard is Tecumseh Court, adjacent to the entrance to Bancroft Hall and the rotunda, located in the extreme bottom right corner of the diagram.

Inset: Satellite photo of College (Dorsey) Creek and Decatur Street Bridge. The A-4 Skyhawk (Scooter) is pictured in the top-left corner.

The (Almost) Great A-4 Heist

Midshipman Second Class
Steve Lambrecht

"Keep your knots up and your powder dry."

—STEVE LAMBRECHT

Nautical Notables:

Scooter: Nickname for the A-4 Skyhawk, due to its small size and impressive agility.

Under the RADAR: To go without being noticed or detected. RADAR has a bottom altitude limit, under which a target may go undetected.

Jimmy Legs: The United States Naval Academy civilian police, who provide security in the Yard. It is also a slang term for "Master-at-Arms," or military police.

Visitors at the Naval Academy will see many jewels of naval history positioned prominently about the Yard, including an A-4 Skyhawk attack aircraft. The A-4 played a significant role in military history as a highly maneuverable and effective aircraft, capable of delivering a nuclear bomb if called upon.

To accommodate such a bomb, this otherwise tiny aircraft was held above the runway or aircraft carrier deck by exceptionally long landing gear. This landing gear also makes a great handle for Midshipmen to grab and push while wheeling a **Scooter** around the Yard, should any choose to do so at 2:00 a.m. We did.

That night, our objective was to push the A-4 from its purchase on Hospital Point, across the College Creek Decatur Street Bridge, up Stribling Walk, and into the middle of Tecumseh Court, where it would await viewing by all members of the Brigade of Midshipmen while they traveled to class the following morning. Much was required to execute the mission, not the least of which was to "fly" this thing **under the RADAR**. We would have to evade capture not only on the way to Hospital Point (the easy part) but also while pushing a not-so-inconspicuous aircraft along a major thoroughfare through the middle of the Yard (the hard part). Once we reached Stribling Walk, the most vulnerable part of the journey would be over, as we could depart the street system in favor of less frequently patrolled walkways.

We had no idea how much the A-4 weighed but figured the engine and a significant portion of the internal equipment had likely been stripped. If we came to a curb, we would need plenty of muscle power to lift the airplane, one wheel at a time, while others pushed. We figured a couple dozen of us ought to be enough to do the job. We mustered the appropriate number, and off we went.

As predicted, getting to Hospital Point was the easy part. The Ho Chi Minh Trail got us to the river, which we crossed using the Sherman Field footbridge to avoid vehicle traffic. The only vehicles likely to be out this time of night were driven by the one or two patrolling **Jimmy**

Legs, and after successfully crossing to Hospital Point, there was no sign of them. This was both a good and a bad thing: good because it might mean they were not patrolling. Bad because it left us wondering if they had come by recently or were due to come by at any moment.

We were a mere 200 yards or so from our objective, but streetlights lit the road and the breath of two dozen clandestinely clad Midshipmen could be faintly seen in the chilly evening air. We moved briskly along the sea wall toward the A-4, and when we reached it, we wasted no time. We quickly unbound the A-4 from her ropes and began pushing her onto the road.

Her weight resisted our efforts, but resistance proved futile. The mighty Skyhawk gave way to our combined efforts, and we inched the aircraft forward off the small concrete pads beneath her wheels and onto the grass, where progress slowed considerably.

We groaned as we pushed her, inch by inch, across the grass until reaching the edge of the road. Then, we pushed her off the curb and onto the street. The struts compressed to absorb the drop onto street level, and we muscled her around the ninety-degree turn to align her with Decatur Avenue, the street leading to Stribling Walk. At this point, we realized we had three major challenges awaiting us.

First, we needed to cross the river. Because we'd have to go uphill for the first half of the bridge, we needed all hands, with a head of steam, to ensure we reached the top. Second, there were guard rails on the sides of the bridge, which might prove to be an obstacle for the wings. We quickly assessed that the abnormally long landing gear on the A-4 facilitated not only nuclear weapons, but also the required guard rail clearance. Third, we had to worry about being ambushed by the Jimmy Legs, an ever-present threat.

"You're good," yelled one of our team members after sighting down the wing tips and seeing that the aircraft could pass between the lights and over the guard rails without impacting them.

"One, two, three, GO!" We all heaved together. The A-4 lurched forward and picked up momentum, rolling more easily on the street than on the grass.

Prior to the bridge, we picked up speed on a slight downhill section of road. Topping out at the pace of a brisk walk, we then began the uphill traverse of the bridge, where our advance slowed despite our efforts to maintain momentum.

We knew if we ran out of steam, it would not end well. The A-4 would almost certainly begin to roll backwards, and we would be powerless to stop it. It would gain momentum, careening into some unfortunate and damaging demise, taking our conduct records along with it. Restriction was always a possibility with these endeavors, but such achievements seldom come without risk!

We kept the aircraft rolling at an ever-decreasing pace until reaching the apex of the bridge. All downhill from here, another hundred yards or so thereafter, and we'd be off the street, onto Stribling Walk, and concealed from the view of traffic.

With that, we were met with the flash of blue lights. Jimmy Legs!

It was pointless to run, and we knew it. The Jimmy Legs rounded the corner and approached us from the direction of our intended path. The only escape route was behind us, the opposite direction from the safety of Bancroft Hall and our rooms. Further, leaving the A-4 to fend for itself meant it might roll down the bridge in either direction. Nothing good could come from that. Best to man-up and face Mr. Legs.

"You folks lost?" said Mr. Legs, backlit by a spotlight and flashing blue doom. We all chuckled and replied with silly responses, laced with a glimmer of hope emboldened by a security officer who didn't seem to be bent on destruction. After a brief discussion, he inspired us to return the A-4 to its appropriate resting place and get to bed before the OOW heard about it and decided to spring into action.

We did so promptly, with all the tender care one expected of a group of young adults attempting to remain under the RADAR. After returning the A-4 to precisely the same spot where we had found her and tying her back down, we returned to our rooms disappointed, yet undefeated.

Some years later, I returned to the Yard to discover that they had finally tied the A-4 down using metal anchors and turnbuckles. My small legacy to the Yard.

The kiddy tractor pull competition is a popular event at Ivanhoe's Polska Kielbasa Days celebration. The size of the sledge alone has to be intimidating to a seven-year-old!

Steve and Ron at the parade and tractor pull. Ivanhoe Polish Days, August 2021.

Polska Kielbasa Days

Ron

"I was as sober as the next guy. The only problem is the next guy was Dean Martin."

—RED SKELTON

Nautical Notables:

Up Spirits: The "Up spirits" call was piped by the bos'n (pronounced: boe-sun) every day at noon throughout the ship. It was the call to muster for the daily issue of rum. Today, many of those familiar with this tradition sign their correspondence with the closing salutation "Up spirits!" followed by their signature.

Drinking a Toast: This phrase for drinking to one's health, or in one's honor, was coined in the early days along the waterfronts. At that time, it was customary to place a small piece of toast in the hot toddy and the mulled wine, which was popular with seamen of the day.

Splice the Mainbrace: An order given aboard naval vessels to issue the crew an alcoholic drink. Originally an order for one of the most difficult emergency repair jobs aboard a sailing ship, it became a euphemism for authorized celebratory drinking afterward. It then became the name of an order to grant the crew an extra ration of rum or grog.

Ivanhoe's sole reason for existence is its location. Centrally located in Lincoln County, with a population of 765 in 1980, it boasts the county seat, courthouse, jail, and County Road Maintenance Department. Today's population is 552, and all that remains are a couple of churches; a bowling alley that is doing okay due to the long winters; a small grocery store, bank, and liquor store; and a couple machine shops supporting the local farmers. Cafes open every few years, but the town is not large enough to sustain one, and inevitably, the proprietor is forced to close.

Today, Ivanhoe is primarily a bedroom community whose residents are widows and families with heads of households employed by the county or in neighboring towns. It is not uncommon to drive down Main Street on a weekday and see only two or three parked cars. (The town council approved the removal of many of the vacant buildings along the two blocks comprising Main Street, losing the character of the town in the process.) You can imagine my surprise, then, when Mom called one day and informed me that someone backed into her as she was driving down Main Street. I guess they were not expecting traffic.

Ivanhoe, however, is also the center of the Minnesota Polish universe. Tykwinski, Lipinski, Popowski, Skorczewski, Ochocki, Stanasheski, Rybinski, Shaikoski, Chihanski, Joworski, and Lasnetski are all common family names. For a while, those of us not having a name that ended in "ski" had fun telling jokes at the expense of our Polish classmates. (The humor ended when we heard about a comedy team in Minneapolis who told a Polish joke. The next morning they were found in an alley with their heads tied together, shot through the hands...but I digress.) All joking aside, there's an old Polish saying, "No work, no cake." The Poles in Ivanhoe knew how to work and how to play.

When it comes to throwing a party, New Orleans has nothing on Ivanhoe. Ivanhoe hosts an annual event called Polska Kielbasa (Polish Sausage) Days, when the beer gardens and Municipal Liquor Store average 127 kegs of beer (2,032 gallons) and the call for **up spirits** runs from 4:00 p.m. Friday to 12:00 p.m. Sunday (or later). That is a lot of beer for a town of 765, especially because not everyone drinks. It is quite possible the words "You can't drink all day if you don't start in the morning" originated at Polish Days.

Polish Days festivities include a softball double elimination tournament, where teams from North and South Dakota, Iowa, and towns across Minnesota compete. Often over one hundred teams are present, making the cause of the record beer consumption obvious. Tractor pulls, beauty and talent contests, craft fairs, dancing, karaoke, and a parade are all part of the celebration. Polish Days is the one annual event that brings those of us that have moved away to far-flung places back to our roots, as we know many of the kids we grew up with are likely to be home.

During one Polish Days event while home on leave, Dad rousted me out of bed on a Saturday morning to attend the tractor pull. I reminded him the tractor pull contest always occurred on Sunday afternoons, but he said that this year was different. Despite my best efforts to cling to my pillow, I found myself being encouraged to get out of my rack.

The night before, I had **drunk a toast** or two, as **splicing the mainbrace** was part of the Polish Days ritual. (Of course, the Polish Days attendees didn't call it that, but the concept was universally practiced.)

After I ate a couple cloves of garlic to improve my breath, we headed to town. There, a polish sausage and high-octane Coke provided hope for my survival.

Sure enough, a new category had been added to the competition schedule, consisting of a robustly built John Deere pedal tractor with a miniature heavy sledge. The sledge is a weight transfer sled; as it is pulled down the track, weight is transferred from over the rear axle and wheels to the front of the sled. Friction increases with increasing distance. The kid in each age category who pulls the sledge the farthest down the track with their pedal tractor wins the competition.

I had forgotten how big and strong seven-year-old Polish farm kids can be, especially the boys. Kids with thighs the size of my waist, strong enough to raise the front wheels of the tractor off the ground from pushing on the pedals, were cheered on by their proud parents. It was appropriate that the pedal tractor was a John Deere, for just as the old two-cylinder John Deere tractors chugged along with the firing of each cylinder, so did the miniature tractor with each push of a pedal.

This was a "bragging rights" event, and it occurred to me that these tenacious kids were United States Marines in the making. Tenacity, it turns out, is a trait not uncommon in those who hail from humble beginnings—and I was no stranger to humble beginnings.

Bulldog

Midshipman First Class Steve Lambrecht

Midshipman Company Commander, 15th Company, USNA

"Old breed? New breed? There's not a damn bit of difference so long as it's the Marine breed."

—GENERAL CHESTY PULLER, USMC

Nautical Notables:

Reserve Officer Training Corps (ROTC): A program for students attending college on a scholarship paid for by the military, given in return for years of service (usually five) upon graduation and commissioning.

Opportunity to Excel: A disagreeable job without the time or resources to properly complete, or an otherwise undesirable task with little or no reward.

Throughout my first three years at the Academy, I was always impressed by the Marines who were stationed there. The Marine instructors, Marine gate guards, and Marine Company and Battalion Officers always looked sharp and conducted themselves in the most professional of manners. They had an intensity about them that I found appealing.

Since the Marine Corps also had fighter aircraft, it felt like a natural fit. The risk of ending up in helicopters was real, but the USMC and I seemed destined for one another. I didn't want to fly helicopters, but I was willing to accept the risk.

At the time, the Corps had been acquiring what it considered to be low-quality Officers from the bottom of USNA graduating classes. This was the byproduct of the service selection process; by the time the bottom-ranking members of each class had their turn selecting the career field they wanted on Service Selection Night, the only choices left were usually Marine Corps and Surface Warfare (ship drivers).

Surface Warfare meant a life at sea as a Naval Surface Warfare Officer. For those who had no such sea-going aspirations, the thought of five years in the Marine Corps, followed by an exit from the military, seemed like the more desirable route.

As a result, the USMC annually acquired a handful of the bottom-performing Officers from USNA who never really wanted to be Marines in the first place. The problem came to a head when it was discovered that several USNA graduates had failed to be promoted to the rank of Captain, which should have been more or less a given following the first five years of service after graduation. Failing to make Captain was exceedingly rare for anyone, regardless of commissioning source.

Secretary of the Navy James Webb had a solution: all those at USNA intending to join the USMC upon graduation first had to attend Marine Officer Candidate School, also called "Bulldog." Bulldog is a six week boot-camp-style course on steroids for those aspiring to be Marine Officers. Historically, only **ROTC** graduates had to attend Bulldog; this was a first for USNA.

Attendance at Bulldog occurred in the summer before senior (First-Class) year. Failure to graduate from Bulldog meant the individual had to select a different occupation on Service Selection Night, which was held in the spring of First-Class year. Marines at USNA put together a training program for all of us aspiring USMC Officers and administered it to us in preparation.

So, despite my brother's warning about their lifestyle, I was off to Bulldog in the summer of 1988, armed with a new requirement and a desire to be a Marine. Bulldog was yet another **opportunity to excel**, and it is where I would receive my third, and final, self-identity-eliminating head shave.

* * *

Bulldog, as with most courses of military indoctrination, was everything one would expect. Morning wake-up included the music of metal garbage cans being hurled through the barracks, accompanied by the harmonious screaming of Marine Drill Instructors (DIs). No uniform or gear inspection could be passed. No bed made well enough.

Our daily physical training (PT) was long and brutal. Speed marches, obstacle courses, and grueling gear-laden humps through the hills of Quantico, Virginia, separated those who would be allowed to lead Marines from those who would not. We crawled through the mud, waded through swamp water, and slept in holes we dug in the ground. When we weren't in the field, PT was conducted on the PT courses, which were many, varied, and daunting.

This program was different in that it stressed and evaluated the ability of each would-be Marine Officer not just to lead, but also to lead under the most austere and challenging circumstances the DIs could muster. Screaming unrelentingly at the candidate who, on a rotating basis, was placed in a leadership position, they observed how the candidate reacted. They wanted to see who remained calm under pressure and could get the job done. Get the job done and the enlisted DIs might allow you to lead them in combat one day.

For all of us Academy Midshipmen, the harassment package inherent to Bulldog was hard to take seriously. While the ROTC students in attendance had not yet faced a similar crucible, the Mids had already endured, at a minimum, Plebe Year and two additional years of stress and harassment. This was simply another six weeks of the same ordeal.

I had the distinct pleasure of bunking across from Tim Goering (no relation to the Nazi Luftwaffe General), an USNA classmate. He was one funny mofo. While standing at attention across from me, he never passed up the opportunity to make a goofy face or otherwise absurd expression while the DIs were not facing him, hoping to crack us up and get us into trouble. It worked.

"Oh! Oh! Oh! You think this is funny, do you?" the DIs screamed.

Then, we all dropped and did push-ups or sit-ups, or struck an uncomfortable pose until pain removed the funny from our funny bones...almost. Like I said, it was hard to take the harassment package completely seriously. We learned our lesson and straightened up, at least until next time.

The program had the desired effect. While there were only two people who washed out of Bulldog from our entire platoon, one ROTC and one USNA, the number of USNA classmates seeking a commission in the USMC was cut by a third. Turns out Bulldog discouraged those who weren't really interested in the Corps from applying in the first place. Mission accomplished.

Steve graduates from Annapolis, receiving his commission as a Second Lieutenant in the United States Marine Corps. Certificates were presented by Admiral Hill (Superintendent) and The Honorable Richard Cheney (Secretary of Defense).

The Final Exam

Midshipman Lieutenant Steve Lambrecht
Company Commander, 15th Company, USNA

"A computer once beat me at chess, but it was no match for me at kick boxing."

—EMO PHILIPS

Nautical Notable:

Brain Housing Group: Mock-technical term for the skull, the part of the body that houses the brain and keeps one's ears from slamming together.

I was selected as Company Commander for my First-Class (senior) year. Despite having superb professional scores and rankings, with my two previous conduct offenses, my Company Officer knew a position any higher in the Brigade was unobtainable. A great honor, I was proud to have the position.

I had a lot of fun First-Class year, but I was also maxed out. Between being a Company Commander, boxing, and studying aerospace engineering, I had plenty on my plate. Still, I managed to find ways to blow off steam and enjoy the experience; in particular, I enjoyed poking the bear. The "bear" was a very good friend of mine named Steve Laabs.

Laabs's father was a retired Navy Captain and USNA graduate who raised his son with a strict code of ethics and discipline. Laabs was a beast of a man. At around six foot five, he earned the nickname "Sky Laabs," and won the NCAA Heavyweight Boxing Championship two years running. He knew not the limits of his own strength. I was undeterred. Laabs was big, athletic, and strong, but his speed and agility were no match for either me or his roommate, Steve "Floyd" Formella.

Laabs made a habit of taking a nap after dinner before the evening study period, sleeping like the giant of *Jack and the Beanstalk* fame. On such occasions, Floyd and I borrowed fingernail polish from our female classmates and set out at doing our best makeover. We silently, aside from our insuppressible giggles, painted his finger and toenails every color of the rainbow.

Upon awakening, often when we were partway through the task, Laabs sprang from his rack and lunged at us from the top bunk. This gave us an automatic three-step lead in the ensuing chase, but occasionally Laabs caught one of us, and he did not spare the whip. The pain was soon forgotten, however, and judged to be worth the experience. After all, nail polish is removable.

On another occasion, I, a model aircraft builder, found myself in possession of a one-forty-eighth scale plastic fighter pilot. I determined there was a place outside the cockpit to better display its magnificence, so with a smirk on my face, a small plastic pilot in one hand, and a bottle of super glue in the other, I waited for nap time. I then set out for Sky Laabs's room.

After the deed, knowing better than to return to my room where I could be found, Floyd and I waited in a stairwell down the hall. Several classmates waited outside their rooms, having been informed of the shenanigans afoot (pun intended).

Suddenly, the door to Laabs's room crashed open. The enraged giant emerged, having awoken from his slumber with a miniature pilot affixed firmly to his big toenail. Neither "Fee," nor "Fi," nor "Fo," nor "Fum" was necessary to convey his desire to thrust his anger upon me.

A short-lived pursuit began. Quickly realizing he was unable to reach maximum speed due to his newly acquired companion, Laabs secured fingernail polish remover from a female classmate and reluctantly returned to his room, where he could contemplate the time and place for his revenge. Needless to say, I laid low and remained elusive until Laabs's laughter replaced his anger.

* * *

In the late winter of 1989, Service Selection Night arrived, when we would choose our career path beginning after graduation. Firsties chose in class-rank order, except those who did not complete Bulldog were not eligible for the USMC.

As was tradition, those selecting Marine Corps, upon returning to their company area, got their head shaved by the Plebes. Not, however, without a proper Marine Corps fight! I chose Marine pilot. Upon my return to company spaces, followed by a respect-earning struggle, I received my fourth, and this time *self-identity-validating,* head shave. The Marine Corps and I chose each other; it was the right fit.

One final obstacle stood between me and graduation: Electrical Engineering. EE ("Double E," as it was known) proved a major hurdle for many at USNA. There were two versions: the easier version, nick-named "Wires," was for those in non-technical majors. The harder version, nicknamed "Cables," was for those in technical majors.

Cables had notoriety for causing Midshipmen to lose their major, graduating as a General Engineer. For this reason, Cables was typically taken junior year, thereby affording a failed student the opportunity to retake the course either in summer school or during senior year. Not so with my class. I had to take it senior year, offer-ing me only two options: pass or fail. Failure would result in not only a loss of my major, but a loss of my ability to *graduate*, as I would not have fulfilled the academic requirements to graduate with *any* major.

EE further challenged me in that I simply had no interest in electrical circuitry or other associated witchcraft. It didn't interest me; there-fore, I didn't give it due diligence. I didn't give it due diligence; there-fore, I sucked at it. It was a vicious circle.

During the first semester, I received a "D" in EE. Now, it was second semester, and I was two weeks away from taking the final. My average in EE going into the final exam was 60.0; the minimum grade to pass and graduate was 60.0. I was reminded of Ron's old saying, "If seventy wasn't good enough, it wouldn't be passing."

Leading up to the exam, I was sweating bullets. I worked like a bomb defuser with ten seconds left on the timer as I tried to cram into my **brain housing group** that knowledge which I had lacked the disci-pline to acquire in a timely manner.

When the fateful day arrived, I went into the exam with a feeling of impending doom. I was a great memorizer, but the deeper concepts of EE still eluded me. I knew it was going to be a close call.

The exam commenced, and I dove in with determination. I knew the best way to take a test was to go through it, seeking to find all the problems I knew how to do first, which I could knock out immediately. Much to my dismay, there were precious few.

After knocking those problems out, I went back to the beginning and began to slog my way through. The clock ticked, but my brain barely clicked. I was able to muscle my way through significant portions of most problems but was unsure if I had completed them correctly.

I left the exam with a tremendous feeling of unease. Everything rode on this one exam. *Everything.*

Two days later, the time came to return to class and get the results. Nervous does not begin to describe my trepidation on that day.

The professor was a Navy Commander, a superb Officer and probably a fine instructor, although I was not qualified to have an opinion on the matter. When I received my blue booklet, which was used to answer the questions on the final exam, I quickly paged to the end.

"60.0. Have a great career" was written.

For me, Double E was a double D. I was happy to have it!

To this day, I cannot empirically state with absolute certainty whether or not I received a legitimate 60.0 or if it was a gift from a visionary Officer and professor who knew I was painted into a corner with no way out. In any event, I *do* think I am qualified to have an opinion on the matter, and I know what my opinion is.

And so, on May 31, 1989, USNA graduated 1,064 Ensigns and Second Lieutenants, including 125 of the original 250 aerospace engineering majors. Steven S. Lambrecht, 2LT, USMC, was one, finishing in the middle of his class.

With that, once again, this midwestern country boy was a dot.

Steve takes a ride in the helo dunker at NAS Pensacola, Florida (1990).

Steve next to a T-34C Mentor at Whiting Field, Florida (1990).

Young Dog, New Tricks

Second Lieutenant
Steve Lambrecht
Student Naval Aviator, VT-2

"Repetition is the Father of Knowledge"

—STEVE LAMBRECHT

Aeronautical Notables:

Signal of Difficulty (SOD): A grade assigned to a flying or simulator event in flight school where the student failed to perform up to minimum standards, meaning the entire flight or simulator event had to be repeated. Also referred to as a "Down."

Chair-Fly: The act of mentally thinking through all aspects of a flight before ever getting into the aircraft. The act may include the physical simulation of motions.

After graduating from USNA, I proceeded to Quantico, Virginia, for six months of training, the standard for all newly commissioned Marine Corps Officers. The Basic School (TBS), as it is not-so-cleverly named, trains officers in the basics of all Military Occupational Specialties (MOSs). There, Marines learn the combat skills of infantry, artillery, and armor, as well as legal, intelligence, logistical, and administrative functions—but above all, every Marine is trained to be "first a rifleman."

TBS is, to a large degree, an extension of Officer Candidate School, replete with plenty of physical fitness challenges, obstacle courses, strength and endurance events, forced marches, land navigation, uniform inspection, and all things USMC. Marines refer to the rite of passage that is TBS as "The Big Suck."

After TBS, with a six-month delay to begin flight school, several of us took the opportunity to attend the Infantry Officer Course (IOC). IOC was a graduate-level course in infantry and combat tactics, a superb course that included such exciting events as firing mortars, training with tanks, and Special Insertion/Extraction (SPIE) rigging. In SPIE training, we were suspended below a helicopter while being inserted and extracted from a landing zone. We also learned fast roping, where we slid down a rope onto a rooftop from a helicopter, without being physically attached to anything. The course was exhilarating and challenging, and it appealed to my basic senses of leadership and the grandeur of ground combat.

Adding to the prestige of the course was the incoming Commander of IOC, then-Major John R. Allen. Ensconcing the warrior scholar ethos, Allen won the Leftwich Trophy for outstanding ground combat leadership in 1988, was a former instructor of mine at USNA, and later went on to become a four-star General.

Immersed in such a euphoric setting, I entertained the thought of giving up my flight guarantee and going infantry. After much contemplation, however, I resisted the temptation. I rounded out my six-month delay by spending the last three months at Patuxtent River Naval Air Station and Test Pilot School, Maryland. I then proceeded to Pensacola Florida for Aviation Indoctrination (AI).

AI had little to do with flying and everything to do with weeding out those who lacked the requisite acumen. There were fitness events o'plenty, including an obstacle course in the sand and an altitude chamber. Academic courses on basic aeronautics were absorbed, and there was swimming galore.

Swimming included rides down the Dilbert Dunker and the helicopter (helo) dunker. There was also parasailing, where we practiced parachute landing in the water, followed by detaching and escaping from the parachute. All of these tests were identical to the ones Ron had already faced in 1979, using undoubtedly the very same contraptions.

The helo dunker, which required four rides to pass, was particularly entertaining because riders never knew which way the device was going to roll. The graduation ride was done wearing blacked-out goggles while having to unstrap, find your way to a single point of escape, and then ascend to the surface.

After the six-week AI course, it was off to Primary Flight Training. My chosen destination for Primary was Whiting Field in Milton, Florida, a mere forty minutes up the road from Pensacola, and upon reporting for duty, I was assigned to Training Squadron Two, the VT-2 "Doer Birds." *Doer Birds—now there's a mascot to rally behind!*

Primary was the true proving ground for pilots, where we learned to fly the T-34C Mentor. Everything was a competition, both between student pilots and with oneself. A student typically received no more than three **SODs** before washing out of the program and being offered the opportunity to pursue other career endeavors outside of aviation. If you made it to the end of training, though, you were ranked according to grades. Aircraft selection followed, with the choices being jets, props, or helicopters—but class rank was not the only deciding factor.

During the Tiger Cruise at age fourteen, I had set my sights on becoming a fighter pilot. That meant I had to first earn jets, but there was a chance jets would not be available the week one graduated, an unavoidable curse to those with bad luck. In addition, there was "quality spread," where assignments were allocated across the talent pool so that the best pilots were not exclusively assigned to jets.

The only way to control one's destiny and to have a shot at one's first choice was to finish first in one's class. The top graduate always picked first and chose from whatever was available. Finishing first gave me the best shot at earning jets, so I set about the task.

While there were periods of formal instruction, with all students expected to be in a classroom, naval aviation flight training was predominately a self-guided affair. During the flying phases of training, the onus was placed on the student to spend their time preparing for not just the next flight or simulator evaluation, but the next few. You had to be ready in case another student was sick or there was a vacancy in the flight schedule.

I was advised, before ever showing up to flight school, of a couple study tricks that had proven useful to aviators who went before me. We were given paper foldout replicas of all the instrument panels in the aircraft. I adhered them to cardboard and turned my home office into a cockpit. Seated in my office chair, I had the side instrument panels affixed to the armrests, and the front instrument panel, with two semi-circles cut out to accommodate my legs, rested on my lap and leaned against my desk. With this configuration, I could **chair-fly** my sorties as many times as desired, becoming accustomed to the location of all instruments and switches in the cockpit. Students were expected to locate all of these with their eyes closed, ensuring they were capable of executing emergency procedures should the cockpit be filled with smoke.

I was also advised that I should practice multitasking while reciting standard operating procedures and emergency procedures.

Multitasking took many forms, such as exercising, juggling, or bouncing a tennis ball against a wall and catching it. The purpose of this endeavor was to ensure one could execute proper procedures and handle emergencies while simultaneously flying an aircraft safely. Armed with this knowledge, I taught myself to juggle and set about spending countless hours at the altar of repetition.

Extra simulator sessions were available to the students, should they desire to gain additional instruction, and I took full advantage of the opportunity. I sometimes signed up for three, or even four, extra simulator sessions in a day, when I wasn't otherwise engaged in formal instruction. This served to further my expertise and proficiency, as well as established my reputation with the instructors as a hard worker and eager student. Undoubtedly, it also helped tip the scales in my favor when it came to being formally graded on events.

I created flashcards, attended group study sessions, and made audio tapes of memory items, which I listened to while exercising and driving back and forth to work. Soon, struggling friends were seeking me out for help with study and preparation for events. So effective are these learning strategies that I still use them today in my commercial airline job or when preparing for checkrides with Federal Aviation Administration (FAA) evaluators.

It wasn't all work and no play, by any stretch. Being married, I was better equipped than my single peers to resist the temptations of Pensacola nightlife. Regardless, I partied heartily with neighbors and spent plenty of time escaping reality in the base woodshop. There, I could clear my head while utilizing the trade-skill genes my dad had bestowed on my brother and me.

However, the woodshop is also where a table-saw accident nearly ended my flying career.

Not adhering to best practices while cutting small pieces of wood, my thumb challenged the blade to a duel, and I nearly suffered the same fate as the famous fighter pilot Joe "Hoser" Satrapa. Satrapa's big toe was removed and grafted to replace his thumb, which had gone missing after an experimental gun accident, leading to his nickname "Toeser."

While this procedure would have undoubtedly made hitchhiking simpler, the thought of putting Odor Eaters in my gloves seemed a cumbersome way to go through life. After an excruciating trip to medical, twenty-four stitches, and six weeks on the sidelines, I kept all of my fingers and toes in their original location. I returned to training with the knowledge that I was not, in fact, bulletproof.

* * *

The First Gulf War broke out during my Primary Training, so several of us Marines approached the Senior Marine flight instructor on base and asked if we could take a break in training to go fight the war. We were concerned this might be our only opportunity to fight for our country. We didn't want to sit it out in flight school, particularly those of us who had taken the time to get our Infantry Officer's MOS, while our peers were in Kuwait and Iraq doing the work.

The Senior Marine told us to go away and get back to our studies. "There will always be another war," he said.

It was not the answer we were looking for. Though we went away, disappointed, he was more right than any of us could have imagined at the time.

After months of working (and playing) hard, it was time to make my selection of flying machines. Jets were available, and having made the Commodore's List with Distinction, I was the first to choose. I was soon off to Kingsville, Texas, and the next phase of flight school: jet training.

View of the aircraft carrier landing zone from astern the ship. The Fresnel Lens with centered "meatball" can be seen along the left edge of the flight deck. Parked left of the landing zone are two F/A-18 Hornets and one F-14 Tomcat. Along the right side, from near to far, are an A-6 Intruder, an EA-6B Prowler, a Tomcat, an E-2C Hawkeye, two Tomcats, and two S-3 Vikings. Vulture's Row faces left from the superstructure on the right. (Photo Credit: Wiki Commons open source)

I Wanted Her. Badly.

First Lieutenant Steve "Curly" Lambrecht
Student Naval Aviator, VT-23

"Obviously, I was challenged by becoming a Naval Aviator, by landing aboard aircraft carriers and so on."

—ALAN SHEPARD

Aeronautical Notables:

Flare: The nose-up landing attitude normal for most land-based aircraft. Carrier aircraft do not flare due to increased landing distance caused by float time.

Fresnel Lens: The primary optical landing device on the carrier. It consists of two green horizontal lights with a single circular light in between them, called the "ball" or "meatball."

LSO: Landing Signal Officer. Squadron member with considerable experience in carrier landings, responsible for assisting others onto the deck and for grading their efforts. Also known as "paddles." Positioned directly adjacent to the landing zone.

Clara: Clara is short for "clarification" or, more bluntly, "Tell me where I am on glide slope 'cause I can't see the ball." The LSO's response after Clara is normally a position call (e.g., "Clara high," telling the pilot they're high).

Groove: Perfect position on approach in relation to glide slope, aircraft angle of attack, and the meatball.

Kingsville, Texas, was nothing to write home about. Like Ivanhoe, Minnesota, it was a small town in the middle of nowhere, a hefty drive from civilization. The weather was generally good, and the training airspace plentiful, as the countryside below was infested with little more than mesquite trees and javelinas. You either loved it or you didn't; I made the most of it, using my spare time to hunt and to haunt the base woodshop.

Once again, the objective was clear: this was a competition-based race for aircraft selection. At each advancing stage of flight school, the level of competition increased. Having made it to jet training, clearly no one was so dumb that they couldn't put together a one-piece puzzle. Quite the contrary—all were bright and talented, and we would be competing for which jet we would fly.

As a Marine, there were three choices of jets available: the EA-6B Prowler, the AV-8B Harrier, or the F/A-18 Hornet. Everyone loves the airplane they fly, but having said that, in the world of combat aviation, it is customary to razz one another. So, here we go:

The Prowler served a highly important purpose: jamming and attacking enemy surface-to-air missile systems. Considered to be a high-value airborne asset (or HVAA), the electronic warfare platform was protected from enemy fighters at all costs. No one wanted to go into enemy territory without one or two Prowlers in support.

That glowing praise, however, should not be confused with a desire to fly one. They were capable of only subsonic flight, not aerial combat, and had a face only a Grumman Ironworks engineer could love. They resembled a turkey drumstick flying through the air with the fat end up front. Further, they carried a crew of four, the aviation equivalent of driving a minivan. Sure, it's practical and serves an important purpose, but no one wants to be seen driving one.

Next was the Harrier, best known for its ability to take off and land vertically. Also, *the Harrier could take off and land vertically.* Finally, the Harrier was capable of horizontal flight at subsonic speeds, with unimpressive maneuverability, but *it could take off and land vertically.*

Lastly, there was the Hornet. The sexy, capable, supersonic, death-doling, magnificent, extravagant, elegant, Lamborghini of fighter jets: the Hornet. If a pilot were to marry a fighter jet, they would choose the Hornet; it is a pilot's airplane. It harnesses all that is best about technology and delivers it to the pilot in an elegant and intuitive manner.

The pilot becomes one with the machine; it does what you tell it to do. Even by today's standards, the Hornet is capable of things no other aircraft is capable of. It was criticized for not carrying enough gas... but only by people who flew turkey drumsticks backwards and by people who could take off and land vertically.

The Hornet was the best, and I wanted her. Badly.

* * *

The Harrier was the most difficult of the three aircraft to fly, and because the Harrier community had historically gotten pilots from the bottom of the class, the mishap rate was unacceptable. The USMC's solution was to institute quality spread. This meant the bottom 40 percent of the class were assigned to fly Hornets, and the middle 40 percent were assigned to Harriers.

There was typically one Prowler spot. The perfect candidate for Prowlers was someone who was average in jet training but did well at carrier qualification, since landing on a carrier was difficult. Someone with talent at carrier operations was a nice fit.

Finally, the individual who finished at the top of the class always got their first choice, and that person almost always chose Hornets. Finish second, and you were headed to Harriers.

When instruction began, I set about applying the same study techniques I had used in Primary. First was ground school and then simulators. Training in the aircraft followed, starting with the T-2C Buckeye, a.k.a. "Thunder Guppy."

A plump little jet, with two small engines slung below the fuselage and a straight wing with wingtip fuel tanks, the Thunder Guppy incorporated old technology, having entered service in 1959. Like the Prowler, it was subsonic and had a face only a blind engineer could love. However, it was stable and served the purpose for which it was intended.

The first phase of jet training was called Familiarization (FAM), where the student and instructor flew alone in the same airplane. The Formation Phase followed, where the student learned to fly alongside another aircraft. Next came the Instrument Phase, where the student flew predominately in the back seat with a hood pulled over the rear of the cockpit, allowing the student to see only the instrumentation and not outside. This phase finished with the student having an FAA

Instrument Qualification, enabling the student to fly in bad weather utilizing only instruments.

As a jet pilot in an aircraft capable of pulling more than about four Gs, one is adorned with about forty pounds of equipment. In addition to a flight suit and boots covering the entire body, except the hands and head, a G suit is worn from the abdomen to the top of the boots. It is plugged into the aircraft, which meters pressurized air into the suit as a function of Gs pulled. The higher the Gs, the higher the air pressure in the suit. The bladders in the G suit inflate, squeezing blood from the lower half of the body to the upper half and increasing the availability of oxygen to the brain. The net effect is to ensure the pilot remains conscious under high G loads.

Next is the harness, a system of straps and buckles attaching the pilot to the ejection seat and parachute. Over the top of everything else is the survival vest, containing day and night signal devices, water, a knife, flashlight, survival radio, and a multitude of other essentials, should the pilot find themselves with a sudden loss of motorized transportation. A helmet is worn on the head, with integrated speakers and a retractable visor. Attached to the helmet is an oxygen mask, covering what remains of the pilot's face. Finally, a set of gloves is worn, completely covering the hands. All told, the hot, heavy ensemble leaves no more than about an inch of exposed skin around the pilot's neck.

Wearing all of this equipment in the hot Texas sun, on a black asphalt airfield in an archaic aircraft, results in significant discomfort. However, the stress of evaluation and the desire for success pushes aside this discomfort as the sortie progresses. A busy mind has only so much capacity.

* * *

Training went well, but the final phase was always the most challenging—and often resulted in some students being washed out.

The Carrier Qualification Phase is where students have their first opportunity to land on a ship at sea. Carrier aviators take great pride in landing on a ship, and they never **flare** to land. Instead, they always maintain 700 to 800 feet per minute rate of descent, all the way until slamming down on the runway or carrier deck (the proper procedure).

The work-up phase to prepare for going to the carrier is extensive. Entire sorties are dedicated solely to the task of practicing landings at the airfield, on a small landing zone painted on the runway to replicate the landing zone on the carrier.

To land on the carrier, a light system called the **Fresnel Lens** provides visual guidance for the pilot to solve glide slope, which is the angle of descent (three degrees) to land at the desired point on the carrier. The pilot has to line the aircraft up with the landing zone, flying at the proper airspeed and glide slope. Finally, an **LSO** provides adjustments on the radio and has the authority to signal a "wave-off," should the circumstances warrant it. These circumstances include a "fouled deck" (where aircraft or personnel are in the landing zone, prohibiting a safe recovery by the landing aircraft) or general buffoonery (where the aircraft is outside of safe parameters, usually due to poor pilot performance).

The entire endeavor is understandably dangerous and has resulted in untold numbers of deaths over decades of operations, including on the ship itself. Two of my three friends to whom this book is dedicated lost their lives during carrier operations. Performance has to be strong; there is little margin for error.

The first pass begins with the break, where the pilot approaches the stern of the ship (or landing zone at the field) at 800 feet above sea level and 350 knots (403 mph). This is followed by a turn to downwind and a position abeam the landing zone, gear and flaps extended, at 600 feet above sea level. From there, an abeam call is made by the pilot, and a turn toward final approach begins.

When established on downwind, individual aircraft will descend to pattern altitude of 600 feet, perform landing checks and closely monitor the abeam distance. The carrier landing pattern is illustrated in Figure 2-5.

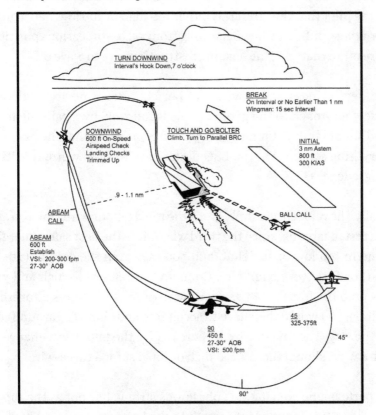

Figure 2-5 Carrier Landing Pattern

 f. **Touch and Go/Bolter.** The procedures for touch and go landings and bolters are identical. Continue to fly the ball all the way to touchdown. Upon touchdown, simultaneously advance power to MRT, retract speed brakes, and rotate to optimum AOA. Maintain wings level and verify a positive rate of climb and maintain optimum AOA. Once a positive rate of climb is established and your aircraft is abeam the bow, use a shallow right turn to parallel the BRC. Take interval on any aircraft that

Rounding the corner toward the landing zone offers the first opportunity to see the **ball** or **meatball**. Seeing the ball is paramount, as it
provides instant feedback to the pilot about where the aircraft is in
reference to glide slope. If the pilot doesn't see the ball, a confession
ensues by making the radio call, "**Clara** ball." The LSO might then
provide radio feedback, such as "Clara high" or "Clara low," informing the pilot that the aircraft is either too high or too low. Salvaging a
pass is very difficult when beginning from such a precarious position.
More often than not, the ensuing instructions are to wave off.

The perfect pass starts with the perfect abeam position, then a
perfect approach to the **groove**. This is followed by a ball call and a
dead silent landing for an OK three-wire, meaning that the pilot did
everything *so* well that the LSO didn't have to say a word, resulting
in a grade of "OK."

Ideally, the pilot successfully grabs the third of four wires for a "trap,"
or arrested landing, since the third wire offers the best safety margin.
Come in too low or too slow, and you may grab the second (not as
good) or first (very bad) wire. Come in too fast or too high and you
may grab the fourth (not as good) wire or miss the wires altogether
(bolter); you would then have to accelerate and climb (go around) for
another try. The fourth wire is there to give the pilot a last chance to
grab a wire, should they be too high or too fast for a three-wire.

My performance during this phase was strong, but not at the top of
the class. Still, one student came into the break and entered his first
pass having forgotten to put his landing gear down! "You might need
your rollers," came the radio call from the LSO. I knew there was at
least one person doing worse than me. As the saying goes, "If the heat
is on someone else, it's not on you."

After multiple sorties and countless passes at the field, being graded
and debriefed on every pass, it was time to go to the ship and put what
we'd learned into practice. There was just one twist, a variable none of
us had yet seen: next time, the landing zone would be moving!

USS Enterprise and an AEGIS escort ship UNREPPING and VERTREPPING. Ron served as an enlisted S-3 AW on the Enterprise (Photo from DVIDS, Open Source).

NAS Cubi Point Officers' Club, Philippines. When the naval station at Cubi Point closed, the club was considered to be so iconic that it was meticulously disassembled and reassembled in the National Naval Aviation Museum, NAS Pensacola, Florida, where it resides today. (Photo from DVIDS, Open Source)

Monkey Business

Ensign Ron "Warhead" Lambrecht

"If you're not making waves, you're not under weigh."

—Chester W. Nimitz

Nautical Notables:

Call Sign: Most call signs play on or reference the aviator's surname. Other inspirations for call signs may include personality traits or past exploits during the aviator's career. Aviator call signs nearly always come from a member or members of the aviator's squadron, training class, or other cohort; it is considered bad form to try to give oneself a call sign. It is also common for aviators to be given a fairly derogatory call sign, and the more they complain about it, the more likely it is to stick.

Bull Ensign: The Bull Ensign is the senior Ensign of a Navy command (ship, squadron, or shore activity). In addition to normal duties, the Bull Ensign assumes various responsibilities, such as teaching less-experienced Ensigns about life at sea, planning and coordinating wardroom social activities, and making sure that the Officers' mess runs smoothly. Though the position seldom has any formal authority, the Bull Ensign serves as the focal point for the unit's expression of spirit and pride. A Bull Ensign will often be recognized by their uniform's oversized gold ensign collar device, engraved with the word "Bull" or "Heifer" as applicable.

Another Fine Navy Day!: An expression voiced (in a very cheery manner) on occasions when, in fact, it's not that much of a Fine Navy Day at all.

August (aw-GUST) Chief Petty Officer: A description of any Chief Petty Officer who exudes majestic dignity or grandeur. Such an individual is recognizable by their dominant yet dignified gate and stature. It may be used in a sentence as follows: "An angry primate, when taunted by the actions of Junior Officers, may exude characteristics consistent with those of an August Chief Petty Officer."

You know you have been accepted into a squadron when someone assigns you a **call sign**, and there is no limit to cleverness when aviators find free time on their hands. Examples of call signs include:

"Barely," the call sign for Lieutenant Able.

"Wedge" had a last name of O'Toole and was the simplest "o' tools."

"SWIM" stood for "Stupidest WSO (Weapons and Sensors Operator) in the Marine Corps."

"Wrong Way" got lost and landed in Mexico.

"Jabber" could humble an auctioneer.

"Atho" was missing his two front teeth (think about it).

"Crawl Space" came from a family of plumbers.

"Pig" had a last name of Guinee.

"Paradox" was a name shared by two flight surgeons (flight docs); one was tall and rotund, the other short and thin.

"Speed Brakes" wore clip-on sunglasses. He and I were running mates back in my Ensign (O-1) and Lieutenant Junior Grade (O-2) days.

"Warhead" (me) was an Intelligence Officer with a propensity for "an expansion in which energy is transmitted outward as a shock wave." Soon enough, even the nametag on my flight jacket read "Warhead."

* * *

The training pipeline for pilots and Naval Flight Officers was about twelve months longer than for Intelligence Officers because of the required flight training, so Junior Officer pilots and NFOs arriving in the squadron were normally Junior Grade (O-2) or Lieutenant (O-3) level. That made me an immediate **Bull Ensign** upon arrival, a position I assumed with pride.

Young debonair Officers like me were always concerned with our image, an image that required haircuts that pushed the limits of acceptable military standards. Although military barbers are plentiful, they knew only one haircut (A.J. squared away), so many military men employed the services of civilian barbers. The North Island Air Station was located on Coronado Island, which is separated from downtown San Diego by a bridge and a bay, so whenever we needed a good "at the edge" haircut, we would go to Hightower's Barber Shop in downtown Coronado.

Hightower was well-liked by the military, and he was always good for a joke or two. One day, Speed Brakes and I headed to Hightower's for a haircut, probably in preparation for a personnel inspection, and when Speed Brakes' turn in the chair came, Hightower asked him how he wanted his hair cut. Speed Brakes pondered for a moment and then said, "On the right side, I would like about a quarter inch white wall above my ear with a fairly abrupt taper along the back. On the left side, leave the hair long enough to slightly cover the upper portion of my ear and block the back."

Hightower looked at Speed Brakes in bewilderment and asked, "What the hell kind of haircut is that?"

Speed Brakes responded, "Well, it's how you cut it last time!"

It took about a month before Speed Brakes stopped looking like a "Jarhead Marine."

* * *

When not on deployment, the Officers' Clubs provided a festive venue for entertainment. The San Diego circuit consisted of the Miramar (of TOPGUN fame) "O" club on Wednesday night, the North Island "O" club on Thursday night, and either the Amphibious Base "O" club (Coronado, SEAL training base) or the US Marine Corps Training Center "O" club on Friday. Saturdays usually consisted of a party hosted on a rotational basis by a squadron mate. Sunday was beach day. Monday and Tuesday were recovery—uh, work—days. Every Junior Officer (JO) worth their salt owned two covers (hats): one to place on their desk so it appeared they were in the area but not at their desk, and another to wear when they were nowhere near their work area.

Pre-deployment workups and deployments were another story. Life becomes all business when on deployment. Even the commute from our stateroom to one's watch station is quite short.

Albeit a dangerous occupation, the lifestyle for the aviators was the envy of most Surface Warfare Officers (SWOs) or "Shoes," as they were fondly called (they wore black shoes, not the brown shoes worn by aviators). SWOs are the men and women who drive and maintain the ships. Eighteen-hour days, seven days a week are the norm for most, and some work longer hours. Because of the mandatory crew rest an Aircrewman is required to maintain between flights, it was the belief of the SWOs that aviators slept until they got hungry and ate until they got tired, with the routine only interrupted by an occasional flight. I can neither confirm nor deny.

JOs tend to still be at the stage of frontal lobe development, so opportunities to let off steam are seldom overlooked. Port calls were meant to provide crews with some rest and relaxation (R&R)—sometimes referred to as rest and *rehabilitation*.

During the first years of my career, it was routine to port in Subic Bay, Philippines, for a five- to six-day R&R period before transiting to the Indian Ocean, when we would spend three to four months on patrol on GONZO Station (Gulf of Oman Naval Zone of Operations). Liberty in Subic Bay was one last opportunity for Sailors to "set their hair on fire" before the long at-sea period that awaited them.

Olongapo City, located adjacent to the Subic Bay Naval and Cubi Point Air Bases, was a nonstop party town because of the never-ending arrival and departure of Navy ships. The beer of choice, because it was the only beer, was San Miguel. No two bottles tasted the same.

One afternoon, several of us JOs were relaxing at the pool at the Cubi Officers' Club when a couple juvenile monkeys appeared from the adjacent jungle. They looked friendly enough, so one of the guys threw a roll in their direction as a peace offering. Instantly, a burly old male appeared from the jungle and grabbed the roll. *Okay, now that he had a roll, let's throw a couple more in the direction of the juveniles,* we reasoned. The grumpy male immediately scooped up the two rolls. After a period of time, he was carrying five or six rolls, and it didn't appear he was about to share.

Speed Brakes grabbed a roll and, ensuring the alpha male was watching, headed for a dumpster located behind the Cubi "O" Club kitchen. He placed the roll in the dumpster and stepped a few feet away. The old male took the bait and jumped into the dumpster. Speed Brakes slammed the lid closed. This bad monkey needed a time-out. At that point, things got really quiet inside the dumpster, so we went about feeding and entertaining the juvenile monkeys while reflecting on how clever we were.

About ten minutes passed when a Filipino cook walked out the back door of the kitchen to dump some trash. He threw back the lid on the dumpster, and the angry inhabitant popped up like a jack-in-the-box, with neither rolls nor sense of humor. Someone was going to pay, and the cook was a target of opportunity.

I do not know if the cook was a student of Maslow's theory, but he understood the concept. He levitated, rotated, and while expressing his situational discomfort in high pitch Tagalog (the Filipino language), sprinted toward the kitchen door. The grumpy male answered in high-pitched monkey. I assumed the cook's four-letter disparaging words about the monkey's mother only added to the animal's determination.

Fortunately, the cook had a five-foot lead on the angry primate because the race was on. The cook cleared the screen door a half second before the monkey, though it appeared to be only a matter of time before the monkey would eat his way through the screen. We were enjoying the spectacle when the enraged monkey looked over his shoulder in our direction.

It was, by definition, **another fine Navy day**. With a vengeance, the angry creature propelled himself in our direction, causing us to vacate our observation posts with vigor for the safety of the deep end of the pool. A period of time passed while the angry male strutted around the pool's edge to show off his moxie and to reflect upon how clever *he* was. **August Chief Petty Officers** had nothing on this monkey!

The monkey eventually retired to our recently vacated beach chairs to finish our lunches. I must admit, until then, I did not know monkeys drank San Miguel.

Photos taken by Steve from his T-2C during carrier qualifications. Top: marshaling overhead prior to commencing. Bottom: on the deck of the USS Forrestal.

YGBSM

First Lieutenant
Steve "Curly" Lambrecht
Student Naval Aviator, VT-23

"If seventy wasn't good enough, it wouldn't be passing."

—RON LAMBRECHT

Aeronautical Notables:

You've gotta be shitting me (YGBSM): YGBSM is a lot like saying, "Hey, watch this." The biggest difference is that "Hey, watch this" means it is your idea; YGBSM means it isn't.

Bolter: The tailhook fails to engage a cable, either due to pilot ham-fisting while landing or due to a "hook-skip." In this most unfortunate of circumstances, the pilot gets another opportunity to excel and be graded for the effort. In other words, it's another opportunity to fail.

Ham-Fisting: A description of poor control inputs by a pilot. Envision a pilot trying to fly a plane with large hams where their hands should be. Adopted by pilots during WWI.

Marshalers: Incredibly skilled personnel capable of directing aircraft around a flight deck, sometimes within inches of the edge, which in turn resides nearly one hundred feet above the water.

March 21, 1992 was a partly cloudy day, and I was about to face the biggest challenge of flight training: landing on an aircraft carrier for the first time!

Our instructor was the lead in our formation of five. He had four wingmen, and I had the privilege of being "dash five," meaning the fifth airplane in the formation. Also known as "dash last," the last person in the formation has certain obligations, such as being timely in joining up and visually verifying that no aircraft in the formation have lurking mechanical defects (e.g., leaking fluids or panels that have opened unexpectedly).

The position also comes with certain privileges. The main privilege is that you don't have to worry as much about being in perfect formation. Other positions, like "dash two," require solid, predictable, and smooth flying so that those on the outside of you (dashes three through five) can have a steady reference when flying formation. As dash five, there's no one counting on you for the same. You can relax. You might even be able to look around a bit.

It was a relief to be able to relax on the way out to the carrier. We were roughly thirty miles off the coast of Texas, in the Gulf of Mexico, a five-minute flight. Only five minutes, but given the challenge ahead, a welcome respite. I could chill. *What a great deal,* I thought. What a dumbass I was.

Until recently, students had always qualified on the *USS Lexington,* a WWII relic used exclusively for carrier qualification training. Having retired *Lexington,* the Navy rotated combat carriers through the assignment. Our assigned ship was the *USS Forrestal,* a ship of war that was noticeably larger than *Lexington.*

Upon arrival above the carrier, we were told to hold at 10,000 feet and wait our turn. The delay might be caused by aircraft ahead of us, which were completing their qualification landings, deck crew changes, heading changes by the ship, or even equipment issues. For this trip, we had an extra five to ten minutes to kill.

I had little else to do as dash five, so I figured I may as well sneak a glimpse at the carrier 10,000 feet below me. I was certain it would be a cool scene: a huge vessel of American power parting the seas before her, patiently awaiting my arrival. I had sailed on the *USS Kitty Hawk* during the Tiger Cruise a mere ten years prior and recalled how immense the ship was, stretching 1,069 feet in length and carrying a compliment of 5,600 Sailors and 85 aircraft.

And so, I relaxed my formation-keeping and looked down. I saw nothing. *She must be beneath a cloud,* I reasoned. As I proceeded around the holding pattern, my glances became more rapid. I figured there were enough gaps in the clouds to allow for me to behold American sea power in all of its magnificence, but alas, no joy. Then, in a moment of simultaneous shock, terror, and realization, I became informed.

My perspective was...in error.

As you read this, I invite you to hold your arm out fully extended, with your fist clenched—like my butt cheeks were in that moment—and your thumb raised. Just like a thumbs-up sign. Look at your thumbnail; its size represents the size of the carrier. Now, imagine parking your car on it while driving 150 miles per hour. Hard to imagine? Me too.

As I looked down from my comfortable position as dash five, I saw this sliver of a postage stamp moving through the water. The largest visual clue of its presence, by far, was its extended wake.

The ship was over 1,000 feet long. I was going to land on an area one third its length, *but at least it would be **moving** in three dimensions!* One-third of a sliver of a postage stamp. Watch this? Not so much. **YGBSM**? Hells yes!

When I was underway on a carrier during the Tiger Cruise, I saw it all, up close and personal. It seemed like a huge ship when I was fourteen. Enormous. I even got lost in it multiple times. From this perspective, however, I knew it was going to be a whole different ball game!

"Luckily" for me, with five to ten minutes to kill, I had the opportunity to behold the sliver multiple times. Each time, instead of inspiring study and contemplation, it filled me with terror anew. Then came the inevitable: it was time to meet my fate.

We were directed to descend and enter the break. The break, if you recall, is the initial approach to the back of the ship, conducted at approximately 350 knots (403 mph) and 800 feet above the water. As we spiraled down, the ship, and therefore the landing zone, became larger. Did it grow comfortably large? Not even a little.

We needed to complete two touch-and-goes, piloting the aircraft within acceptable parameters for a safe touchdown, without the tail hook extended. We would then apply full power to ensure a takeoff and back around the pattern for the next pass. Following two touch-and-goes, we would do the same thing with the tail hook extended, catch a cable and stop (called a trap), then proceed to the catapult for a launch (called a cat).

Two touch-and-goes. Four traps and cats. Six total passes, provided you didn't screw them up and be made to repeat any.

There are as many ways to screw up a pass as there are carrier pilots, but the most common are to be either unsafe or to have a **bolter**. Unsafe means exactly that: if the pilot cannot demonstrate a confidence-inspiring approach to the back of the carrier, the LSO will demand a wave-off, whereby the non-confidence-inspiring pilot will command full power, climb away from the ship, and cease to threaten the lives of all those contained therein. To accentuate the point, the ship is equipped with either a pit to duck into or a safety net to roll into over the side of the ship, in the event the doubt-inspiring pilot motivates the LSO to utilize either.

I can tell you two things. First, the trap (cable catch) and the cat (catapult launch) are absolutely, positively, make no mistake about it, the most amazing things I've experienced. Second, given the proper amount of thrust and buffoonery, an overwhelmed, wide-eyed aviator can laugh at himself—even after the thrill of his first ever catapult launch.

I tried my best to concentrate only on my instruments and to not be distracted by staring at the ship. Doing so, I feared, might cause me to shit my pants. Still, an occasional glance was necessary in order to ensure proper positioning in the pattern.

After completing the break, I used my instruments and a quick glance outside to maneuver into the abeam position, properly configured with gear and flaps extended and at the proper speed for approach. This was a good start. I made the "abeam" call, and then the easy part was over.

I began my descent and turned toward the final approach, but halfway through the turn, I noticed I was a bit high and eased off the power. The next milestone was to see the ball as I rounded the corner to final. The ball was visible, which was a huge relief (I was not "Clara"), but the ball informed me immediately that I was higher than desired.

I called the ball, "Blazer seven, Buckeye Ball, 5.7, Curly." The call included my flight call sign, visual acquisition of the ball, fuel state in thousands of pounds, and my personal call sign (I was nicknamed "Curly" in honor of my shrinking hair line, or growing forehead, whichever you prefer).

"Roger ball, you're high," came the response.

The LSO told me what I already knew. I was not inspiring confidence.

If a pilot is too high, they have to be "back on the power" (throttles back and engines delivering less thrust than usual) and descend at a higher-than-normal rate to get back on glide slope. It is not uncommon, when being high, to be late bringing the power back up, causing the aircraft to pass through the proper glide slope and end up too low. As I approached the proper glide slope, the LSO called "Power," inspiring me to add power as to not end up low.

The proper line-up eluded me. I began the final approach by slightly overshooting the landing zone and, from there, proceeded to **ham-fist** back and forth, never being perfectly stable with the alignment.

Landings are made on the angle deck, which is canted nine degrees from the ship's direction of travel. This means the landing zone is traveling away from the pilot in two dimensions. As Dad used to say while watching me cut boards with a circular saw, "The only time you are on the line is when you are crossing it!"

So it was with this pass, and several others that followed.

Adding to the variables of landing the Buckeye on the carrier is that the engines hang below the centerline of the aircraft. Because of this, every addition of power results in a nose-up pitch; every power reduction results in a nose-down pitch. The overall effect is to "porpoise" the aircraft as power is adjusted.

More variables. Just what I needed.

While fighting line-up, power setting, and glide slope, hurling myself at the ocean—with a horrifyingly small postage stamp trying to suck my eyeballs away from the task at hand—and the LSO doing his best to keep me from taking my final bath, I touched down, added full power, then took-off again. I knew it wasn't pretty, but I was one down. Five to go.

The next pass, my second and final touch-and-go, was not remarkably better. This was a lot like playing pool as a kid in The Club, except the pool table was moving and I was riding my chair at 350 miles per hour!

The next pass was a trap. There's a lot going on in the two seconds it takes to decelerate from 140 knots (160 miles per hour) to zero in just 344 feet. Upon touchdown, I had to add power, in case of missing the cables, while hoping to feel the telltale deceleration resulting from a successful cable engagement.

Confirmation came when I was thrown forward in my shoulder harness and my helmet nearly bounced off the instrument panel. It was just pretty frickin' amazing, all around, but there was no time to revel! The landing zone had to be cleared immediately for the next aircraft.

I gave 100 percent of my attention to the **marshalers** (yellow shirts) directing my aircraft around the flight deck. As they marshaled me to the catapult, I briefly contemplated what was about to happen. I was about to be hurled off the front end of the very hunk of steel I had worked my ass off to land on in the first place. YGBSM!

Imagine, if you will, sitting in the cockpit of one of the most amazing pieces of engineering man has ever created, looking at 300 feet of steel before you and the limitless expanse of ocean waiting to swallow your soon-to-be dead carcass. Now, imagine the kick in the ass that accelerates the total weight of pilot and machinery (approximately 12,000 pounds) from zero to 150 knots (173 miles per hour) in that same 300 feet. Talk about being along for the ride!

The catapult launch is sometimes compared to an amusement park ride, which is both fair and accurate. At least fair and accurate in the same way that comparing a sunburn with traveling to the center of the sun is fair and accurate. The catapult launch is simply the most breathtaking, exhilarating experience there is! Period.

What makes the experience breathtaking (literally) is that you are simultaneously piloting a remarkable piece of engineering and placing your life in literal peril. A great many things can go wrong, each with a high potential to result in death. Arguably, it is worth it.

There I was, on the pointy end of the ship, eyes wide open and throttles at full power. My hand was behind the throttles to prevent their movement aft as a result of the force from the launch, which would reduce the thrust below the minimum required for flight. The jet was "in tension," meaning the catapult was in contact with the launch bar, applying immense force toward the front of the ship. At the same time, the holdback, a device contrived to prevent launch, was literally holding the aircraft back from the force of the catapult.

The net effect was that the aircraft "squatted" against the opposing forces as it was compressed against the deck. *Everything* was "in tension," including my seat cushion. You could not have driven a sewing needle up my asshole with a sledgehammer; if I had been holding a lump of coal in my sphincter, I would have created a duplicate of the Hope Diamond!

I saluted the catapult Officer, affectionately called the "Shooter," who then touched the deck and pointed toward the bow. This act signaled the catapult operator, protected in a recessed compartment on the side of the deck, to hit the launch button. With that, the pistons of the steam catapult were released, shearing the hour-glass shaped pin holding my Buckeye back against her fully powered engines. The total weight of man and machine was hurled into pure acceleration.

From that moment, and until flight was achieved, intervention was no longer possible. Either everyone had done their job correctly, or they hadn't. It was the moment of truth. The moment of reckoning. A proving ground for everyone involved, myself included.

As I was "enjoying" the ride, which is too short and terrifying to truly enjoy, the force of the launch caused my thumb to activate the radio transmitter switch on the throttle. All those within one hundred-plus miles and tuned into the carrier frequency were free to hear the sounds a twenty-four-year-old master diamond maker makes while hurling toward certain death. I wish I had the audio recorded—I'd be YouTube famous! It must have sounded like a combination of spitting, coughing, and being kicked in the junk. Despite my terror, the absolute thrill of the launch and appreciation for my own buffoonery caused me to laugh at myself as I set up for my next pass.

Three touch-and-goes and four traps/cats later, I was qualified to land the mighty T-2C Buckeye on America's aircraft carriers. Three touch-and-goes because I had one hook-skip bolter.

I won't lie to you—it was all a complete blur. To this day, I can't recall the specifics. I relied heavily on my training, coupled with Marine Corps grit. Failure was still not an option.

The minimum required score for qualification was a 2.4, and not everyone in my class made it. I finished with an adequate but less-than-convincing 2.4. At the bottom of my grade sheet, my LSO wrote, "A qual is a qual." Qualified is qualified.

I had flashbacks of the "double D in Double E" experience from my days at USNA. On the one hand, I was reminded of what my brother had said: "If seventy wasn't good enough, it wouldn't be passing." On the other hand, the minimum wasn't going to get me into my dream jet, the F/A-18. Another chance to prove myself at carrier qualification awaited me in the TA-4J Skyhawk, and I intended to take full advantage of it.

Later in life, I discovered the only thing more terrifying than YGBSM. It is YGBSM, only at night. Thus, YGBFSM. That story will greet you soon enough.

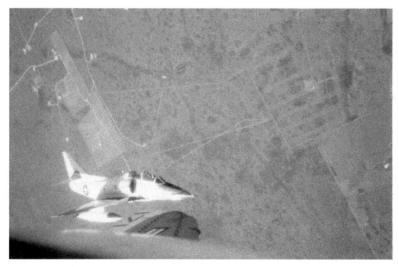

Steve on the wing of a tactical maneuvering sortie in a TA-4J over southern Texas.

First Lieutenant Steve Lambrecht on the day he received his Naval Aviator Wings of Gold at Naval Air Station Kingsville, Texas (1992). Steve was winged with a class of nineteen fellow pilots shortly after this photo was taken.

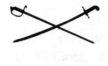

Wings

First Lieutenant
Steve "Curly" Lambrecht
Student Naval Aviator, VT-21

"I have not yet begun to fight!"

—Captain John Paul Jones

Aeronautical Notables:

Navy Standard Score (NSS): A representation of any score relative to the average score. The scale is artificially centered at 50 (that is, 50 is average).

For the Math Geeks: NSS = (((grade - avg grade)/SD)10) + 50 rounded. Grade = any student grade; avg grade = the mean grade for the distribution in question; SD = standard deviation for that distribution.

It was now time to move on to the TA-4J Skyhawk, so I had to redouble my efforts.

The TA-4J was a training version of a tried-and-true combat aircraft: the A-4 Skyhawk, the same aircraft I pushed around the Naval Academy in an attempted heist. Affectionately nicknamed the "Scooter," the Skyhawk was a fun, maneuverable aircraft, unlike anything I had flown before. The cockpit was tiny, as was the entire aircraft.

Beginning in the '60s, the Soviets created highly maneuverable aircraft that the larger, less agile US fighters could not easily compete with in a dogfight. The A-4 helped reverse that trend. Designed largely by John Boyd and Pierre Sprey, the A-4 was a nimble warfighting machine, flying far better than it rolled over the College Creek Bridge at USNA!

The tactical application of flying the A-4 was new, and it whetted my appetite for more. Once, while practicing basic tactical maneuvering against an instructor, we began with myself in the defensive position. I maneuvered in such a way as to become offensive, pulling a lead-turn for a shot with the gun. Lead is required to employ the gun, as the bullets need to be fired in front of a moving target. It was a skill I had perfected during my childhood hunting endeavors. Simultaneously, from the instructor's radio in the other A-4, and the intercom from the instructor in my backseat, I heard the words, "Nice move." In that moment, I knew I had chosen the right vocation.

Advanced Jet Training went very well for me, and my experience on the boat during Carrier Qualification on the USS Dwight D. Eisenhower in the Scooter went far better than it had in the Buckeye. With repetition, the carrier aviation lightbulb was beginning to illuminate. Once again, I finished first in my class and achieved Commodore's List with Distinction.

When it came time to select the aircraft I would fly (ultimately in combat), I chose my dream jet: the F/A-18 Hornet! Rumor has it I had come close to setting a record for an **NSS** in flight school, but my Buckeye boat experience may well have kept me from doing so.

No matter. On October 22, 1992, I received my Navy Wings of Gold and moved on to my next assignment as an F/A-18 student at Cecil Field, Jacksonville, Florida.

Sons and Daughters of Neptune

Ensign Ron "Warhead" Lambrecht

"To those mariners courageously sailing waters unknown

Those brave with weeping mothers at home

Sing your song and let it be known

I've crossed the line into Neptune's throne"

—UNKNOWN

Nautical Notables:

Shellbacks: Sailors who have crossed the equator.

Pollywogs: Sailors who have not crossed the equator.

No Room to Swing a Cat: The entire ship's company was required to witness floggings so that all may learn from the endeavor. If the crew crowded too close to the Bosun's Mate, he might not have enough room to swing his cat-o'-nine-tails.

Shellback Initiation is the ceremony that converts **pollywogs** to shellbacks. The ceremony is said to have dated back to the early days of the British Royal Navy and was originally created to test a new sailor's ability to withstand long, hard days at sea.

Early Shellback Initiation ceremonies involved beating "wogs" with wooden planks and wet ropes and, in some cases, dragging sailors overboard. It is historic fact that some sailors died while participating in Shellback Initiation. My initiation was less dangerous but equally humiliating.

The crossing of the equator is officially recognized by service record entries indicating date, time, latitude, and longitude. It involves elaborate preparation by the "shellbacks" to ensure the "pollywogs" are properly indoctrinated. All pollywogs, even the Commanding Officer if they have not crossed before, must participate.

US Navy practice holds that when a ship crosses the equator, King Neptune comes aboard to exercise authority over his domain. He adjudicates charges brought against pollywogs accused of posing as Sailors who haven't paid proper homage to him. Members of Neptunus Rex's entourage usually include Davy Jones (Neptune's first assistant), Her Highness Amphitrite, the Royal Scribe, the Royal Doctor, the Royal Dentist, the Royal Baby, the Royal Navigator, the Royal Chaplain, the Royal Judge, attorneys, barbers, and other hangers-on. In the day when only men crewed Navy ships, all roles were played by shellback Officers and Sailors, including the Royal Baby and Her Highness Amphitrite.

So it was on my *USS Kitty Hawk* deployment. While in transit to the Indian Ocean, we dipped south of the equator. Upon entering the Strait of Malacca off the coast of Singapore, our forewarning arrived. It was recommended that we pollywogs purchase an inexpensive pair of tennis shoes from the ship's supply store and don clothing we would never need again.

Some shellbacks had over thirty years of naval service, and let me just say, they represented a different era—and in many ways, a different standard for acceptable behavior when it came to creative shenanigans. It was during this shellback ceremony that I gained a real appreciation for the "sailors of old." Once they were unleashed, their inner pirates emerged. (All in good sadistic humor, of course.)

The ceremony was not to start until reveille, but at about 0430, there was no longer "quiet about the decks." Rather, the shellback pirates were causing a commotion like I hadn't experienced since Aviation Officer Candidate School.

We were herded on all fours like cattle to collection areas. Next, we were assigned to pirate "tutors" who personally knew and worked with us. It was an opportunity for them to tailor the initiation to fit the crimes of said wog, and because I was follicly challenged and had been an Aircrewman, I was fitted with a toupee of arresting gear grease (a heavy grease concoction for lubricating the cables used to catch airplanes landing on the carrier deck). This was followed by a compliment from my personal pirate indicating I looked handsome with hair.

That made me nervous. The grease was bad enough, but some sadistic pirate discovered the stuffing in our pillows consisted of feathers. It is common knowledge that grease attracts feathers!

After an intentionally forgettable amount of time dedicated to all sorts of humiliating activities, we were herded to the flight deck, where the real fun began. The gauntlet started with a trip through the garbage shoot. At sea, compostable garbage is dumped over the side through a tapered tube, which prevents garbage from slopping back onto the fantail of the ship. It has a three-foot opening on one end and a two-foot opening on the other. Once inside, there was **no room to swing a cat**.

After entering the shoot, I discovered why we were served skinless chicken the night before: raw eggs and various other slimy items contributed to the experience. Good thing it was dark because I am sure some wogs ahead of me contributed to the contents as they transited the tube. When we reached the other end, the Royal Baby, wearing only a diaper, awaited us.

The Royal Baby was appropriately played by a Master Chief (E-9), who, through ingenuity of some sort, proved it was possible to evade physical fitness tests and body weight standards. He sat on a pedestal with his entire chest and belly caked in lard/Crisco. A cherry, placed in his belly button, was to be removed by a wog by biting the stem. Seemed simple enough, except the Royal Baby grabbed our heads and smeared our faces all over his belly. With another handful of Crisco smeared on his hairy belly, and another cherry inserted, he was ready for the next wog. My pursuit of the cherry resulted in arresting gear grease and feathers being added to the lard on the Royal Baby's ample abdomen. The Royal Baby was not happy!

I could go on, but I will spare you. Probably the most challenging part of the day was trying to remove arresting gear grease from what ended up being all over my body. I attempted to take a shower using soap and shampoo, and all I did was cause rivers of grease to run down my legs. With 3,000 other guys waiting to take a cold shower (all the hot water was depleted), I needed to move on, so I headed to the flight deck wearing nothing but my birthday suit.

There, a station was set up for spraying sea water to "clean" the recently initiated pollywogs. In desperation, I asked others for advice. An unknown shipmate (to whom I am eternally indebted) handed me a bottle of Wisk laundry detergent. Trust me with this: if you ever find yourself covered in arresting gear grease and only have ice-cold sea water to bathe with, find a bottle of Wisk! Five minutes later, I was pink and squeaky clean.

With a few exceptions, those who have been inducted into the "mysteries of the deep" by Neptunus Rex and his Royal Court count the experience as a highlight of their naval career. I am no exception.

USS Dwight D. Eisenhower. (Photo Credit: Photographer's Mate Second Class Miguel A. Contreras, Public domain, via Wikimedia Commons)

Speed Is Life

First Lieutenant
Steve "Curly" Lambrecht
Student, Replacement Air Group, VFA-106

"I've never done THAT before, and I'll never do it again."

—Every Fighter Pilot Ever

Aeronautical Notables:

Speed Is Life: A common saying among military aviators. Refers to the benefit of having airspeed available to escape the threat from enemy fire, either from the ground or from other aircraft. Excess airspeed is always beneficial...or almost always.

Salty: Description of a Sailor or Marine who is highly experienced—or thinks themselves so. Someone who is salty is also referred to as a "Salty Dog." The saying originates from having been to sea multiple times.

Bingo Fuel: A predetermined fuel quantity which, upon being reached, signals the aircrew to end the mission and return to base.

Speed of Heat: A phrase to describe something moving at a supremely fast rate.

Skipper: Squadron Commanding Officer. A Navy Commander.

Carrier Air Group Commander (CAG): A Navy Captain in charge of all aircraft assigned to a carrier air wing.

Editorial note: all names and personal call signs contained in this story have been changed to protect the guilty and innocent alike.

There I was, a bourgeoning young fighter pilot nearing the end of my training in the F/A-18 Hornet. Only Aircraft Carrier Qualification remained, and then it was off to my first active Marine Corps Fighter Squadron. The thought of it intoxicated me.

I had been successful in flight school thus far, training in three previous aircraft and qualifying at the carrier in two of them. But landing on the carrier had proven to be the most difficult portion for me thus far, and this time I had to do it at night!

In Jacksonville, Florida, a small outlying airfield about eleven miles to the north, called OLF Whitehouse, was used exclusively for carrier workup training. We launched from our home station of Cecil Field, proceeded to OLF Whitehouse where the LSOs (Landing Signal Officers) awaited us, came into the "break," and entered the pattern for repeated evaluation.

Airspeed in the break is more or less at the pilot's discretion (much more about that later), but one of many sayings among carrier aviators is "John Wayne in the break, Slim Pickens on the ball." This is in reference to the inherent difficulty of arriving in the landing zone (slim pickings) after breaking at excessive speeds (looking like John Wayne). A target airspeed in the break ranged from a minimum of 350 to a maximum of 450 nautical miles per hour (knots), or 518 statue miles per hour. Anything faster than 450 and the pilot was being a "cowboy," thus the phrase "John Wayne in the break." At this stage of our aviation careers, we had already been to the carrier twice, successfully, and therefore felt a little **salty**.

Typically, as many as twelve touch-and-goes are evaluated in one sortie, sometimes during the day and sometimes at night. Upon completion of the last touch-and-go, usually **bingo fuel** was reached, and we proceeded back to Cecil Field for a final ungraded break to a full-stop landing. This, my friends, is where the trouble began.

The young are often known for their indiscretions, and young Naval Aviators—strapped to high-performance, eye-watering, magical machines such as the F/A-18 Hornet—are known for their brilliance... and occasional indiscretions. For instance, it can be very difficult to determine the speed of an aircraft by looking at it from the ground. It can also be very fun to achieve high speeds in the break. Put the two together, and you have the recipe for indiscretion.

So it began: each pilot in the class became more of an airspeed cowboy than the previous one. Each one whispered about their exploits in the debrief. Day and night, the festivities continued.

Among the many highlights was a French foreign exchange pilot (call sign "We We"), who commented on our frivolities one night during the debrief. With his French accent, he said in broken English, "This, this thing you are doing with airspeed. It is most foolish."

The question followed, "How fast did YOU go tonight, We We?"

We We responded, "587 knots."

The room erupted with laughter. That's 676 miles per hour, in case you are wondering, well into the cowboy regime. That number didn't outlive the frivolities, however.

It continued. Each day, a new unprecedented level of speed was achieved. As it happened, yours truly had proven to be the fastest cowboy of all, with a speed of .93 Mach (93 percent of the speed of sound, or 716 miles per hour). That is, until two days prior to our departure for *USS Eisenhower* in Key West, Florida, for our carrier qualification. On that fateful day, a rival, call sign "Creep," achieved .94 Mach, leaving me with only one day to retake the lead.

For those who are unfamiliar with the dynamic properties of air, there is a region of airspeed called the *transonic region*. It begins at about .95 Mach and ends at Mach 1.0, the speed of sound. In the transonic region, the air passing over certain portions of a vehicle may be traveling faster than sound (supersonic) due to the curvature of that portion of the vehicle. In supersonic flight, a shock wave forms that results in a loud "boom" when heard from the ground. Long story short, there is a fine line between a .95 Mach cowboy and extreme loudness. The loud boom enables those on the ground to determine audibly that which cannot be determined visually: an aircraft is traveling supersonic.

So, there I was, having just completed my final touch-and-go at OLF Whitehouse and on my way back to Cecil Field for a high-speed rendezvous with destiny. I proceeded to the appropriate location approximately seven to eight miles east of the active runway to begin my approach. My heart was pounding. Precision was a must. The margins for error were extraordinarily slim.

I pointed toward the airfield and pushed the throttles to military power, the maximum setting short of afterburner. The aircraft accelerated. In the thick, humid Florida air, military power only got me to about .92 Mach. Extra thrust was requested by the pilot and provided in the form of afterburners. I was approaching the **speed of heat**!

As I neared the runway, I "hawked" the airspeed, scanning it persistently for the slightest changes. All I needed was .95 Mach, nothing more; additional speed would put me soundly into the transonic region, placing me at risk of audible discovery. The aircraft accelerated. .93, .94, .95. The instant I saw .95 Mach, I deselected the afterburners, but alas, the engineers at McDonnell Douglas had designed a magnificent machine, with capabilities far exceeding those of its pilot. The aircraft continued to accelerate for a fraction of a second—.96, .97—then began to decelerate. Damn it!

As I pulled seven Gs in the break, to bleed down the requisite airspeed necessary to turn John Wayne into something other than Slim Pickens, I heard a radio call that made my heart sink. An instructor, on the ground in another Hornet, said to the Squadron Duty Officer, "Hey, Flem, nice supersonic in the break, huh?"

It was a beautiful pass. Without a doubt, an OK three-wire, the highest score achievable. I figured I might as well make it a good one, as it would undoubtedly be my last. I was certain the **Skipper**, and perhaps even his boss, the **CAG**, would be planeside waiting to rip the wings right off my chest.

As I taxied back to my parking spot, nothing appeared out of the ordinary. I parked and shut down. I proceeded into maintenance debrief, where a couple classmates awaited. They said that they had only heard a small "thump," nothing too extraordinary. There was slight hope, but I knew enough to man-up, fess-up, and face the music.

I went directly to the Squadron Duty Officer, Flem (a great American), and confessed my indiscretions. He recommended I proceed directly to the Air Traffic Control Tower and confess to the FAA representative.

I scurried to the Tower, but the FAA rep had gone home for the day. Others in the tower obligingly called him at home and handed the phone to me. I told my story. He replied that no one had complained, and if he was twenty-something and someone strapped a rocket ship to his butt, he'd probably do the same thing. It appeared I had escaped reprisal...for now.

Upon review of my tape, I realized I had momentarily traveled .98 Mach, which equaled 632 knots (755 miles per hour, converted for temperature). Some of my classmates on the other side of Cecil Field at McDonald's said they had heard the thump, but luckily, nothing had broken. I went home that night and awaited the fateful call I assumed would come. It didn't.

The next day, I proceeded to Key West, Florida, where we pre-positioned for both day and night (YGBFSM) carrier qualification in the F/A-18. During the entire ten-day trip, I feared being recalled, should the long arm of Uncle Sam seek to yank me from my purchase. Little did I know the fate awaiting my return.

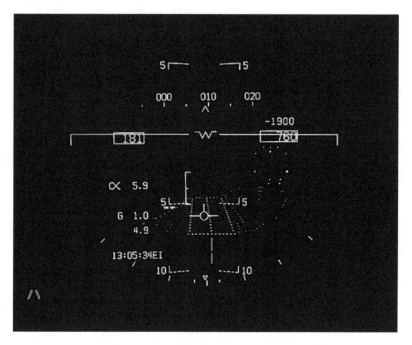

A view of the aircraft carrier landing zone at night, as seen through the heads-up display (HUD) of an F/A-18 Hornet. The vertical row of lights directly below the landing zone are located on the stern of the ship. The two lights forming a chevron to the bottom left of the HUD are angle of attack lights. A matching indicator is located on the nose-gear and is visible to the LSO. In this photo, the pilot is fast, and if left uncorrected, will likely result in either a bolter or a wave-off. (Photo from DVIDS, Open Source)

YGBFSM

First Lieutenant
Steve "Curly" Lambrecht
Student, Replacement Air Group, VFA-106

"I hardly ever die."

—STEVE LAMBRECHT

Aeronautical Notable:

YGBFSM: You've gotta be effing shitting me. YGBSM is to YGBFSM as diarrhea is to catastrophic sphincter failure.

The final exam for every stage of jet training is carrier qualification, but in the Hornet, the ante is upped. In the Hornet, carrier qualification takes place not just during the day, as with the T-2C and the TA-4J, but also at night.

In good weather conditions, believe it or not, daytime carrier operations become fun for the pilot. It's always dangerous, but once the lightbulb comes on and the pilot is comfortable, the "beyond roller-coaster-like" attributes of carrier aviation make the experience both challenging and exhilarating. It provides an adrenaline high like no other on Earth.

During the course of daytime qualifications in the Hornet, the lightbulb came on for me (finally), and I had a blast. Whenever I was offered the opportunity for extra cats and traps, I took them, and I crushed them! I was a legend in my own mind. I made that carrier my big floating steely bitch. The increased confidence, coupled with the familiar smells of steam, lubricants, and greasy cheeseburgers, made me feel as if I were home.

And then came the night.

While daytime carrier operations become fun for the pilot, the same cannot be said for nighttime operations. This is, in part, because the pattern is significantly extended so that each pass takes substantially longer to contemplate and complete. But mostly, it's due to **YGBFSM**.

Imagine, if you will, a catapult from the Middle Ages. You are lying in the bucket, waiting to be hurled. During the day, you can see where you are about to be flung; there is at least a sense of knowing. If you are about to be thrown against the wall of a castle, you will be able to see it coming. At night, the wall is somewhere in the distance, or perhaps it is very close, waiting to greet you shortly after release. It may not be there at all—you do not know. You must wait and see. You only know you will be hurled. Everything else is unknown.

That is a night carrier catapult launch.

The aircraft takes tension. The engines roar. The holdback gives way. You are thrust violently into an unforeseen fate. Then, silence. The violence is over. The motions cease, as if you are suspended in pure darkness. It is one of the most disorienting experiences imaginable—especially if it's a black, humid night under an overcast sky, during calm seas off the coast of Key West, Florida. Unbeknownst to me, these were similar circumstances to the ones that later claimed the life of my roommate at the time, Don Cioffi.

Night flying is instrument flying, and this particular night flying is instrument flying on steroids. No room for flying by the seat of your pants.

On March 19, 1994, there was not a single solitary outside point of reference. None whatsoever. The low cloud layer above my Hornet blocked any possibility of seeing stars or the moon. The humidity in the air created a haze that kept horizontal visibility to only a handful of miles, and I had nothing within those miles to reference.

I knew the sea was below me, but with no light source to illuminate it, the water could've been anywhere, either one foot or thousands of feet below me. I had no ability to judge up from down because looking outside was like being locked in a pitch-black vault. It was complete and utter darkness. The only references available were the instruments inside the cockpit...until I was about halfway around the pattern. Then, I looked outside in the direction my instruments told me the ship should be.

If you recall my previous story about carrier qualification during the day, I compared it to parking your car on a thumbnail while going 150 miles per hour. At night, the thumbnail is a single point of light. In the vast, 360-degree darkness, with no visual references whatsoever, there was a single point of light, upon which I was to hurl my 36,000-pound aircraft at 150 miles per hour and land, without killing or dying. YGBFSM!

I thought I would see a *cluster* of lights. You know, the ship, the landing zone, etc. It's a huge ship! It has a big number on the side that lights up! There must be lots of lights! Not so much. During normal carrier operations, as it happens, the lights are mostly off. Turns out, we don't want the enemy to find our aircraft carriers. A single prick of light in a 360-degree sphere of complete blackness. Awesome.

So, back to the instruments. No point in looking out the transparent part of the aircraft at this stage. Precision flying using only instruments, until turning onto final, which is ten miles directly behind the ship. From that distance and perspective, I thought for sure I'd be able to see more detail and lights, but I was wrong. I beheld a small slightly brighter light source in the middle of nothingness. It dared me to land on it.

Finally, inside of about one mile, I made out all the details I needed. The fantail, or aft end of the ship (also called the stern), had vertical lights to let me know it was below the flight deck and therefore not the place to land the aircraft.

On the flight deck, the landing zone is illuminated by a perimeter of lights, most importantly, the Fresnel Lens, or "meatball." The meatball, or "ball" for short, held the key to success. Without seeing the meatball, there was no chance for a successful landing.

With the aid of instruments and an extended pattern, it was actually much easier to arrive at a good starting position on the ball at night. From there, it became a battle of human versus self. The pilot needs to trust that the ship, with all of its landing area, arresting cables, and goodness, was, in fact, actually there amongst the less-than-plentiful lights. So, we stick to the training, go with what we know, listen to the LSO, and do our best.

Landing becomes more of an act of faith at night than during the day. With little to no visual references betraying the presence of an actual ship, the pilot largely relies on instrumentation and the Fresnel Lens for assurance there is a structure to land on. The assurance comes in the form of the impact of aircraft and carrier, followed by the rapid deceleration inherent with an arrested landing. A quick glance outside at the few lights of the carrier, and the fact they aren't moving relative to the pilot, provides confirmation of a successful trap.

The alternative is either a bolter or a failure of equipment, resulting in a partial deceleration but not a complete stop. The latter condition can be caused by a broken tail hook or arresting cable and is particularly dangerous at night. The pilot can be left without enough airspeed to fly while rolling toward the edge of the ship. Without much visual reference, it can be difficult to determine; either the pilot applies the brakes and is able to stop, or they are forced to eject before going over the side.

All in all, it went fine for me. It was death defying and all that, but I got through it successfully. Not so much for "Wimpy," who was a good guy but, overall, a pretty average pilot. On this occasion, he practically ground his hook off to a nub, executing bolter after bolter after bolter.

At night, a bolter results in an impressive display of sparks as the hook is dragged down the entire length of the landing zone to the end of the carrier, where the aircraft becomes airborne again. That night, Wimpy provided a magnificently sparkly display of YGBFSM.

There comes a point in carrier operations when a pilot may receive the call, "Trick or treat." Trick or treat means the pilot has enough gas for one more attempt at a landing on the ship. Failure results in "treat": flying a "bingo" profile utilizing your remaining fuel to reach an alternate landing location. An alternate landing location almost always means a land-based airport.

When a pilot hears the words "Trick or treat," they are not having a good day (or night). An aircraft in a bingo situation is a troubling thing. Much planning and execution goes into figuring out how to get the pilot/airplane back to the ship. It's also an embarrassment for the pilot, assuming the pilot is the reason for not getting aboard the ship. One wonders why it's called "treat."

That night, Wimpy heard "Trick or treat."

The rest of us students were perched in Vulture's Row on the super-structure, which is the only structure that rises above the flight deck of the aircraft carrier. From Vulture's Row, one has a front-row seat to everything happening on the carrier deck, including Wimpy's highly sparkly YGBFSM show. This was my first return to Vulture's Row since the Tiger Cruise when I was fourteen.

We were all rooting for him. We wanted him to succeed. Anticipation grew, as pilots have more time to complete each pattern at night than in daytime. In fact, the next wave of pilots going for qualification had already launched and were doing their first carrier landings, while Wimpy, a member of the *previous* wave of candidates, was making the final strides toward his destiny.

We listened to the radio calls, knowing he was on his last shot.

"Gladiator 7, Hornet Ball, 3.4, Wimpy. Roger Trick or Treat."

Gladiator 7 was his official call sign that night. Hornet Ball meant he was flying a Hornet and saw the meatball. 3.4 meant 3,400 pounds of fuel remaining. Wimpy was his pilot call sign. Roger Trick or Treat meant he knew this was his last chance to declare victory; if he didn't grab a wire, he was going to the beach, hefting failure with him.

If we had popcorn, we would have eaten it. If we were allowed to have beer, we would have swilled it. We had completed our qualifications, so the pressure was off of us individually. Only one classmate left in jeopardy.

Come on, Wimpy!

From Vulture's Row, we saw his aircraft lights about three-fourths of a mile away. The most distinguishable light on an aircraft at night is the angle of attack indicator, which displays to the LSO what the pilot sees inside the cockpit. If the aircraft is at the proper speed, a yellow light is displayed; if the aircraft is fast, a red light is displayed; if slow, a green light is displayed. As the laws of physics translate into carrier landings, being fast trends toward a bolter. Wimpy showed the mother ship some red.

Undulations followed. Red, then yellow, then green, then red *and* yellow, then a touch of only red, then red and yellow again, then green. At about one hundred meters from the back of the ship, his entire aircraft came into view. Dimly at first, then brighter as he closed the distance. Red, yellow, red, yellow, "easy with it," "right for line up," red, yellow, touchdown, sparks...power up...deceleration...stop.

Wimpy made it!

He inadvertently selected afterburner when he powered up, generating a momentary afterburner plume and greater than necessary thrust for takeoff. Further battling the moment, he struggled against the cable. But...he made it!

As my LSO told me after my first encounter with the carrier, "A qual is a qual." Qualified is qualified. We all made it that night.

Day can be fun, but night is a perpetual proving ground and chance to break even.

An F/A-18 is transonic as it expends a flare. (Photo from DVIDS, Open Source)

The Reckoning

First Lieutenant Steve "Curly" Lambrecht

Student, Replacement Air Group, VFA-106

"We have met the enemy, and they are me."

—COMMODORE OLIVER "HAZARD" PERRY
AND STEVEN S. LAMBRECHT

Nautical Notables:

Flying Colors: A ship that has come through a battle relatively unscathed and with her colors (flag) flying is said to have come through with "flying colors."

Over the Barrel: A common method of punishment aboard ship was flogging, meaning to hit or whip repeatedly. The punished sailor was tied to a grating, mast, or "over the barrel" of a deck cannon.

Jarhead: Slang term for a Marine, borne from the shape of a Marine's head when sporting the traditional "high and tight" haircut. The high and tight haircut originated in WWI, when Marines shaved the sides of their heads to ensure their gas masks sealed properly.

I returned home from Key West after a successful carrier qualification endeavor—and after ten days of *not* being recalled to Cecil Field for my previous airspeed indiscretions. I felt I had come through with **flying colors**. I walked into my house with a sense of accomplishment and relief...that is until I noticed the answering machine blinking like the Vegas Strip. Apparently, the word had gotten out.

With no fewer than twelve messages awaiting me, I was not out of the woods yet, not by a long shot. There were several messages from the XO (Executive Officer, second in command), the senior Marine in the squadron, instructors, the senior Marine on base, and others. The message was clear: my career and future as a Naval Aviator were in serious doubt. The XO, Lieutenant Colonel "Jock" Mach (ironic, don't you think?), made it clear that I was to talk to no one, see no one, and look at no one until reporting to him first. I obliged.

When I saw him, Jock said, "The Old Man (Skipper) is pissed. He wants your wings. You are lucky you've done well in training; the instructors have rallied behind you. So has Colonel Corrigan." Colonel Corrigan was the senior Marine on base and had personally requested that my ass belong to him, an act designed to let Marines simultaneously take care of their own problems and to "take care of their own."

The ass chewings were many and varied. They had me **over the barrel**. I requested audiences with both Colonel Corrigan and the CAG, apologizing for my shenanigans and seeking to assure them I had become a new man, that my days as a cowboy were over. Generally, the conversations went well.

There was one last hurdle to overcome, however. The Skipper, Commander "Muffy" McGee, held the final decision in his hands. In the end, I had to report to him.

I donned my uniform, which I had meticulously prepared, polished my everything, and ensured my grooming standards were such that any **Jarhead** would be proud to see me in his mirror. When I went to see him, though, the Skipper intentionally made me wait for two hours in his outer office with his secretary. The goal, of course, was to make me sweat. Mission accomplished. Mercifully, the moment finally arrived when I was to stand tall and eat the fruits of my labor.

"First Lieutenant Lambrecht reporting as ordered, sir."

"Parade rest, Lieutenant."

Parade rest is a position slightly more comfortable than "attention" but neither as comfortable nor as hospitable as "at ease." Having a superior Officer place me in the position of parade rest reminded me of my experience waiting outside Lt. Col. Kunkle's office at the Naval Academy a few short years before. I once again found myself behind the power curve.

We proceeded to discuss the errors of my ways, how he needed to maintain good order and discipline in his squadron, and finally, how had it not been for the instructors and Marines rallying behind me, my service as a Marine and Naval Aviator would have been part of naval history (a phrase I had heard before at USNA). Speaking is not allowed while at the position of parade rest, so with each response I gave, I had to come to the position of attention, respond to the question posed, then return again to parade rest. I did so with every bit of diligence and bearing deserving of the occasion.

Commander McGee agreed to let Colonel Corrigan's punishment stand, which was to delay my progression to my first Marine Fighter Squadron by one month so that I could have the distinct privilege of being the Officer of the Day (standing duty), 24/7, for the entire next month. I was dismissed. Standing duty 24/7 for a month was about as appealing as drinking a cup of warm spit, but it was a darn sight better than the alternative.

When I finally left Cecil Field one month later, I placed a bottle of the finest Mescal (one of Commander McGee's preferred beverages) on his desk, with a note expressing my gratitude to him for saving me from myself.

What is the lesson? Speed is life, and it is decidedly possible to have too much of a good thing.

PART III

Boundless

USS Kitty Hawk, South China Sea. (Photo from DVIDS, Open Source)

A Soviet Navy Charlie II-class submarine running at periscope depth, photographed by a US Navy S-3A Viking of Anti-Submarine Squadron VS-22 "Checkmates" in the Atlantic Ocean west of Gibraltar, in 1986.[4]

4   Wikimedia Commons. Public domain.

Attacking the Periscope

Ensign/Lieutenant Junior Grade/ Lieutenant Ron "Warhead" Lambrecht
Anti-Submarine Warfare Intelligence Officer

"Without a decisive naval force, we can do nothing definitive."

—GEORGE WASHINGTON

Nautical Notables:

Restricted Line Officer: Officers of the line of the Regular Navy and Navy Reserves who are restricted in the performance of duty by having been designated for supply, engineering, aerospace, intelligence, or other support duties.

Unrestricted Line Officer: A commissioned Officer of the line in the United States Navy qualified for command at sea of the Navy's warfighting combatant units, such as warships, submarines, aviation squadrons, and SEAL teams.

Fitness Report (FITREP): An evaluation form used by the United States Navy and United States Marine Corps to evaluate Officers.

Ready Room: A ready room is a space on an aircraft carrier where on-duty pilots stand by prior to going to their airplanes. Each flight squadron has its own individual ready room. It's also a place for meetings and for camaraderie.

Considering I had over 400 hours in the S-3A as an AW, it made perfect sense to detail me to an S-3 squadron. I knew the plane, tactics, and sensors like the back of my hand, so when I arrived back on the West Coast in January 1980, I was assigned to an anti-submarine squadron (VS-29). The S-3 squadrons were co-located in a single hangar at North Island Naval Air Base. No other Intelligence Officer in any of the anti-submarine warfare (ASW) squadrons had the background, training, and experience in the aircraft I brought to the position.

Having been assigned to North Island as a Second Class Petty Officer a year earlier, I was familiar with the base and knew many of the Officers and enlisted folks still assigned to the squadrons. Soon, some Chief Petty Officers I formerly knew or worked for would work for me.

Most Ensigns are commissioned straight out of college, but as a thirty-one-year-old Ensign, my level of "horse sense" and maturity resulted in almost immediate assignment as a Division Officer overseeing the AWs. As a **Restricted Line Officer**, I was filling a leadership role a junior **Unrestricted Line Officer** coveted in order to break out of the pack when **FITREPs** were due.

Though not all Intelligence Officers subscribe to this philosophy, I believed my sole purpose was to support the Unrestricted Line

Officers (aviators and SWOs). I honestly believe it was because of the Unrestricted Line Officers on the selection boards that I ultimately ascended to the rank of Commander; most of my fitness reports had been written by them.

* * *

From the early '70s until the fall of the Soviet Union in 1991, Soviet submarines were considered the number one threat to US carriers. Without the technology or infrastructure to build and support a carrier force, the Soviets instead built a huge fleet of submarines to counter the American fleet, including its carriers. Their submarine technology was not as advanced as ours, but in the words of Admiral Gorshkov (twice awarded the title "Hero of the Soviet Union" and credited with the expansion of the Soviet Navy into a global force during the Cold War), "Better is the enemy of good enough." Anti-submarine warfare was a big deal onboard carriers, and an incredible amount of national and tactical energy was devoted to countering the threat.

In preparation for deployment, my job entailed training the aircrews on Soviet submarine tactics and known deployment patterns. Aircrews had to know where submarines were home-based, what was deployed, and where they were operating. A firm grasp of oceanography and geography, both land and undersea, was required to anticipate submarine movements.

Early Soviet submarines were built with a limited mission in mind. Some submarines were fast attack and carried torpedoes as their primary weapon; other submarines carried cruise missiles and, in the early days, needed to surface in order to launch. This background knowledge, and an understanding of what type of submarines were deployed at any one time, hinted at which tactics the Soviets would use if we went to war. We focused on search areas and tactics accordingly.

On November 4, 1979, a group of "students" stormed the US embassy in the Iranian capital, Tehran, taking over the compound and seizing the embassy staff. The militants eventually held fifty Americans hostage for a total of 444 days.

VS-29 was assigned to Carrier Air Wing Fifteen and was due to deploy on the *USS Kitty Hawk (CV-63)* in 1981. We were the front-line responders should the American hostages be in imminent danger, and the general temperament aboard ship was that of a rabid dog on a short leash. If unleashed, there would be the Devil to pay.

Although the hostages were released prior to our deployment, all of our workups occurred while they were being held. These workups were intense, consisting of several at-sea missions over a three-month period, which led to a nine-month deployment to the Indian Ocean and GONZO Station (Gulf of Oman Naval Zone of Operations). We set sail on April 1, 1981, and the level of tension between the US and Iran kept us on a war footing throughout our deployment.

The carrier was manned by a crew categorized as ship's company. They were assigned to the ship and remained on the ship for the duration of their two-year assignment. The Air Wing, in contrast, deployed on the carrier for workups and deployments but disembarked when the deployment ended. As an Air Wing Intelligence Officer, I was assigned to the Carrier (CV) Intelligence Center or CVIC. All briefings presented to the flight crews were televised from CVIC and transmitted to the respective **ready rooms**.

There was a separate workspace on the ship called the ASW Module from which ship's company personnel managed the employment of all ASW assets. They remained in radio communication with airborne and nonorganic platforms to provide situational updates and mission changes should they occur. It was a hectic place to work: those manning the radios and overseeing the ASW picture also had to stay cognizant of all other ships' activities happening in parallel with submarine prosecution.

Soon, the ship's company personnel realized I had a strong background in ASW. As a result, I became the point person for most of the mission planning. Since I briefed virtually all of the ASW missions, I knew where the assets were deployed and how they were employed in the overall picture. I proposed strategies, search areas, sensor deployments, and mission options for follow-on sorties.

This routine continued for nine months. Apparently, my performance was acceptable as I was ranked number one out of all the Air Wing Intelligence Officers in my pay grade. Not a bad day's work considering that position was usually reserved for one of the intelligence folks assigned to a fighter squadron.

A few months after the deployment, I negotiated follow-on orders. My performance in the squadron made me competitive for assignment to the S-3 training command, where I would teach prospective S-3 aviators (pilots and Naval Flight Officers [NFOs] Soviet weapon systems and tactics.

First impressions make a difference, so Officers and enlisted who were considered good examples of the ASW community were screened for the instructor positions. I depended on performance and left the politics to others. It worked; I was detailed to the training command.

View inside Tent City. In addition to housing Marines, there were shower tents, a medical tent, chapel, Officers' Club, and chow halls. Placed on concrete pads, these tents were heated, air conditioned, and electrified. For Marines, this was living in relative luxury. The stones between the sidewalks served as drainage and also as projectiles on evenings when it mysteriously "rained rocks."

Political map of Bosnia and Herzegovina, Serbia to the east, and Croatia west and north. This region of the former Yugoslavia plunged into an ethnic civil war after the collapse of the Soviet Union. Ethnic cleansing ran rampant. Udbina Airfield, subject of the painting Moonlighters Over Udbina, is approximately at the center of the concentric circles.

*A Moonlighter Hornet over Tent City, Aviano Air Base, Italy (1994).
Tent City was home to all Marines deployed to Aviano AB. Beyond Tent
City, the tank and hand grenade training range can be seen. At the
bottom of the photo are hardened aircraft shelters with combat loaded
A-10 Warthogs at the ready. Photo credit: Colonels (Retired) Frank
"Jason" Richie and Jeffrey "JAWS" White.*

Bosnia

Captain
Steve "Curly" Lambrecht
Airframes Maintenance Officer,
VMFA(AW)-332

"War is God's way of teaching Americans geography."

—AMBROSE BIERCE

Aeronautical Notables:

Fleet Marine Force (FMF): The entirety of the Marine Corps that is deployable, as opposed to being confined to state-side, such as at a training unit.

The Pointy End of the Spear: On cruise or deployment. Being at the ready and pre-positioned for combat action should the need immediately arise. Also called "Tip of the Spear."

Combat Mission: Mission flown in a designated combat zone. Does not require delivery of ordnance to qualify as a combat mission. A total of twenty combat missions qualifies the aircrew for an Air Medal. Single combat missions may also qualify aircrew for an Air Medal, should they rise to the level deemed worthy by superiors.

Surface-to-Air Missile (SAM): Designed to shoot down aircraft, and their inhabitants, from the ground.

Anti-Aircraft Artillery (AAA): Munitions, often cued by RADAR, then fired at aircraft. Once fired, the munitions are unguided but usually set to detonate at a predetermined altitude.

After nine years of military education and training, it was time to finally serve in the fleet! My first assignment in the **FMF** was to Beaufort, South Carolina, where I joined VMFA(AW)-332, a two-seat Hornet squadron. An NFO, not a pilot, occupied the back seat. The NFO often was someone who didn't have 20/20 eyesight, and therefore couldn't become a pilot, but still wanted to fly. Jokingly, we said NFO stood for "no future outside," as they had little to no hope of ever being an airline pilot. The NFO in the back seat of the Hornet was referred to as a Weapons and Sensors Operator (WSO).

In 1993–94, our squadron, having been decommissioned after their A-6 Intruder aircraft were placed in mothball status, was stood up once again with brand new F/A-18D aircraft. The pilots and WSOs were a combination of former A-6 crew, former F-4 Phantom crew, a few seasoned F/A-18 pilots, and the rest of us, who were brand new pilots and WSOs in the USMC. It was an eclectic mix, to say the least.

Our young guys were an impressive cast of diverse characters. Among them was Steve "Chumley" Hildner, a WSO and king of the one-liners; Tim "Wedge" O'Toole, a pilot who is one of the funniest human beings ever to live; and Tray "Tonto" Ardese, a WSO, half-Choctaw Indian, wrestler, boxer, and third-degree black belt in tae kwon do, built like a tank and harder than woodpecker lips. Also included in the mix was Teagan "SWIM" Yonash, a gem of a man but not the smartest WSO in the squadron. (In fact, SWIM, a name thought up by none other than Wedge, stood for "Stupidest WSO in the Marine Corps." SWIM was a little slow—let's just say it took him an hour and a half to watch *60 Minutes*—but everybody loved him.)

The former A-6 crew members were accustomed to flying low over long distances and carrying large loads of munitions. Because of their RADAR, the A-6 could fly very low in the weather, where they picked their way through the completely cloud-obscured mountains without needing to see them. They were very proud of their former aircraft. However, while they had a great deal of experience dropping bombs, they had no experience whatsoever with the much more complex and dynamic air-to-air missions.

We young guys were not hesitant in pointing this out. We ridiculed them relentlessly for having flown an aircraft with the "pointy end in the back," as opposed to the front, where a *real* fighter's pointy end always resides. Like the EA-6B Prowler, we dubbed her bomb-dropping two-seat A-6 Intruder cousin "The Flying Drumstick." The ridicule apexed when, on our first deployment to Aviano, Italy, all of us outside the A-6 community had T-shirts made with an A-6 on the back, a large red circle and diagonal line drawn across it. On the front it said, "We don't care how you did it in the A-6." Needless to say, the A-6 elders were not impressed, but being Marines, they could take crap as well as anyone. A good thing, given the amount they received.

* * *

Five months after reporting to 332, I was thrust to the **pointy end of the spear**—we deployed to Aviano, Italy, in support of Operation Deny Flight. Our deployed Air Force counterparts lived in Pianco Vallo, a ski resort perched in the mountains above Aviano, where I learned to ski while on deployment. They lived large and earned full per diem.

The Marines, however, would have none of it. We lived in tents on Aviano Air Base, serenely placed between the end of the runway and a tank/hand grenade training range. Fighters took off 24/7, fully combat-loaded, using full afterburner, a few hundred meters from our tents. For those of us who flew at night and slept during the day, the roaring sounds of the Italian Army doing heavy armor maneuvers and the explosions of their hand grenades further serenaded us. Our per diem was $3.50 per day.

I vaguely recalled Ron's words, "Marines live hard and in more austere environments." Turns out, he may have had a point.

All that aside, it was still Aviano, Italy. Our Marine counterparts were typically deployed aboard ship or to some austere corner of the world. We, conversely, were able to dine at superb Italian restaurants and drink phenomenal Italian wine, and we did plenty of both.

"Wow, I feel like a hundred bucks," said Chumley on more than one morning after.

On the weekends, those of us not flying often escaped to Venice, Salzburg, or Munich, all of which were within rental car distance. We piled in with whoever wanted to go and headed off to explore and adventure.

"What's that up on the road? A head?" said Chumley on more than one trip.

Tonto, meanwhile, was an interesting character. Hailing from Oklahoma, he returned each year to compete in their "Tough Man" competition, which he always won. He reveled in his Native American culture, and in his tent, he kept a medicine bag with relics from his life, including the circumcised foreskin of his son.

Highly susceptible to the effects of alcohol, everyone knew Tonto had a three beer limit, which he occasionally exceeded. Thankfully, he wasn't an angry drunk, but he was damn sure entertaining. One night, after imbibing a few too many in our O' Club tent, he proceeded to run up and down the sidewalks in Tent City, doing spinning martial arts kicks...in his tighty whities.

The Operations Officer, Major Mark "Boru" Placey, was a badass in his own right, with a black belt in karate. Boru was a strapping Irishman with a short fuse and a long temper. Seeing Tonto kick the door to his tent open, then dive in, Boru proceeded, full steam, to the entrance, where he also kicked the door open.

A small crowd gathered to witness the event. When Boru was greeted by Tonto, standing in his tighty whities and spinning nun chucks at a blinding speed, Boru said what required saying: nothing. At the sight of him, Tonto's nun chucks spun slowly to a halt. Tonto knew he was outranked and held no cards. He promptly retired for the evening—but not for the entire deployment. His exploits were many and varied.

The **combat missions** in Aviano, however, were no joke.

* * *

After the collapse of the Soviet Union, satellite nations began spinning off and becoming independent. Without big brother USSR around to maintain law and order, old factions and rivalries sprung anew again. This was especially evident in the Balkans, where the Serbs, Muslims, and Croats were at war and engaging in ethnic cleansing. The Serbs had the upper hand with military hardware, namely aircraft, but also in other armaments, which they used in their genocidal endeavors.

Our job was to enforce the UN No-Fly Zone established over Bosnia and Herzegovina, a country I had to research to locate. The mission required 24/7 operations, and we flew accordingly.

We carried sidearms and flew without name patches on our flight suits, to help avoid capture should we be shot down over enemy territory. We also carried a silk map of Bosnia in our gear so that we could point and talk if we encountered friendly civilians along the way. On the back, printed in several languages, was an explanation that we were Americans and any aid provided to us would be rewarded. (Hollywood depicted the war in the movie *Behind Enemy Lines*, a story loosely based on the shootdown of Captain Scott O'Grady, which occurred between my two Bosnia tours in 1995 and 1996.)

Our intrepid Hornets were the most capable aircraft in the theater at the time. We carried an impressive combination of armaments, including air-to-air missiles, LASER-guided bombs, and the HARM (High-Speed Anti-Radiation Missile), which was designed to target surface-to-air missile (**SAM**) RADAR systems. At night, we flew with night vision goggles (NVGs).

Relying heavily on our Intel Officers to help us keep track of the best-known locations for the SAMs, we played cat and mouse with the Serbs. They illuminated our aircraft with SAM RADARs while we were pointed away from them, then shut their RADARs off when we pointed toward them. In all cases, we stayed just outside their maximum engagement zone. They moved their SAMs frequently, but our technology allowed us to locate them again very quickly. By far the biggest threat to our aircraft, we watched for SAMs continuously.

Because they were fond of using their aircraft to bomb Muslim targets, the Serbs were not happy with our presence. In February 1994, US fighters shot down four Serbian Jastreb aircraft after such an attack. Operating out of Udbina Air Base in Croatia, the Serbs bombed targets in the Banja Luka region of Bosnia. My squadron arrived in theater during October 1994 and took our turn in the breech enforcing the No-Fly Zone.

In November of 1994, the Serbs were again using Udbina to attack Muslim targets, this time in the Bihać (Bee-haahch) region of Bosnia. Approval was given to strike the airfield, and our squadron was to participate. The decision was made to stack the deck in seniority order, with the young guys sitting this one out.

Genuine shooting missions were few and far between. The boss took care of the older guys, most of whom had not seen true combat. The Intelligence Officer's briefing was thorough and included locations of SAMs and **AAA**, as well as the targets to be struck. The mission was a perfect success, with no friendly losses, and is immortalized in the famous Mark Styling painting *Moonlighters Over Udbina*.

Three days later, a determination was made to take down an SA-2 SAM site being used by the Serbs. The SAM was a persistent threat to NATO aircraft, and the Serbs were very good at moving and hiding them. This time, the young guys would get their chance. With two waves of VMFA(AW)-332 F/A-18s in the mix, I was in the second wave. Unfortunately, by the time I got there, the work was done. Many years passed, and many things changed, before I had another opportunity to test my wares.

Steve preparing to taxi for a combat mission over Bosnia and Herzegovina. This F/A-18D Hornet is loaded with two AIM-9 air-to-air missiles, one MK-82 bomb, one GBU-12 LASER-guided bomb, one LASER spot search and tracking pod, one infrared targeting pod, two external fuel tanks, and one pod of five-inch rockets for marking enemy targets with white phosphorous.

Take Aim

Captain
Steve "Curly" Lambrecht
Airframes Maintenance Officer,
VMFA(AW)-332

"I hardly EVER crash."

—STEVE LAMBRECHT

Aeronautical Notables:

Piddle Pack: A plastic bag-like device designed for male aircrew to relieve themselves in flight. Their use, while inconvenient, should never be deferred.

Poopy Suit: A dry suit worn by aircrew while flying over cold water, designed to combat exposure to cold water and extend the life of a downed pilot by up to twenty minutes.

Foreign Object Debris (FOD): Any item having the potential to cause damage to an aircraft (for example, a stone being ingested into an aircraft engine or a pen dropped in the cockpit, which subsequently interferes with flight controls or electronics).

Over the course of a five- to seven-hour combat mission, one usually has to relieve oneself at least once. To solve this dilemma, America's engineers colluded to create the **piddle pack**. The piddle pack is a heavy-duty plastic bag, with a wide "fill tube," and looks similar to a miniature hot water bottle. The idea is quite simple, really: open the piddle pack, insert oneself into the opening, and then do what needs doing.

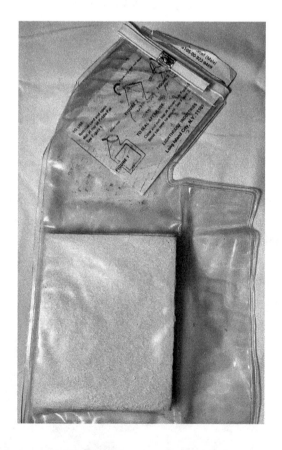

The piddle pack is transparent, because obviously everyone needs to see their own urine, and the early version—which is the star of this tale—had a dried sponge inside capable of absorbing nearly *half* the urine expelled into it. The sponge didn't matter much, though, because the piddle pack itself seems specifically designed to hold no more than 90 percent of the urine a pilot is capable of releasing, regardless of the occasion. It's always best to have two at the ready. Just in case.

Flying a supersonic death-defying magnificent piece of engineering such as the F/A-18 Hornet requires the mastery of many, many things, all at one time. Luckily, the engineers and pilots who collaborated in the design of the Hornet were supremely capable and succeeded in making it as easy as possible for the pilot to master flying the aircraft while simultaneously operating the weapons and sensors. The designers of the piddle pack, however, were not part of that team.

There's an art and a science to many aspects of modern air warfare. However, being able to successfully piss into a piddle pack during a combat mission at night while wearing night-vision goggles (NVGs) and operating a targeting pod over Sarajevo, Bosnia and Herzegovina, coupled with being talked onto a target building by a Forward Air Controller (FAC), is not something anyone takes the time to teach at flight school. Or, as I would find out later, TOPGUN. It can only be learned through experience or by discussing techniques with other pilots around the Ready Room, perhaps over a couple beers.

There are many techniques for using a piddle pack. First, the piddle pack has to be removed from a plastic storage bag, also containing a handy wipe, which—while handy—has never been used in the history of piddle packs. The storage bag and handy wipe must then be secured so they don't wind up on the floor of the cockpit, where the pilot can't reach to pick them up.

Next, the piddle pack must be opened, which consists of unfolding it and opening the funnel tube. For some strange reason, the funnel tube has its own chamber, which first traps the urine before allowing it to drain through holes into the main chamber. This design is dumber than a bag of hammers. If the first chamber is filled too quickly, there's not sufficient time for the contents to drain into the main chamber before overflowing. Before beginning, a wise and experienced pilot reaches in and tears the first chamber open to allow urine to flow freely into the second chamber.

That's the easy part. Next, the piddle pack must be placed in close proximity to the ejection handle, which resides just in front of the pilot's groin, but the ejection handle interferes with the placement of the piddle pack. The pilot has to disarm, or "safe," the ejection seat to ensure there are no mistakes resulting in an unintentional ejection from the aircraft. This accomplished, the ejection handle must be rotated away from the groin to create more room. Finally, the piddle pack can be dangled alongside the ejection handle and below the seat so gravity can do its job.

Proper technique demands the rudder pedals be retracted closer to the pilot. By doing so, the pilot can push against both rudder pedals simultaneously, thereby raising himself slightly out of the seat. Care must be taken to ensure equal pressure is placed on both rudder pedals so the aircraft doesn't turn or roll. In order to raise oneself out of the seat, the lap belts securing the pilot to the seat must first be loosened or released.

Almost there.

Next, the pilot must gain access to the most vital piece of equipment. Luckily, flight suits have a zipper that runs the full length of the suit, from chest to groin, and the zipper operates in both directions. Unfortunately, during cold weather operations, it is commonplace and necessary to wear long underwear. When flying extensive distances over cold water, the wearing of a dry suit, a.k.a. **poopy suit**, further complicates the process.

A word about multi-seat aircraft: aircrew flying multi-seat aircraft with ejection seats must utilize piddle packs in the presence of other aircrew members. This creates a problem for the modest. Fortunately, in the F/A-18D, the two crewmembers are seated in tandem and separated by an instrument panel.

So, there I was. At night, in the winter, wearing night vision goggles, flying over Bosnia. My back seater, Major "Skull" Riedel, a senior and superb WSO, and I had about ten minutes to go before our scheduled midair refueling, and then we would continue our heretofore boring mission on this otherwise uneventful evening in 1994. I felt the urge to use a piddle pack but figured I'd wait until after the tanker so that I would have plenty of time and not be rushed. Off to the tanker we went.

While on the tanker, we received tasking over Sarajevo and were directed there immediately after getting our gas. We did so. I began to wish I had used those ten minutes before going to the tanker more wisely.

We proceeded to Sarajevo, checked in with the FAC, and established a ten-mile racetrack pattern while Skull began manipulating the targeting pod. I informed Skull I'd be adding to the complexity of the mission: this was a two-piddle pack situation. Maybe more.

At our speed, using a ten-mile racetrack pattern, the inbound and outbound legs were flown straight and level, taking about a minute to traverse. The inbound and outbound legs were crucial because we used that time to see the target with the targeting pod and make necessary adjustments. In the turns, the targeting pod was often obscured, and progress ceased. These legs also provided the opportunities to progress through each of the steps toward relief. I did so with great anticipation and haste.

One minute inbound to get the piddle packs out and begin opening them, then one minute in the turn, requiring more or less my undivided attention on flying the plane. One minute outbound to finish opening the piddle packs, break open the inner chambers, and then safe the seat. One minute in the turn to contemplate the insufficient size of my bladder. One minute inbound to loosen my lap belts, rotate the ejection seat handle away from me, then retract the rudder pedals toward me. One minute in the turn to curse my incredibly inadequate use of time. One minute outbound to lift myself out of the seat while unzipping my flight suit and scrambling to get hold of myself while simultaneously reaching for the piddle pack. Good thing I taught myself how to juggle in flight school! I was about seven minutes into the process and rapidly approaching the point where I again had to commence my turn inbound.

Have you ever had to go to the bathroom, and the closer you got to the bathroom, the worse you had to go? Me too.

Finally, with every extremity in full tremble, I leveled the airplane inbound toward the target and, in complete darkness, experienced the sweet release awaiting me. Wow. That was *close*.

Knowing the first piddle pack had to be getting full, and having taken a significant edge off the problem, I approached the turn outbound. Enabled by a youthful prostate, I ceased my flow. I used the time in the turn to ease myself back into my seat, give my legs a rest, secure the used piddle pack, and retrieve the second one. I had this stuff wired. *I should write a book.*

After establishing the turn, I eased myself down into my seat and lifted the used piddle pack up to close it and put it away. I was surprised to discover the piddle pack was only about a third full and, at the same time, shocked to discover how wet and warm my legs and butt were. It seems I had missed the piddle pack with most of my first expenditure and instead deposited it onto my ejection seat.

I didn't have time to fully survey the damage; there was still more work to be done. I sealed up the partially filled piddle pack and put it away, then reached for the second one I had prepared, which had conveniently fallen onto the floor between the ejection seat and the side instrument panel. It was irretrievable, as if placed there by the enemy. I was inconsolable.

Erratically, I scrambled for my helmet bag, which held the balance of my piddle packs. Apparently, I was no more tactful in my endeavors than I was when I peed on the windows of The Lakeview Supper Club at the age of three. A voice chimed in over the intercom.

"Everything alright up there?" Skull inquired.

Searching for the intercom switch so I could answer him wasn't my highest priority in the moment. I found a piddle pack, my last one! Ripping it free, I tore open the inner chamber, hoisted myself into the air, and let loose the cannons. The force nearly blasted the piddle pack out of my grasp!

This was all getting quite tedious. I was ready to be done with it and put my focus back where it belonged. That is until my fingers started to get wet. I had filled the second piddle pack, and it was overflowing! YGBFSM! Prostate, do your thing!

To secure a piddle pack, there has to be "head space." That means there has to be room above the level of urine so that the top can be folded over and clamped shut with a metal clasp. No way that was happening. I proceeded to fold the top over, spilling more all over myself and the cockpit, and clamped it shut. Mission not yet complete. No more piddle packs.

Remembering the first one I used to be only about a third full, I found it, opened it, and finished the job.

With the better part of three moist and humiliating hours to dry out, I directed every available air vent toward my nether regions and ejection seat. I hoped like hell I didn't need to use another piddle pack that night and swore to never again break the surly bonds of Earth without enough piddle packs to equal any possible task.

There is a tradition in aviation: should an aircrew drop something in the cockpit and be unable to retrieve it, thereby **FOD**ing the cockpit, the offending aircrew is obligated to buy the maintenance team, who has to retrieve it after the flight, a case of the beer of their choosing. So, too, it is with soiling an ejection seat cover, requiring replacement by the maintenance team. The beer was on me, but they needed to bring their own piddle packs.

Last Training Opportunity to Fail

Lieutenant
Ron "Warhead" Lambrecht
Air Anti-Submarine Squadron-41

"Live as if you were to die tomorrow. Learn as if you were to live forever."

—Mahatma Gandhi

Nautical Notables:

Fleet Replacement Squadron (FRS) (formerly known as Replacement Air Groups [RAGs]): A unit of the United States Navy and Marine Corps that trains Naval Aviators, Naval Flight Officers, and enlisted Naval Aircrewmen on the specific front-line aircraft they have been assigned to fly.

Captain's Mast: Captain's Mast is the Navy term for non-judicial punishment (NJP). It is used when there has been a violation of the Uniform Code of Military Justice (UCMJ), but it is only used when other options to correct deficiencies have been unsuccessful or when the violation is fairly egregious. Examples include underage drinking, drinking and driving, UA (unauthorized absence), integrity violations (cheating/lying), and assault. There are no rules of evidence for NJP; the Captain will review the Sailor's entire record before holding Mast. The Sailor appears in front of the Commanding Officer (CO) in dress uniform, and their entire chain of command is posted along the left-hand side of the CO. The Captain ensures the Sailor is aware of their rights and gives the Sailor the option to have the case resolved at Captain's Mast or a trial by court-martial. The Captain will ask the Sailor questions about the incident and consult the chain of command about the Sailor's abilities, potential, and effort. The CO will then adjudicate and award punishment, if appropriate. The term "award" is used for both positive (medals) and negative (fines), as they are both earned.

As I reflect back on my tour at VS-41, I consider it to be the most enjoyable of my twenty-six years in the Navy. The job was hard to beat because my fellow instructors, both Officers and enlisted, were the crème de la crème. Plus, we had the mission of training extremely high-energy young aviators.

I taught students an introduction to the Soviet Navy, the Soviet strategy for countering US naval forces, and tactics that could be used to exploit their limitations. It was fun. The subject matter was interesting to the students, and they fully understood its importance.

Capable of carrying conventional bombs, cluster bombs, rockets, air-to-ground missiles (AGM-84 Harpoon or AGM-65 Maverick),

Mark 46 torpedoes, or Mark 54 depth bombs, the S-3 Viking could also drop mines. Aircrews had to understand the characteristics of each weapon system and aircraft sensor. Once they did, the aircraft became a formidable tactical asset.

VS-41 logged in excess of 10,000 flight hours per year, qualifying approximately fifty pilots and eighty NFOs trained to perform mission management as Tactical Coordinators (TACCOs), along with eighty AW sensor operators (SENSOs). As is the case with all military schools, information was delivered to the students as though they were being fed through a fire hose; the screening process we all went through to get this far in our respective training pipelines presupposed we were up to the task.

There were exceptions, of course. Not everyone made it.

Shortly after arriving at the **FRS**, I was designated the Division Officer for the AW Branch. The instructors were easy to manage, but it was not so easy managing the AW students destined to be S-3 SENSOs. Most of them were in their teens and very green. It was unrealistic to expect a first tour AW to function as a seasoned SENSO. For instance, the P-3 Orion community had a crew consisting of several AWs, and young SENSOs were paired with more seasoned Sailors. This gave them the opportunity to make mistakes while learning on the job. The first tour S-3 SENSO was the lone operator in the four-man S-3 crew. Through no fault of his own, he lacked operational experience.

As mentioned, three Officers and one enlisted man comprised the S-3 crew. When it came to hunting submarines, the Officers were at the mercy of the young SENSO and his ability to detect and assist in tracking a hostile submarine. I directed the instructor staff to expect and accept nothing less than full comprehension of anti-submarine warfare and a full working knowledge of the SENSO position. As a result, we had a high attrition rate, and I was not popular with the AW Enlisted Detailer charged with the assignment of Sailors to commands.

On average, we trained eighty SENSOs a year, and they all fell under my charge. San Diego offers many opportunities for young teenage men to get into trouble, and being just across the border from Tijuana, Mexico, does not help.

Almost every Wednesday morning, the Commanding Officer reserved a spot for me to the left of his podium as he engaged in **Captain's Mast**, which invariably included one of my AW students. That part of the job was painful, and the cost to the taxpayer should a student be dropped from training for disciplinary reasons was significant.

I gained valuable leadership experience while at the FRS, but I wish some of it had been more positive in nature.

* * *

During my second year at the FRS, I met my future wife, Anne. Shortly after we married, I visited her parents and relatives living in the Annapolis, Maryland, area.

As mentioned, Anne's dad retired as a Navy Captain and graduated from the Naval Academy in 1941. During our visit, we were invited to her aunt and uncle's home for an evening of "triple F" (Forced Family Fun). There, I noticed three framed Marine recruiting posters that he had placed along a hallway. In his younger days, Anne's uncle was commissioned as a Marine Second Lieutenant, and I immediately recognized one of the posters as the awe-inspiring billboard I saw as a young boy during our family trips to Marshall.

My wife informed me that the Marine Officer in the posters was her uncle, who served as the USMC poster boy shortly after his commissioning. Who could have ever predicted that a rural Minnesota farm boy, inspired by a billboard, would actually meet that very same billboard Marine in Maryland after marrying his niece?

Later, when I was midway through my third year at the FRS, I started negotiating orders with the Detailer. I was competitive when ranked against my peers in the past, and I did well in my two squadron assignments. Several excellent opportunities were then presented to me, including a two-year assignment at the Naval Postgraduate School (PGS) in Monterey, California, where I could earn a master's degree in international studies.

At this point in my career, I did some serious soul-searching. Things were going well professionally, and I seemed to have a bright Navy future. The logical decision was to accept postgraduate school, but I was also offered an instructor position at Fleet Intelligence Training Center Pacific (FITCPAC), located in San Diego.

Back-to-back instructor duty would do little to broaden my experience base, so I consulted with a few senior Officers, who indicated that I would be taking a career chance by declining postgraduate school. I decided to take the instructor job at FITCPAC anyway. There, I would be competing against other Intelligence Officers.

After nine years (three enlisted, six as a JO), I departed the anti-submarine warfare community for good.

Graduating class of TOPGUN, including adversary instructor students and combat controllers (1995). Steve is standing in the second row, third from the right. His WSO, Mike "Twistin'" Shoup is kneeling in the front row, third from the right. This was the last TOPGUN class to graduate from Miramar Naval Air Station before the school was moved to Fallon, Nevada.

Ron and Steve standing in front of the TOPGUN training building while Steve was attending the program (1995). The aircraft silhouettes etched into the glass blocks represent aerial victories achieved by TOPGUN graduates. Each block contains the type of aircraft shot down, as well as the pilot's name, type of aircraft flown, and date of the event.

TOPGUN

Captain
Steve "Curly" Lambrecht
Airframes Maintenance Officer,
VMFA(AW)-332

"Whatever you can do, I can do better."

—EVERY FIGHTER PILOT EVER

Aeronautical Notables:

TOPGUN: United States Navy Fighter Weapons School. Formerly located at Naval Air Station Miramar in California. Now located at Naval Air Station Fallon in Nevada.

Basic Fighter Maneuvers (BFM): A fight to the "death" between two aircraft. Also known as 1 v 1.

Knife Fight in a Phone Booth: Close-in, slow-speed aerial dogfight.

Bogey: The term was originally coined to describe a phantom or a ghost in sixteenth century English. For fighter pilots, however, a bogey is an unidentified aircraft spotted in the sky. It could be a friendly aircraft, an enemy aircraft, or a neutral aircraft.

Furball: A large aerial engagement with many combatants. Multiple aircraft engaged in tight air combat maneuvering in the visual arena.

Merge: The coming together of two or more aircraft in a visual fight.

RADAR Warning Receiver (RWR): A piece of equipment capable of detecting RADAR transmissions and informing the pilot of their existence.

Our squadron consisted of an eclectic group of pilots and WSOs: most of the A-6 elders lacked fighter experience, while the F-4 crews were mostly older folks. Because of this, the door opened for us young, capable, and hungry crew to have professional opportunities unusual for our level of experience. With a shortage of instructors in the F/A-18, the door opened further.

The first step in becoming an instructor is passing a gauntlet of study and flights called the Air Combat Tactics Instructor (ACTI) Course. ACTI involved reading and memorizing the contents of the Tactical Manuals, **TOPGUN** Manual, threat manual, aircraft software manual, and other documents. In total, north of 2,000 pages of information.

While studying this material, a crew also had to learn to brief, lead, debrief, and instruct to proficiency three types of air-to-air sorties.

They were 1 v 1 **BFM**, where a single aircraft engages in a **knife fight in a phone booth** to the death with one other, a 2 v 2 intercept sortie flight, and a 4 v X flight, where the X meant an unknown quantity of **bogeys**.

Finally, instructors from the Marine Aviation Weapons and Tactics Squadron (MAWTS-1) in Yuma, Arizona, arrived at the aspiring instructors' base to administer a written closed-book examination of 150–200 questions, then fly each of the aforementioned sorties with the upgrading crew before certifying them as ACTIs. Much to the dislike of some elders, several of us younger crew were selected to participate in the program. Though we had less than a year in the squadron, we advanced to a position customarily reserved for those with two years or more of experience.

My WSO, Mike "Twistin'" Shoup, and I, along with Tim "Wedge" O'Toole and John "Saint" Langford, were the first of the young crew chosen. After a grueling three months, requiring many fourteen-plus hour days and working weekends, we all passed.

It was good to have such capable and humorous cohorts with whom to endure the suffering, and our buddy Chumley hovered about, lightening the mood. Wandering in during our study sessions, he asked, "What are you doin', something?"

Shortly after completing ACTI, Twistin' and I were chosen to attend TOPGUN, a tremendous honor and something we looked very much forward to. I had seen the movie featuring Tom Cruise twice before. The glamour and notoriety heaped upon graduates was renowned across the globe.

With ACTI and one six-month combat tour under our belts, Twistin' and I headed for Miramar, California, home of the fighter pilot. It was heady times. TOPGUN proved to be one of the most formative experiences of my flying career.

The level of instruction at TOPGUN was off the charts. The first couple of weeks consisted of superb academic instruction, including a lecture by Vietnam ace WSO William "Willy Irish" Driscoll. He recounted a fight where he and his pilot, Randall "Duke" Cunningham, encountered (unbeknownst to them) North Vietnam ace Colonel Nguyen Toon. A renowned and respected pilot, Toon had clearly been trained by the Soviets. He had thirteen kills in his MiG-21 Fishbed.

The fight did not begin well; Duke and Willy's F-4 was outmatched in maneuverability by the nimbler MiG-21. However, when both aircraft were nearly out of gas, Colonel Nguyen Toon disengaged first, a decision that cost him his life. He was unable to outrun the AIM-9 heat-seeking missile Duke and Willie gave him as a parting gift.

Not long after, during one training sortie, I became engaged in one of the largest **furballs** I had ever seen. It was a fourteen versus X sortie, meaning there were fourteen of us against an unknown number of adversaries. The X turned out to be fourteen adversaries. None of that was unusual, except as the fight developed, all twenty-eight planes found their way to the same visual fight in the same phone booth! Approaching the **merge** from about eight miles away, I saw airplanes spiraling everywhere, as everyone dove in with their fangs out. From that distance, it looked like a swarm of bees circling a hive.

I, too, joined the fun. After jumping in and getting a few kills, I decided it was just too dangerous. We exited the fight, and shortly thereafter, a wise instructor made a timely radio call, terminating the entire engagement.

This was definitely the big leagues. We flew every type of combat training mission the Navy was ever likely to encounter: large-scale air-to-air missions over water, missions against complex integrated air defense systems at China Lake, California, and strike missions in Fallon, Nevada. In the process, we incorporated every airborne asset in the USN inventory.

The final sortie at TOPGUN was perhaps the most exciting of all. It was a 1 v 1 Unknown. Unknown, because there was no way of knowing what type of aircraft you were fighting until arriving at the merge. Aircraft and pilots from all over the world were invited to participate. There were F/A-18s, F-14s, F-5s, F-15s, F-16s, and even an older but highly maneuverable Soviet fighter, a MiG-17! We all hoped to not get the MiG-17; getting shot by one, given its 1950s technology, would be an embarrassment difficult to live down.

The MiG-17 was known for its ability to turn tight circles without losing energy. The other students and I whispered strategies on how we might defeat it, should we have the unlucky draw. The only thing we knew with certainty was that we would not be fighting another TOPGUN student.

Each of us received an envelope with one page of instructions telling us where to be, at what altitude, and on what radio frequency. It also told us what *single* munition we would carry, in addition to our gun. I drew an AIM-9 Sidewinder heat-seeking missile. The same instructions gave us each a single expendable, which could be used to defeat any air-to-air missile. The catch was, in order to use it effectively, we would have to recognize we were in the defensive envelope of our opponent, correctly guess that he had launched his one-and-only missile, then call "expendable" over the radio during the missile time of flight. Make the call too early, and the expendable was used prematurely, leaving you unprotected against future attacks. Make the call too late, and, well, it was too late.

We all knew what menu of aircraft we could potentially encounter at the merge. Each of them had strengths and weaknesses; the challenge was to have a game-plan ready for each of them, to make an identification at the merge, and then to employ the game-plan effectively during the ensuing fight.

Twistin' and I arrived at our appointed place and altitude, then checked in on frequency. Our opponent had not yet arrived, but a few minutes later, they checked in.

Our holding points were twenty miles apart. We were to meet in the middle and fight "to the death." After the fight, there was further humiliation to endure (grandstanding to conduct): the winner returned to the airfield and entered the break, a normal recovery procedure, and one that could be conducted with one's dignity intact. The loser, conversely, had to shoot an instrument approach, broadcasting their call sign at the initial approach fix over the TOPGUN squadron frequency for all to hear. In other words, the defeated had to conduct a humiliating straight-in approach, with one's "tail" between one's legs.

"Ready east," I transmitted.

"Ready west," responded my foe.

"Inbound," we both called.

Twistin' found him on the RADAR immediately. Shortly thereafter, the enemy did the same, as my **RWR** informed me. Once we acquired each other visually, we called "Tally ho." We were forbidden from beginning maneuvers until we had merged. We did so and called "Fight's on!"

It was another Hornet. Twistin' and I both knew immediately what this meant: it had to be a TOPGUN instructor! The only Hornet pilots present at the brief, other than students, were current and former TOPGUN instructors. *Alright, "best of the best" bitch. Let's see what you've got!*

We "turned and burned," but I was patient. I knew the type of fight I needed to fight. The other Hornet was an older model with less powerful engines. I would fight a two-circle fight, a technique allowing me to keep my energy up, provide additional separation from the enemy, and force him to bleed his energy down.

My opponent, conversely, tried to force me into a phone booth. He knew a slow-speed fight offered his single-seat Hornet a slight advantage over our two-seat model, as the larger canopy on our aircraft was a slight hindrance to maneuverability at slower airspeeds. I didn't take the bait. All those years playing foosball at The Club taught me to be patient, precise, and to seize a moment should it be presented to me.

We fought viciously. No one, and I mean *no one*, wanted to shoot the instrument approach of shame back at Miramar. Twistin' kept our opponent in sight, called out our airspeeds, and announced the enemy's moves.

As the fight continued, we lost altitude and energy, approaching the "hard deck." The hard deck is the minimum altitude above which the fight can continue. Anyone breaking the hard deck, which simulated the ground, was considered dead immediately. As we approached the hard deck, I had the advantage in altitude, airspeed, and position. I pulled for a shot with my AIM-9, and my opponent, noticing the hard deck approaching, leveled his wings and pulled to avoid busting it. My simulated AIM-9 impacted his aircraft as he flew through the hard-deck.

"Knock it off, knock it off," he called.

We *won*!

After many sorties, intense study, and instruction, Twistin' and I graduated from TOPGUN on September 1, 1995. Upon completion of TOPGUN, I felt as though I could make the Hornet sing. I had mastered the aircraft to new levels, particularly in the realm of air-to-air combat. But one challenging course remained: WTI.

WTI

Captain
Steve "Curly" Lambrecht

Pilot Training Officer, VMFA(AW)-332

"The Marine Grunt: the sole reason for the existence of Marine Air."

—EVERY MARINE AVIATOR EVER

Aeronautical Notables:

United States Marine Corps Weapons and Tactics Instructor Course (WTI): The Marine Corps' equivalent of TOPGUN. Located in Yuma, Arizona. To adorn the coveted WTI patch, a pilot must complete ACTI, TOPGUN, and WTI.

Close Air Support (CAS): The Marine Corps' bread and butter aviation mission, where aircraft support the troops on the ground.

Forward Air Controller (Airborne) (FAC[A]): Aircrew qualified to provide terminal control and to authorize weapons release from other aircraft, naval gunfire, and ground artillery onto targets.

The **WTI** is conducted in Yuma, Arizona, a location that was chosen as a USMC air base, undoubtedly, for its clear weather, ample military airspace, and bombing ranges. It is well-suited for the task. Yuma is home to MAWTS-1, the squadron of instructors hosting WTI, who had previously certified Twistin' and me as Air Combat Tactics Instructors (ACTIs).

While WTI is not as well-known as TOPGUN, the latter having been immortalized in a movie, the course is absolutely superb, nonetheless. The major difference between the two was that while both contained training and instruction in air-to-air *and* air-to-ground missions, TOPGUN was focused more on air-to-air, and WTI more on air-to-ground. The Marine Corps' primary mission, after all, is to close with and destroy the enemy using fire and maneuver on the ground.

WTI provided some of the most dynamic and challenging flying I ever encountered. We fought our way into targets protected by F-5 Tiger II aggressor aircraft, then attacked defensive missile systems and targets with our air-to-ground weapons. We also flew against mobile SAM systems, while coordinating close air support **(CAS)** missions, both day and night.

Twistin' and I were both Forward Air Controller (Airborne) **(FAC[A])** qualified, which placed additional demands on us throughout the course. We flew at low altitude, at night, using night vision goggles, while simultaneously coordinating strikes against mobile SAM systems, coordinating CAS missions, and providing terminal control and weapons release authority. Three hundred feet above the ground, lofting illumination rockets into a target area based on timing, then visually acquiring and marking targets with white phosphorous rockets for the CAS aircraft to see. Finally, visually acquiring the CAS aircraft to ensure they were pointed at the target, we provided "Cleared Hot" calls, authorizing them to deliver their munitions. In between missions, we refueled at low altitude from a C-130, again, while using night vision goggles. This was varsity work, and as difficult as it gets in a fighter.

A few years prior, those of us who knew him were deeply saddened by the loss of Lt. Bobby "McFly" Forwalder, a friend of mine from my days at USNA. Lost at sea on his way to Bosnia, his E-2 Hawkeye impacted the water during low visibility carrier operations. Now, during WTI, I lost my second close friend, Lt. Don "Stump" Cioffi, in a training mission.

Donnie and I had lived together while I was in Hornet training in Jacksonville, Florida. An S-3 pilot, Donnie trained at Cecil Field at the same time as me, and he was there for me every step of the way during my "Speed Is Life" indiscretions. We spent countless hours together in the woodshop, drinking beer, and building great memories.

He died in a night catapult shot off the *USS John C. Stennis* and went down with his plane. It was a heavy blow. I still imagine Donnie with his plane, which softens the blow ever so slightly. I'm sure he would agree: it's better to be entombed in a multimillion-dollar machine he loved to fly than in a mahogany coffin. The instructors gave me permission to leave WTI for a couple days to attend his funeral. Although I missed one sortie in the course, they allowed me to finish and graduate.

Upon graduating WTI and receiving our WTI patches, Twistin' and I joined our squadron for our second tour fighting the war in Bosnia. We had mastered our craft in all possible ways and felt supremely ready for combat. However, I would not experience combat in a meaningful way for another decade, in a war not yet thought of.

Knowledge Matters

Lieutenant
Ron "Warhead" Lambrecht
Fleet Intelligence Training Center Pacific (FITCPAC)
Collateral Duty Intelligence Instructor

"A ship in port is safe, but that's not what ships are built for."

—REAR ADMIRAL GRACE HOPPER

Nautical Notables:

Knee-Knockers: A passageway opening through a bulkhead, designed to enhance structural integrity. The lower lip of the opening sits at shin height.

CASREP: Inoperative, casualty reported; OOC (out of commission).

Sally Ship: Sally ship was a method of loosening a vessel that ran aground from the mud holding her fast. A grounded ship was freed with little or no hull damage if she was rocked out of her muddy predicament. To free her, the order was given to sally ship. The crew gathered in a line along one side and then ran from port to starboard and back and forth until the vessel began to roll. Often the rolling broke the mud's suction, and she was pulled free and gotten underway.

FITCPAC's mission is to train naval intelligence professionals and operators in intelligence analysis, technologies, and processes to ensure they prevail in combat operations at sea and ashore. Shortly after arriving at FITCPAC, I was placed in charge of a course of instruction targeting Officers and Sailors assigned to ships without a resident Intelligence Officer.

Cruisers, destroyers, frigates, supply ships, and amphibious ships—other than those carrying an Admiral or Commodore's staff—did not have intelligence personnel assigned, so our job was to train collateral duty Intelligence Specialists. With an enrollment averaging 120 students/year, it was FITCPAC's premier course.

It was a good course, but I thought the training materials, order of curriculum, and practical application of skills needed improvement. After reworking the curriculum, I created realistic, scenario-driven exercises incorporating videos of Soviet platforms, and then broke the students into teams similar to staffing on ships. Then, we held competitions between them. We delivered information as if through a fire hose, and since course material was classified, students remained after hours to study or prepare for the various tests. The training days were long, but in a two-week period, students learned naval geography (choke points, transit lanes, patrol areas, etc.), Soviet naval platforms and weapons, and intelligence reporting protocols.

The course became so successful and in such high demand that we more than doubled the number of class offerings. Since instructors were experts in specific areas and schedule conflicts prevented their availability to convene two classes simultaneously, we staggered the two-week classes with a new class beginning each week. We averaged 280 students per year during the second and third years of my tenure.

Once a year, for six weeks, we hosted Intelligence Officers from countries friendly to the United States. These included Japan, South Korea, Germany, Mexico, Kenya, Saudi Arabia, Morocco, United Arab Emirates, and several others. We provided instruction in "foreign releasable" intelligence applications, but in reality, we only gave them an overview of what we were capable of. I am sure they felt the same way. With our hands tied due to "release-ability limitations," not much intelligence application value was learned by our guests. We painted them "Red, White, and Blue" (tongue in cheek, of course) and sent them home.

Each of the instructor staff sponsored one of the foreign Intelligence Officers, and it was our responsibility to ensure they enjoyed their stay. The Fourth of July normally occurred during the six-week course, so they participated in all of the usual US celebrations. One summer, we held a picnic at a local park and challenged our guests to a softball game. They were not good at softball but agreed to play only if we also played a game of soccer. It was ugly...for both teams. We had our way with them on the softball field, and they dominated us on the soccer field.

During the soccer game, which we played almost entirely on our defensive end of the field, I engaged in a joust against a South Korean. A **knee-knocker** would have been a gentler opponent. A spiral fracture to my tibia and three fractures to my fibula resulted in game-over—I was no longer a weapon! I was **CASREP**'d. It took a significant amount of **sally shipping** to pry me loose from the grass I clung to. After a couple days in the hospital and three months in a cast, I swore off soccer forever.

If you haven't guessed by now, we are driven by fitness reports (evaluations). Shortly after arriving on board, my fitness reports began to read "top two" and evolved to "Top Lieutenant" shortly thereafter. Performance in billet, as I had been previously advised, saved my bacon. I was promoted to Lieutenant Commander (O-4).

VMFA-451 Hornet in the vertical during a photo shoot. Photo credit: Randy Jolly from the back seat of a two-seat Hornet piloted by Steve (1996).

Tonto

Captain
Steve "Curly" Lambrecht
Pilot Training Officer, VMFA(AW)-332

"He who laughs last didn't get the joke."

—CHARLES DE GAULLE

Nautical Notable:

Semper Gumby: A play on the traditional motto of the Marine Corps, Semper Fidelis, which means "Always Faithful." Semper Gumby means "Always Flexible."

In the year between my two deployments to Aviano Air Base, Italy, flying missions over Bosnia, much transpired. I graduated from TOPGUN and WTI, Captain Scott O'Grady had gotten himself shot down in Bosnia, and a peace treaty had been signed between the warring factions. A tenuous peace was in place.

On my second deployment to Aviano Air Base, the change was visible, even from 25,000 feet. During the first deployment, the entire country was blacked out at night; the only visible light came from the glow of ammunition shot at opposing sides. This time, the entire country was lit up, and airliners were flying in and out Sarajevo, the capital.

Our new mission as part of "IFOR," short for Implementation Force, was to maintain a presence to ensure all parties adhered to the terms of the new peace treaty. Peace had broken out, which made our jobs much more mundane. We sarcastically referred to the entire endeavor as "WW Bosnia." **Semper Gumby.**

Occasionally, to blow off steam, we attended the Officers' Club at Aviano Air Base. Since it was a multinational operation, there were aircrew from all over the world in attendance, which made for fun times and expanded horizons.

"What are you doin', something?" asked Chumley one evening.

I replied I was not, so off we went with the crowd to the Aviano Officers' Club, where we challenged the Brits to a game of crud.

For the uninitiated, crud is a fast-paced game played by two teams around a pool table. There are only two balls: the cue ball and the eight ball. The game begins when a member of one team launches the cue ball at the eight ball, placing the eight ball into motion. Players rotate from defense to offense, then out.

The objective of the game is for the next defender to prevent the next offender from successfully hitting the eight ball with the cue ball before the eight ball stops rolling. Shots can only be taken from the ends. If the eight ball stops rolling, the offensive player loses a "life." Each player has three lives.

The game often gets physical. Sometimes very physical.

We had some large Marines in our squadron, so we put together our six biggest and brawniest players. Our team's average height was well north of six feet, and our team included Tonto, of "harder than woodpecker lips" fame. The game with the Brits commenced. The action quickly intensified. The physicality escalated. The noise from the crowd practically deafened.

That's when it happened. Tonto, moving from defense to offense, picked up the cue ball and sprinted to the end to take a shot. At the same time, the British defender rounded the end from the opposite side, knowing he must prevent Tonto from taking an accurate shot. The Brit lowered his shoulder and drove himself with full force toward Tonto. The Oklahoma Tough Man and martial arts expert was quick to defend.

They collided, and the room fell silent. We could not believe what had just happened, nor what we saw before our very eyes. When taking up a defensive position in order to absorb the impact, Tonto had raised his hand with the cue ball in it. The Brit impacted the cue ball, full force...teeth first. It didn't just knock his teeth out, it shattered them, and uncountable pieces were strewn across the red felt of the pool table! We were speechless.

Tonto, being Tonto, clandestinely began to walk around the pool table collecting a few pieces and putting them in his pocket for his medicine bag! The Brit took it all in stride. He laughed with his newly adorned jack-o'-lantern teeth, ordered another beer, and proceeded to pick up as many pieces as he could find, intending to take them to his next dentist appointment, undoubtedly the following day.

When Tonto attempted to apologize for the catastrophe, the Brit said, "Just buy me a shot of tequila, mate." When the intense blast of alcohol hit the exposed nerve-endings of his shattered teeth, he howled in pain. After recovering from the shock, the Brit shouted, "That was *good*!"

In 2006, I discovered Tonto had abandoned his relationship with alcohol, while retaining his tenacity as a war fighter.

Serving as a Forward Air Controller with a Joint Special Ops Task Force in Iraq, Tonto encountered the enemy while on the front lines. Having been severely wounded in the shoulder with shrapnel from an IED, Tonto called in friendly air support, saving his unit from the enemy and earning the Purple Heart and Bronze Star with "V" for Valor. He retired as a Colonel and now serves as an evangelical preacher.

Tu-95 Bear bomber. (Reprinted through UK OGL 1.0, 83352)

F-14A of VF-111 with Soviet Il-38 in 1984. (Open source)

Libyan MiG-23 Flogger. (Open source)

All Hands on Deck

Lieutenant Commander
Ron "Warhead" Lambrecht
USS Constellation
Assistant Intelligence Officer

"The task ahead of you is never as great as the power behind you."

—RALPH WALDO EMERSON

Nautical Notables:

Shot: A shot, one of the forged lengths of chain joined by shackles to form an anchor cable, is usually fifteen fathoms long (ninety feet). A ship is held in position by the weight of the chain lying on the bottom. After the anchor is down, several lengths (shots) of chain are paid out.

Forecastle (abbreviated fo'c'sle): The upper deck of a sailing ship forward of the foremast, or the forward part of a ship used as a shelter for stores, machinery, or as quarters for sailors. It is the space where the anchor chain passes through on its way to a storage void located belowdecks.

Fathom: A fathom is a unit of length in the imperial and US customary systems, equal to six feet. The word is also used to describe taking measure (e.g., "to fathom something").

A promotion to Lieutenant Commander meant a return to sea, and I was detailed to the *USS Constellation* as the Assistant Intelligence Officer. I worked directly for a Commander (O-5), and we were subordinate to the Operations Department, led by an alumni Squadron Commanding Officer (Captain, O-6) who served as the Department Head.

In addition to the intelligence work routinely performed on a forward-deployed carrier, I found myself in the position of co-managing approximately ninety personnel. We had three branches under our charge: the Intelligence Branch, consisting of Intelligence Officers and enlisted Intelligence Specialists; the Cryptologic Branch, consisting of a Cryptologic Officer and enlisted Cryptologists; and the Photographic Branch, consisting of a Photographic Officer and enlisted Photo Mates.

An aircraft carrier with 5,000 personnel on board is a microcosm of society as a whole. Within a two-year tour, some shipmates/Sailors may die or end up with significant medical problems. Some lose loved ones. Some Sailors excel, while others will be consistently in trouble. Some marry, while others have marital problems and get divorced. Some find themselves in financial trouble, while others succumb to drug and alcohol abuse.

I consider myself a good shepherd of people, and as a counselor, listener, empathizer, and disciplinarian, I found my judgment to be trusted on board. My humble beginnings, occasional living off the "grid" in Fargo/ Moorhead, struggle to find my way in life in my early years, and experience as an enlisted man resulted in a persona that earned the confidence of those under my charge. That persona served me well as I progressed in my military career—and later as a federal employee.

* * *

Going to sea on a United States ship of war is a global affair. One never knows what may be encountered, whether scheduled or otherwise. Plans change based on emerging events, sometimes as they occur.

On December 1, 1988, the *USS Constellation* departed North Island, San Diego, for a six-month deployment to the Western Pacific and Indian Ocean. While in transit, our schedule included a missile firing exercise northwest of the island of Kauai, Hawaii, in an ocean area known as the Pacific Missile Range. In preparation for these exercises, the Navy, as routine, posted a "Notice to Mariners" to stay clear of the area.

On the day of our exercise, an Indian-flagged vessel named the *Jag Vivek* was notified by radio that it was in the restricted waters of the Pacific Missile Range. The Navy gave the ship a new course to clear the area, and two or three hours later, Navy aircraft control personnel gave the Indian vessel an "all clear." Believing the missile range to be clear, an F/A-18 Hornet attack fighter from the *USS Constellation* fired a twelve-foot-long unarmed Harpoon missile toward a target hulk ship positioned several miles from the aircraft launch point. As the Harpoon proceeded toward the target hulk, it instead locked onto the Indian merchant.

Since the F/A-18 pilot was not carrying live ordnance, he couldn't shoot the missile down. All he could do was follow the missile to its destination point. The missile tore through the living quarters near the top of the pilot house and eventually landed in the water forward of the ship. One Indian crewman was killed.

The Navy took responsibility for the incident, but as we left Honolulu a few days later, we saw that the *Jag Vivek* was positioned pier-side awaiting repairs. It was not the last time our paths crossed.

Despite the Cold War drawing to a close, decades of training and "cat and mouse" with adversaries created habits that would die hard. During the remainder of our transit, Soviet submarines and reconnaissance aircraft used us as a "training aid," and we used them back. Both sides were good at our respective missions, and we continuously battled for supremacy. Given the politics of the time and the thawing of relations, it felt like a game. Deadly, but a game.

During our six-month deployment (typical during that time) at GONZO Station, tensions rose on several fronts. The Soviets kept us busy with their Tu-95 and Il-38 long-range reconnaissance aircraft (NATO nicknamed them Bear and May respectively) and their never-ending presence of submarines. Meanwhile, we were also tracking Iranian and Iraqi military vessels in the Gulf.

The US, a superpower with global interests, has to give attention to actors on many stages. At the time of our deployment, Saddam Hussein was saber rattling with an eye toward Kuwait and had positioned more than 100,000 Iraqi troops along the Iraq-Kuwait border. He threatened Kuwait with an all-out invasion (which occurred in August 1990, after our deployment).

Then there was Gaddafi, the Gulf of Sidra, and the Line of Death. On January 4, 1989 (one month into our deployment), two *USS John F. Kennedy* F-14 Tomcats shot down two Soviet-manufactured Libyan MiG-23 Floggers. The F-14 pilots believed the MiGs were attempting to engage them. The event took place over the Mediterranean Sea about forty miles north of Tobruk, Libya. Granted, the Gulf of Sidra is in the Mediterranean, but an American aircraft carrier is on constant ready alert when it's within a couple days' steaming time from a conflict. We were functioning on a hair trigger.

Although the eight-year Iran–Iraq war drew down in 1988, oil tanker escorts in the Persian Gulf continued during my deployment in 1989. In 1987, the US-flagged Kuwaiti oil tanker *Bridgeton* hit an Iranian mine. As a result, the US and other allied nations began tanker escort duties in the Gulf.

Both Iraqi and Iranian naval vessels were active during our deployment, and we were constantly monitoring their potential for mining activities. Minefields were still in place as a result of the Iran–Iraq war, and it was not uncommon to find free-floating mines that had come loose from their moorings. Two years later, both the *USS Tripoli* and *USS Princeton* hit mines in the Gulf.

All mission planning originated in the Carrier Intelligence Center (CVIC), which was the first place aviators were required to be when the mission was over. We analyzed information gleaned from the aircrews and applied the results to follow-on missions. Information collection was a constant task, as we used what we learned to predict future enemy movements and then plan our actions accordingly.

In concert with our carrier operations, Special Operations units patrolled the Gulf while attack helicopters searched for Iranian mining activities. One evening, a helicopter crew spotted an Iranian-flagged ship dropping mines into the shipping lanes. Two US gunships engaged with mini-guns and high-explosive anti-personnel rockets. The badly damaged vessel was subsequently boarded by a team of SEALs, who searched the ship and took several Iranian prisoners. The SEALs eventually scuttled the Iranian vessel by detonating explosives in its hull.

There is no "high ground" at sea level, so our F-14 and F/A-18 pilots took the high ground over the Gulf, serving as a formidable deterrence to Iranian fighter aircraft attempting to penetrate the air space. Iranians still had a few American-made F-14 fighter aircraft in their inventory, and they posed a significant threat to ships operating in the area.

In 1979, shortly before I attended Aviation Officer Candidate School in Pensacola, a major revolution broke out in Iran. As the revolution unfolded, all training of Iranian student pilots in the US, and those who were attending Aviation Officer Candidate School (AOCS) while I was there, was halted. Iranian student pilots remained in Pensacola throughout the summer of 1979, while the US decided what to do with them.

Human nature being what it is, many became friends with the US instructors assigned to provide them training. The pilots flying the Iranian F-14s in 1989 were these same students, and many were personally known by our pilots who were instructors at the time. When the pilots recognized each other, the banter became somewhat humorous, but always occurred while the Iranians maintained a safe distance.

As deployed life became routine again, we learned to react when we had to but tried to anticipate events before they occurred. After close to three months, we passed the baton to our on-coming relief carrier and headed home. Our flight operations continued while in transit in order to keep the pilots at the top of their game, but also as a line of defense for the ships in the battle group.

As we were transiting through the Straits of Malacca off the coast of Singapore, one of our pilots received a call from a ship in route to the Indian Ocean. It was the Captain of the *Jag Vivek*, the ship one of our pilots hit with an inert Harpoon off of Hawaii.

"American aircraft, please stay away from my ship. You are scaring my crew." Wow, and who could blame them?

* * *

After returning to San Diego, I negotiated with the Intelligence Detailer for orders to my next duty station. Again, I had several excellent career options, including a three-year tour in Hawaii at a Joint (all services represented) Command.

The intelligence community had a self-imposed set of hoops each of us needed to jump through in order to be well-rounded and competitive for promotion, and a joint tour was one. Other "career enhancing tours" included a Washington tour, maybe an attaché job at an embassy somewhere, a sea tour in every rank, and, oh yeah, whatever you do, do not homestead in one location your entire career. Misery loves company, and homesteading was viewed as not paying one's dues.

Up to this point, I had never left San Diego proper except for training commands and deployments, so I was becoming promotion vulnerable. I was penciled in to go to Hawaii when I got a call from the Commander, Naval Air Force, Pacific (COMNAVAIRPAC) staff Intelligence Officer, who offered me the Operations Intelligence position on the staff, working for a three-star Admiral. He had requested me by name. I accepted the position and remained in San Diego for yet another tour.

This occurred a few months before my actual transfer date. Meanwhile, life aboard ship continued. I was one of two Lieutenant Commanders on the *USS Constellation* qualified to serve as Command Duty Officer (CDO) while in port; all other CDOs were the rank of Commander or Captain and were Unrestricted Line Officers. On my duty day, and when serving in the absence of the CO/XO, I was in charge.

Upon returning from our Western Pacific/Indian Ocean deployment, we prepared the ship for an overhaul to take place in the Philadelphia shipyard. After transiting around South America, we headed north along the East Coast to Philadelphia. While in transit, we conducted a port call in Rio de Janeiro, Brazil. I had duty on the first day in port and received a call from the Quartermaster notifying me that we were dragging an anchor at the rate of three knots. Fortunately, we were sufficiently separated from land and other obstacles and had time to react.

Option A included letting out several additional **shots** of anchor chain. Option A worked, but stopping a 60,000-ton ship traveling at three knots with an anchor chain can cause some interesting sounds to emanate from the **fo'c'sle**. As I stood in the passageway gazing through the fo'c'sle hatch, I saw the chain, consisting of 300-pound links, stretch tight. We began to slow and eventually stopped. Reflecting back, had the chain snapped, I was probably not standing in the safest place on the ship.

Option B was to get underway. "Lieutenant Commander 'Warhead' Lambrecht, Intelligence Officer extraordinaire, at the helm of one of the mightiest warships in the world, underway at three knots against the current!" Now *that* would have looked good on my résumé! It is hard to **fathom**. Alas, it did not happen, but since the Commanding Officer is responsible for all things under his command, it was fun seeing the rooster tail behind the Captain's liberty boat as he headed back to the ship.

We arrived at the Philadelphia shipyard, and shortly thereafter, I transferred to COMNAVAIRPAC. Little did I know one of the most incredible experiences of my career as an Intelligence Officer awaited me.

Steve working as a "mercenary" and is seen here on a camel, with an "unmilitary-like" beard (1999).

Instructor cadre poses in front of a Kuwaiti Air Force F/A-18C Hornet at the Ahmad al-Jaber Air Base (1998).

Mercenary

Major
Steve "Curly" Lambrecht
Contract Pilot, The Boeing Company

"Majors: They are like Lieutenants, but with none of the potential."

—STEVE LAMBRECHT

Aeronautical Notables:

Life-Force Sucking Happiness Vampire: Any person, place, or event serving to attack the morale of an individual. While not yet a Famous Naval Saying, it *is* a Steve Lambrecht original saying.

Envelope: The maximum performance parameters of an aircraft. Flying at the edge of the envelope means to utilize the max speed, Gs, or altitude of an aircraft.

Functional Check Flight (FCF): Various systems are tested by the pilot using a scripted checklist; the FCF is a validation flight conducted after significant maintenance has been performed on an aircraft.

Split S Maneuver: A "Split S" maneuver is when a pilot rolls inverted and pulls, resulting in a pure vertical turn of 180 degrees.

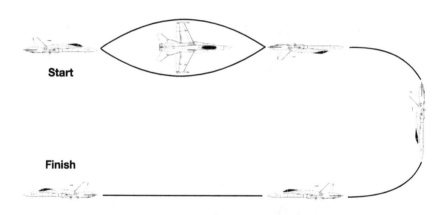

Start

Finish

After a superb stretch in the USMC, flying Hornets in combat and off of carriers, flying combat missions in Bosnia, and graduating from ACTI, TOPGUN, and WTI, I found myself unwilling to commit to twenty years of active duty. I had witnessed too many cases where politics influenced decisions, and I was not good at politics. I was good at performance.

I generally finished well in performance-based competition, but I generally came in second when popularity contests were in play. It took time for my performance to overcome a popularity deficit, and there was no guarantee it ever would. All I ever wanted was to be a Fighter Squadron Commander, a Skipper of a gun squadron, but at the age of thirty-one, I decided I wouldn't risk another ten years in the prime of my life hoping for dreams to come true.

My decision was aided, in part, by a three-week August deployment to Twentynine Palms, California, for a Combined Arms Exercise (CAX). The purpose of CAX is to allow Marine forces to perfect the employment of all combat resources upon an enemy. (Resources include infantry, artillery, armor, air power, and naval gunfire.) Perfection is attained when, by protecting themselves from one resource, the enemy becomes vulnerable to another. It is a magnificent orchestration of firepower and maneuver.

CAX is a superb training exercise, and Twentynine Palms is a superb range—but it is also a **life-force sucking happiness vampire** of heat, sand, and forbidding conditions. The crappers were a community affair, occupying an entire bay of the restroom facility, with no dividers in between them. Rolls of toilet paper hung on a wire strung across the room and could be slid to a fellow Marine upon request. I was reminded, yet again, of my brother's observation regarding Marines' austere living conditions.

While briefing for a flight in one of the many floorless tents we occupied in the desert, a windstorm blew through and filled every orifice in my body with sand. As the storm passed, I looked at my Skipper, who was crawling out from under the four-by-eight-foot briefing board that had fallen on him, sand stuck to the sweat pouring from every pore in his body.

I asked myself, *Do I really want to be doing this when I'm forty, hoping that performance will out-distance politics?*

With airlines hiring like crazy, I decided to throw my hat in the ring. Service still ran in my veins, and since I was halfway to a military retirement, continuing until at least twenty years only made sense. I wanted to continue serving in either the Reserves or Air National Guard, so I looked into multiple military flying units across the country. I received several offers, but unfortunately, I had not yet been hired by an airline, which would be the prime bread-winning job. The Guard/Reserve would be supplemental. I was nearing the end of my time in the USMC and needed to win some bread!

Through an odd happenstance of events, I found myself in contact with McDonnel Douglas. They had a contract with the Kuwait Air Force, teaching Kuwaitis to fly F/A-18 Hornets...in Kuwait. A fellow Marine Aviator and former TOPGUN instructor, with whom I was stationed in Beaufort, South Carolina, had preceded me there less than a year prior. I contacted him, and after an interview in St. Louis and a phone interview with the Chief Pilot in Kuwait, off I went to the Middle East.

It was 1998. Adventure awaited, and the money was good.

* * *

The first Gulf War began in 1991 and "ended" in 1992, six years prior to my arrival, but Kuwait still suffered from the ravages of war. Their resources and facilities had been scavenged and destroyed by Iraq, and the physical scars were still highly visible. The United States flew missions over Iraq, enforcing the No-Fly Zone after Saddam Hussein gassed the Kurdish citizens of Iraq. Still considered a threat to Kuwait, Hussein's intentions remained unclear.

I arrived in Kuwait in August 1998, and though it was approximately midnight local time, I exited the air terminal into a blast furnace of heat—well in excess of 100 degrees Fahrenheit. I caught my ride to the hotel where I stayed while searching for more permanent living arrangements.

It was a very foreign and exotic land. The Kuwaiti wardrobe consisted of dishdashas for men and abayas for women. Camels walked along the roads. Shepherds tended their herds of sheep and goats, pushing them across busy highways as their needs required. I certainly knew of this place, having studied it extensively, but studying it and living it were two very different things.

The next day, a McDonnel Douglas employee retrieved me from my hotel, and I began my in-processing to Kuwait. After I had obtained work visas, physicals, etc., the McDonnel Douglas employee escorted me to my new place of work, al-Jaber Air Base. Roughly an hour's drive west of Kuwait City, in the middle of the desert and far from civilization, it was not uncommon for temperatures at my new workplace to exceed 140 degrees Fahrenheit during the peak of the summer months.

There, I connected with a fellow new-hire pilot, Jeff "Junior" Hancock. We had arranged via email to share an apartment in Salwa, a suburb of Kuwait City, and we found a great apartment with a balcony overlooking the Arabian (Persian) Gulf from across the street. It was a two-bedroom refuge—and the stage for many fine memories to follow.

We also purchased a car from a souk (local market) that became our trusty steed: a used, light green Caprice Classic. (There's a reason you've never seen a king driving one.) We wanted something slightly beefy, yet economical, with a trunk big enough to contain our valuables and the dishdashas we kept handy in the event we needed to disguise ourselves and head for the border. Every morning before going to work, we thoroughly inspected our vehicle for explosives. Such was life in Kuwait in 1998.

Before I get to the flying portion of this story, I have to talk about driving in Kuwait. There is no way I can sufficiently describe driving in Kuwait in 1998, but I will try. The Kuwaitis were somewhat new to cars, and almost daily, we saw vehicles overloaded with people and livestock, flipped over, on fire, or traveling at speeds far exceeding any reasonable margin of safety.

At night, traveling on the freeway in pitch black conditions, at speeds in excess of seventy miles per hour, one became aware of another vehicle approaching from behind by the sudden appearance of head-lights no more than two feet from one's back bumper! Why the sudden appearance of lights where before there was only darkness? Common belief among Kuwaitis at the time was that leaving the vehicle's lights on depleted the car's battery, even while driving. Upon passing, the lights again were turned off.

You probably dismissed my statement about vehicles on fire earlier, but you should not have. It happened almost daily. On one occasion, I even saw a vehicle suspended no less than fifteen feet in the air, wrapped around a light pole! It was the Wild West of driving.

The flying was more disciplined. Because all Kuwaiti pilots were trained either in the US or the UK, the standards were much higher in aviation than on the freeways, but cultural norms did have a way of creeping in.

Upon my arrival, I was assigned as the Assistant Air-to-Ground Phase Head, which meant I had the job of standardizing all air-to-ground munition delivery academics and instruction. The normal flow for students is to start with familiarization, where they are first learn-ing to fly the airplane, then on to formation, where they learn to fly alongside and in formation with other aircraft. I showed up at the end of formation, with most of the heavy lifting of instructing complete. The students already knew how to fly the airplane, and the tactical phases of air-to-ground and air-to-air that followed were far less stressful and far more interesting and enjoyable for both student and instructor.

Instructing in Kuwait was a new experience. With little to no guidance from the State Department as to what we were allowed to discuss, we resisted the temptation to share everything we knew, understanding that we *could* discuss anything in the publications they had on hand and to those classification levels. There was also the question of diplo-macy. Asians, in general, are less accustomed to the brutal frankness of the American fighter pilot debrief; delivery of truth required finesse and prowess in order to inspire improvement.

We created our own weapons school, a six-month course designed to teach advanced tactics, techniques, and procedures. We were very proud of the course. Not only did we provide a superb tactical learning environment for the students, but we also taught them to teach. No one knows the material better than someone able to teach it; the flight path to excellence for a pilot comes from learning to extract lessons from each sortie, with the aim of continuous improvement.

Kuwait also offered the opportunity for me to fully explore my skills as an aviator, unencumbered by many of the rules and regulations designed to protect me from myself in today's enlightened flying environment. Certain things, when done in an airplane, will get a pilot fired, but those "things" vary by country. The United States is generally very strict where the rules are concerned; Kuwait was, shall we say, less so. That's not to say they didn't care about the rules—they did. They just didn't have many of them.

The published altitude and airspeed limits of the aircraft provide a comfortable margin of safety when compared to the actual physical capabilities of the aircraft. For instance, the F/A-18C has a published maximum speed of Mach 1.7 and a max operating altitude of 50,000 feet, but other restrictions are applied in order to constrain the pilot and to increase safety margins.

One example? When practicing unrestricted air-to-air combat, the pilot is not allowed to descend below 5,000 feet above the ground; this altitude is defined as the "hard deck." Another example is absolute minimum altitude restrictions: during low altitude training, which includes restricted air-to-air training, the United States Marine Corps limits operation to no less than one hundred feet above ground level (AGL) during daylight operations.

As fighter pilots, we often wonder about the real limits. They are different for each of us, and they differ from day to day. How does the airplane, and me as a pilot, perform when unrestricted by altitude and airspeed regulations? Familiarity beyond the published restrictions is limited to a review of engineering specifications and physics charts; one is not truly free to explore the edges of the flight **envelope**. However, the enemy hasn't read our regulations—they could not care less about them. In combat, the "hard deck" becomes the ground, and survival dictates the airspeed limit.

In the F/A-18, we had one particularly boring sortie called a functional check flight (**FCF**). An FCF profile is flown as a single aircraft, and the pilot has a laundry list of systems to check throughout the course of the flight. It includes shutting down and restarting engines, cycling the landing gear, and more. When done thoroughly, efficiently, and expeditiously, the pilot has enough gas remaining for a little fun. The FCF, with a side order of desire to validate personal and published limitations, seasoned with a minimal amount of regulations, is a recipe for varsity fighter pilot expertise.

How fast *does* the airplane go? The physics diagrams show a **Split S** can be performed below the hard deck of 5,000 feet without impacting terrain. *Can it be?* Can it be performed at *4,000* feet, as shown on paper? Lower? What does it feel like? What does the maximum sustained G limit look and *feel* like when performed just above sea level, as opposed to at 5,000 feet? Airshow pilots get to know this, albeit without external fuel tanks, missiles, and bullets loaded, but the average fighter pilot doesn't train in this regime. British pilots, meanwhile, are renowned for their piloting exploits below one hundred feet AGL. What does it look and feel like to be that low if I ever *must* be to avoid enemy fire?

In Kuwait, I was privileged to explore these limitations. It was not about breaking rules; it was about becoming better. It was about feeling fear and overcoming it in a peacetime environment, before it really mattered. I can attest to the validity of the envelopes and diagrams, the engineered margins of safety, and I came to know what it felt like to operate within them.

* * *

Kuwait was also the place where I came closest to dying. At the time, I was evaluating a Kuwaiti instructor-in-training during an air combat maneuvering (ACM) sortie. An ACM sortie is a *very* dynamic sortie.

The premise is as follows: the good guys have failed to kill everyone while using long-range missiles beyond the visual arena. One or more bad guys has survived and made it to within visual range (about ten miles), followed by the merge. This is where the proverbial rubber meets the road. It's pilot vs. pilot. Airplane vs airplane. By proxy: nation vs. nation. These are the scenarios made famous by the movie *Top Gun.*

There are many scenarios we use to set this up, but it always amounts to a visual discovery of the enemy, at a point of vulnerability, requiring extreme maneuvers and coordination in order to achieve success. Sometimes the scenarios involve two bad guys alive at the merge. Mostly, we train with two good guys and one bad guy, formally known as the "bogey." For this scenario, I was the bogey.

My job was to alternately, on each set-up, attack either the flight lead or the wing man. The instructor's job, the Kuwaiti instructor in this case, was to brief, teach, fly, then debrief each set. When he was attacked, it was his job to stay alive, while his wingman's job was to kill me. When I attacked his wingman, it was the instructor's job to teach his wingman to stay alive, while his job was to kill me.

The main danger in ACM is deconfliction, which means ensuring no one collides with another aircraft. It can be very difficult to maintain sight of multiple aircraft in an ACM environment, so the two aircraft engaged with each other are only responsible for ensuring they deconflict from one another. The other friendly aircraft, not engaged by/with the enemy, termed "supporting," must maintain deconfliction from the other two. Hence, the "supporting" fighter must have sight of the other two before pitching into the fight. In the engagement that nearly ended my life, I was the bad guy, the student was engaged with me, and the instructor was the supporting fighter.

The instructor was a superb pilot. Among the US instructor cadre, we talked about his having a "great set of hands," meaning he had great natural skills and maneuvered the airplane as well as any of us. I can attest to this personally, as he is the only pilot in the Kuwaiti Air Force ever to achieve a valid gun "snap shot" against me!

I attacked the friendly formation from their six o'clock, high. I pointed first at the instructor, then decisively committed to the wingman. After wrapping him up in a rolling scissors, we continued in a descending spiral, persistently threatening each other with our noses. The student was decisively defensive and was likely to lose the fight within fifteen seconds.

After rolling over the top and threatening the student with my nose, I unloaded, pushing forward on the stick to take all pressure off the control surfaces, resulting in G forces of less than one. As I was regaining airspeed, suddenly and without warning, a Hornet *flashed* through my heads-up display. It passed directly across the nose of my aircraft, close enough to make me gasp for air! My Hornet "thumped" as I flew through his jet wash. It was nearly a blur!

Over the radio, I screamed, "KNOCK IT OFF! KNOCK IT OFF!"

"Knock it off" is the call made to end *all* training in progress, usually due to a safety situation. I knew exactly what had happened: the instructor had pointed into the fight without having both his wingman and the bogey (me) in sight. It was an amateur mistake made by a very good pilot.

I handled the debrief diplomatically, a requirement for this environment; culturally, brutal honesty needed to take a backseat to saving face. I did confront the instructor after the formal debrief, however, and showed him the video. Maintaining a state of denial, he never admitted to his lapse in judgment.

I reconstructed the event further using stadia metric ranging and good old-fashioned Ivanhoe and Annapolis math. We had passed within 125 feet of one another, the equivalent of two and a half aircraft lengths, at a closing velocity of 350 miles per hour. One fourth of a second was likely the difference between me living to write this story or not.

In summary and in retrospect, I'd say the Kuwaitis were and are doing well, especially considering their relative timeline with respect to military advancement and requirements. However, as a word of caution, I would also say that when it comes to national defense, you either get serious about it or you just get by. There is a reason why America has the best fighter pilots in the world, and I say that without reservation, pride, or humility. It's simply a fact. We have them because we accept nothing less than excellence, we strive for it daily, and we give no one a break, least of all ourselves. That, coupled with the incredible resources made available to us courtesy of the tax-paying American citizen, makes us unstoppable. Whether talking about pilot vs pilot, airplane vs airplane, or nation vs nation, by proxy or by direct conflict, the US reigns supreme.

In February of 2000, after one and a half years as a "mercenary," I returned to the US, began my new job as a newly hired pilot with United Airlines, and awaited my start date with the Vermont Air National Guard (VTANG). Kuwait was a neat adventure, and I'm glad I did it, but I swore I would never do it again.

No longer in the active duty military, I wasn't sure if I'd ever get to apply my newly refined fighter pilot skills in combat. Boy, was I wrong.

USS Constellation returns to San Diego after a cruise. (Photo from DVIDS, Open Source)

Fo'c'sle Follies

Lieutenant Commander
Ron "Warhead" Lambrecht

USS *Constellation*
Assistant Intelligence Officer

"The question who ought to be boss is like who ought to be the tenor in the quartet. Obviously, the man who can sing tenor."

—HENRY FORD

Aeronautical Notable:

Fo'c'sle Follies: At the end of each grading period for landings (called a line period), the awards for Top Hook and other accomplishments are handed out during Fo'c'sle Follies. The name comes from the location on the ship where this ceremony takes place (ship's fo'c'sle), where crazy, funny, and sometimes "straddling the line of political correctness" skits are performed. It is a great camaraderie-building event that normally happens before a port call or just prior to the end of a long cruise so that spirits are high.

Undeniably, the dirtiest space on an aircraft carrier (and any other modern ship) *should* be the fo'c'sle, as it is the space where the anchor chain passes through on its way to a storage void located below decks. An incredible amount of rust, mud, and debris is carried into the space by the 300-pound links of chain housed below.

However, instead of being filled with rust and debris, the Boatswain's Mates, with pride, make the fo'c'sle the showcase of the ship. All brass fittings are polished to a brilliant shine, anchor links are freshly painted, and an artist's rendering of some nautical theme usually adorns the bulkheads and deck. The entire space is impeccably clean and often serves as the location for church services, social events, and gatherings.

On board, occasional moments of decompression occurred between levels of high intensity. The **Fo'c'sle Follies** is one such venue. Per tradition, Fo'c'sle Follies is scheduled a couple days prior to a port call. All squadrons participate.

A typical airwing in 1989 consisted of F-14 Tomcat and F/A-18 Hornet fighters, A-6 Prowler ground attack aircraft, E-2C Hawkeye early warning aircraft, S-3 Viking anti-submarine warfare and tanker aircraft, and SH-3 Sea King anti-submarine warfare and logistics helicopters. Arguably, the helicopter pilots are the hardest working and least appreciated aviators on the ship. Their most important job is to serve as "first responders" (Navy term is "plane guard") during flight operations in case of a down-aircraft. In other words, they are the first to launch in the morning and the last to land at night. In addition, they perform anti-submarine warfare missions, personnel movements between ships, and logistics missions between ships and shore.

As logistics haulers, helicopter pilots are frequently required to fly while the ship is in port and the rest of the crew enjoy liberty. A day or two before arriving in port, the ship is often within helicopter range of land. Helicopters make frequent runs to the beach carrying supplies, as well as advance parties to conduct port coordination and, if room is available, other passengers from the airwing and ship who contrive an excuse for getting off the ship early. While helicopter pilots normally don't have a lot of clout (since they fly aircraft that beat the air into submission in order to stay airborne), when within range of land, they rule supreme.

The helicopter guys had had enough, and Fo'c'sle Follies was the perfect venue for revenge. In order to tell this story, I have to set the stage, literally. The helicopter skit consisted of a couple two-foot by six-foot tables positioned in front of the audience. A blanket held up in front of the tables served as a curtain that prevented the audience from seeing what was going on behind. A sheet was then held behind the curtain and in front of the tables. Two butt-size holes were cut side by side out of the sheet, positioned at table-top level. You might see where this is going.

Four smaller holes were cut in the sheet below the table for a couple 'copter guys to place their arms through. Two other 'copter pilots dropped trousers, laid on their side on top of the table, and positioned their butts into the holes. Lips were painted directly onto the butt cheeks above and below the cracks of their asses, and eyes added on the upper cheeks. Ears were painted on either side of the holes directly onto the sheet, and hair was painted on the sheet above the holes. The "F-14 Butt Heads" were born.

The front row of the audience, positioned five feet from the stage, consisted of the Admiral, Chief of Staff and other staff members, Carrier Air Group, his Deputy, and the Commanding Officer of the ship and his Executive Officer. Positioned directly behind them were the Commanding Officers of the squadrons, as well as their Executive Officers and Operations Officers, and behind them in descending pecking order were the Department Heads and other mid-level Officers, with the airwing pilots and Intelligence Officers at the back of the room.

When the curtain was removed, a two second pregnant pause blanketed the room until everyone recognized the spectacle before them. Then, the entire place collapsed in uncontrollable laughter. Laughter persisted for about two minutes until the place somewhat quieted down, at which point one of the 'copter pilots positioned below the table pulled out a cigar. The place relapsed into uncontrollable laughter. A minute or two passed, and then the guy with the cigar attempted to blindly lodge the cigar into the ass crack of the Butt Head. We convulsed. After about a minute of fishing for a place to lodge the cigar, he was finally successful, at which point he pulled out a lighter. Some in the audience may have lost control of their bladders at that point!

When the crew finally regained composure, the dialog began. A 'copter pilot positioned at the podium began talking to the Butt Heads. He asked a question, and then one of the Butt Heads provided a response. The "owner" of the Butt Head pulled and pushed on his upper cheek, behind the curtain, causing his ass crack to spread and close as if it was talking. This also caused the end of the impaled cigar to move up and down. More convulsive laughter.

The 'copter pilot asked, "What makes you so important that you need to hit the beach a day before everyone else?"

The Butt Head replied, "Well, let me think about that for a minute." At this point one of the guys below the table reached up and blindly attempted to rub the "chin" of the Butt Head as if the Butt Head were engaged in deep thought. The Butt Head continued, "My Commanding Officer wants me to wire flowers to his wife on his behalf."

"Yeah right," said the 'copter pilot. "You just want to go to town and get crap-in-your-pants shit-faced!"

The dialog continued with the banter back and forth between the 'copter pilot and the Butt Heads until an arm of one of the Butt Heads reached up and started to fan the Butt Head.

"Ew, what is that smell? Did you burp?"

We spent the vast majority of the skit on the deck, convulsing in laughter. Every Navy guy in attendance that day remembers the F-14 Butt Heads. I suspect the level of levity permitted then is somewhat curtailed in today's Navy. "Butt," then again...?

Photo of Lt. Col. Barent "Bear" Rogers in a VTANG F-16 over Ground Zero. Photo credit: Lt. Col. Terry "Trap" Moultroup (September 12, 2001).

The first aircraft (F-16 from Vermont) takes off to defend the homeland, September 11, 2001, at 1345 hours, EST, kicking off Operation Nobel Eagle.

9/11

Major
Steve "Curly" Lambrecht
Assistant Weapons Officer,
134th Fighter Squadron

"Forgive your enemies, but never forget their names."

—JOHN F. KENNEDY

Nautical Notables:

Improvise, Adapt, and Overcome: A Marine Corps phrase rooted in the knowledge that the USMC typically has less money, fewer resources, and larger challenges to conquer than the other services. It means exactly what it says.

September 11, 2001 was the perfect fall day. Crisp air. Not a cloud in the bright blue sky.

I had just returned to the Vermont Air National Guard (a.k.a. The Green Mountain Boys) from F-16 training in Tucson, Arizona. For an experienced fighter pilot, it was two months of training spread across *four* months; it was not an efficient program and could have been delivered in half the time, but it served the purpose. I returned from training in July of 2001 and received the finishing training touches necessary to declare me a "Combat Mission Ready" pilot in the F-16. Then, I returned to United and commuted to New York City.

At the time, I was a First Officer on the A320, and being very junior, I was sitting reserve, a fate I do not wish upon anyone. The bottom 20 percent of pilots on the seniority list sit reserve (on call) in case they are needed to fill in for a pilot who calls in sick—or for another of several reasons.

Since I didn't live in New York, I had a choice: I could either stay in a hotel on my own dime or rent what's called a "crash pad." Crash pads come in many varieties, but generally it involves renting the right to a bed, in a run-down apartment, in some older neighborhood. Either you rent a bed exclusively, meaning it's yours and no one else sleeps in it, or you rent a slot, whereby you keep your bedding in a closet and choose an open bed when you need it. Having done the latter previously, I had not yet decided whether to rent a crash pad or stick with a hotel. On 9/11, I was in a hotel on Long Island.

My hotel was economical. Since I was paying out of my own pocket, while making $24,000/year as a first-year pilot at United, I didn't have money to spare on the extras. This hotel smelled like Carpet Fresh, and I kept my socks on to avoid having to feel the carpet's greasy texture on my feet.

On September 11, 2001, I woke up at about 8:55 a.m. and turned on the TV. Live on CNN, I saw footage of one of the World Trade Center

Towers on fire, with reports that a plane had crashed into it. Immediately, I supposed it involved some kind of pilot error, either by someone sightseeing in a small airplane or perhaps a helicopter tour gone wrong. Then, as I watched live, a large jet crashed into the South Tower. Immediately, I knew this was no accident. As an airline pilot, it was clear to me the jet was a large passenger aircraft. It was later identified as United Airlines Flight 175, a Boeing 767.

As with most of America, I remained glued to the television, seeking more information about the events at hand. The hotel was about four miles away from the World Trade Center. Finding an open door and stairway leading to the rooftop, I observed the carnage clearly enough.

My cell phone was virtually useless; the cell towers were overwhelmed. Finally, after a couple hours, I was able to contact the United Airlines Crew Desk. Their instructions were simple: "You are released. Do what you need to do." I managed to get a text to my sister informing her that I was okay and to please contact everyone and let them know, which she did.

All of this ranked subordinate to my military DNA. I was in the Air National Guard and needed to return to Vermont as quickly as possible, but with work to be done in defense of our nation, how was I to get back to Vermont? I called all the rental car companies and Greyhound Bus. Everyone was sold out. Appropriately, the government grounded all airlines.

At 9:45 a.m. on September 12, I remembered Amtrak served Essex Junction, Vermont, once daily, so I contacted Amtrak and discovered that the train was scheduled to depart Grand Central on Manhattan Island at 11:30 a.m. Being on Long Island, I needed to get to Manhattan, fast. I had no choice. It was time to **improvise, adapt, and overcome**.

Quickly cramming my belongings into my suitcase, I ran for the subway station. The routes were all disrupted due to damage around the World Trade Center, so I found the open lines and pieced together a path to get there.

At 11:00, I emerged from the subway. My heart sank. A line of people extended out of Grand Central and down the street for over a block. No way was I going to make an 11:30 train.

Without an alternative, I walked past the line to the ticket booth and showed my military ID. I explained I needed to get on the 11:30 to Vermont. Mid-sentence, the lady in the ticket booth emerged from behind the counter and escorted me directly to the train. No ticket— she just put me on it. I don't even remember what she said.

To this day, this particular event brings tears to my eyes. I wish I could meet her again so that I could say "thank you." The sense of urgency and kindness to our fellow man blanketed all of America.

After nine hours, I arrived in Vermont. It was evening, and I needed to report for duty the next morning. I went home and attempted to sleep, but adrenalin had been coursing through my veins for thirty-six hours.

The next morning, I awoke, put on my uniform, and commenced my ten-minute drive to work, tuning in to NPR during the middle of an interview with a New York City firefighter. He was a Station Chief, or some other high-ranking firefighter in charge of many others. A salt-of-the-earth, true American classic, his New York accent rang prevalent as he described, in heart-breaking detail, what it was like to lose a fellow firefighter. They were a family, he said. They lived together, ate together, and knew each other's wives and children. Some were godfathers to their team members' children. Some were relatives. He described how hard it was to lose someone that close, and how no matter how hard they trained, no matter how hard they tried, they all *knew* they would someday lose another.

That was the conclusion of the interview. The commentator came on and explained that it was a previously recorded interview and that the firefighter had been killed in the World Trade Center on 9/11. I lost it.

Three blocks from my home, I pulled over to the side of the road and sobbed uncontrollably. The combination of the previous forty-eight hours, coupled with the shock and unexpected loss I felt at that moment, was more than I could withstand. The entirety of the event came to bear.

War followed. Plenty of it. For the next seventeen years, I protected the homeland and fought in Iraq. A fellow United pilot and friend calls the decade that followed 9/11 the "Lost Decade." Our lives changed forever.

Nineteen years later, as I write this, I fly the 757/767 for United Airlines. The irony is not lost on me.

The Soviet Navy destroyer Vinogradov sails under the Coronado Bay Bridge in San Diego, California (1990).

A US Navy Commander talks with a Soviet Navy Captain Second Rank near the Soviet guided missile destroyer Boyevay.

Captain Alexander Mikhailovich Zuyev (left) in the cockpit of a MiG-29 like the one shown on the right. (Photo credits: Creative Commons)

Comrade

Lieutenant Commander
Ron "Warhead" Lambrecht
COMNAVAIRPAC

Operations Intelligence Officer

"I was an Intelligence Officer, not a policy-maker."

—Cofer Black (Directorate of Operations at the Central
Intelligence Agency [CIA])

Nautical Notables:

21-Gun Salute: The most commonly recognized of the customary gun salutes that are performed by the firing of cannons or artillery as a military honor. The custom stems from naval tradition, where a warship fired its cannons harmlessly out to sea until all ammunition was spent to show that it was disarmed, signifying the lack of hostile intent. As naval customs evolved, twenty-one guns came to be fired for heads of state, or in exceptional circumstances for heads of government, with the number decreasing with the rank of the recipient of the honor.

17-Gun Salute: Salute to Generals and Admirals, Assistant Secretaries of Defense (Army, Navy, Air Force), and chairs of congressional committees.

After decades of animosity, sometimes taking us to the brink of a world war, the relationship between the US and the Soviet Union began to thaw. The two countries agreed to host reciprocal military ship visits. Heretofore, my entire military career had centered on countering the Soviet threat, and now I found myself fully entrenched in preparations for hosting three Soviet ships in San Diego!

At the time of my assignment to Commander, Naval Air Force, Pacific or COMNAVAIRPAC (CNAP), the Admiral commanded all USN aviation units in the Pacific area of operations. The Intelligence Division handled equipping, coordinating training, evaluating/inspecting, and administratively supporting the intelligence assets assigned to aviation units under CNAP's purview, including carriers. We managed installation of intelligence-related computer systems, staffed emergent personnel assignments (including positions vacated due to performance issues, humanitarian requirements, or "needs-of-the-Navy"), performed readiness inspections, and ensured training qualifications were achieved.

It was my first experience working on a three-star Admiral's staff, and I must admit our office spoke with a fair amount of authority! Among the seven San Diego naval bases, Vice Admiral John Fetterman, CNAP, served as Senior Officer Present Ashore (SOPA), so his staff oversaw all Navy activities impacting the civilian community as well.

For the Soviet Navy's visit to San Diego, I was charged with recruiting interpreters. The goal was to have one interpreter for every two Soviet Sailors, so with 850 Sailors visiting, we needed 425 interpreters. We advertised in the Los Angeles and San Diego papers, as well as on local TV and radio stations, and professional interpreters arrived from Washington, DC, to interview those who volunteered.

We recruited the entire cross-section of American life, from college-aged adults with purple hair to Farmer Jones in his bib overalls. Volunteers included white-collar professionals and factory workers, cab drivers, and 7-Eleven employees. We took anyone who spoke fluent Russian. Since there was no dress code for the volunteer interpreters, they were quite a sight to see at the various formal events, such as banquets and military cocktail parties.

Three Soviet warships, *Admiral Vinogradov*, *Boyevay*, and *Argun*, sailed into the once-forbidden waters of San Diego Harbor, the first such military visit to the West Coast in more than a century. It was an amazing sight, and the Soviet Sailors' excitement matched our own.

The two Soviet destroyers and an oiler arrived pier-side at the 32nd Street Naval Station after exchanging **17-** and **21-gun salutes** with their US counterparts. The Soviet military band played. Lines of Soviet Sailors formed at the rails as they took in their first glimpse of Southern California.

The scene quickly evolved into friendly acknowledgments, photo ops, and gift exchanges between US and Soviet Sailors. Initially, the Soviets were reluctant to trade or sell their uniform pieces, as one Soviet Officer explained, their Sailors were not allowed off the ships out of uniform, but that rule lasted less than a day. By the second day, it appeared there were not enough uniforms left for even the watch standers.

While top-ranking Naval Officers for each country made speeches expressing their hope for improved relations, many of the 850 Soviet

Sailors had other plans. We positioned three US ships of comparable size and mission on the opposite side of the pier from the Soviet ships, and the crews on board those ships were designated escorts for their Soviet counterparts during the five-day visit. It was heartening to see the relationships mature between the Sailors as the week progressed.

We scheduled visits to typical San Diego attractions, such as the zoo, Sea World, picnics on the beaches, and sightseeing adventures. In fact, with a tape prepared in advance of the Soviet Sailors' visit to Sea World, the whale, Shamu, lip-sync'd a welcome message in Russian. On another afternoon reserved for shopping at a local Navy Exchange, the Soviets bought every boom box in the store and completely depleted the store's inventory of batteries. On several occasions, Soviet Sailors counted their US dollars to buy a camera or portable radio only to discover they were short, and then their US Sailor escort slipped them the extra cash needed to make the purchase.

On the first evening of the visit, CNAP hosted a reception at the Admiral Kidd Officers' Club located on the bay in downtown San Diego. Attendees included senior Naval Officers, the mayor, and other local government officials, along with dignitaries from both countries and attachés from the Soviet Embassy in Washington, DC. I was provided a new name tag for the event, since we all agreed it would be bad form to use my CNAP name tag, which read "Intelligence Officer." My new name tag read "Interpreter," but since I do not speak Russian, all of my conversations with the Soviets included interpreters.

Once, I engaged in a conversation with a senior Officer from the Soviet embassy, so I knew he spoke English and could read my name tag. The fact that I carried on a conversation through an interpreter did not compute, so he began to tell jokes to see if I laughed from the punch line before it was relayed through the interpreter. I passed that test! I am sure to this day that that Russian has a healthy respect for my poker face.

On the fourth day of the visit, translators fussed over the address to be given at the Marine Corps Recruit Depot. Intending to treat the Soviet senior leadership as though they were actual recruits arriving for training, a Drill Instructor, using a Russian interpreter, gave the visitors a version of his usual opening pitch. "I wonder if there is a Russian equivalent of 'Get your eyes off me, maggot,'" one Marine mused.

Having lived through a couple similar introductions (enlisted boot camp and AOCS), I understood the nervous responses observed on the faces of the Soviets. They were directed to exit the bus, place their feet on yellow footsteps painted on the sidewalk, and follow the Drill Instructor's every command. Later, Admiral Genadiy Alexandrovich Khatov, Commander of the Soviet Pacific Fleet, asked Vice Admiral Fetterman to explain how we got young men to volunteer and put up with this treatment. Admiral Fetterman explained that we teach our Marines pride, respect, and confidence, while meeting their basic needs, such as wages, clothing, and food. The tenor of Admiral Khatov's response suggested Soviet conscripts received no such care during their two-year enlistment.

The Marines hosted the Soviets for one day of activities, which included a beach party, riding jet skis, parasailing, and water skiing, plus a barbeque and an afternoon rodeo on the Camp Pendleton Marine base, located north of San Diego. There, Marines were engaged in bronco riding, calf roping, bull riding, etc., and it did not take long for the Soviets to want to participate. "If American Yankee can ride bull, Russian can ride bull." No, they can't. But they tried.

I will never forget that week. On the morning of the Soviets' departure to their home base at Vladivostok, there were damp eyes on both sides of the pier.

* * *

Unfortunately, one port visit did not end decades of Cold War, and my duties as CNAP's Operation Intelligence Officer continued. This included serving as the Contact Officer for a Soviet MiG-29 Fulcrum pilot by the name of Captain Alexander Zuyev.

In May 1989, Alex flew his plane to Turkey (defected) and requested political asylum in the US. As one of approximately one hundred pilots selected to fly the then top-secret MiG-29, he was one of the Soviets' best pilots, and they wanted him back.

The Soviets claimed Alex shot and killed a guard during his defection. A gunfight *did* occur between Alex and the guard, and both were shot. Alex emerged with a bullet lodged in his shoulder, and he broke his thumb in the ensuing hand-to-hand combat.

Fortunately for Alex, Soviet leader Mikhail Gorbachev instituted two initiatives: *Perestroika* and *Glasnost*. *Perestroika* meant "restructuring," referring to the restructuring of the Soviet political and economic system. *Glasnost* meant "openness" or more open, consultative government and wider dissemination of information. Because of *Glasnost*, the Turks were able to dial into a local Soviet television station and discovered the guard did not die in the gun battle; he was being interviewed in the hospital.

The next day, Alex was on a plane to Frankfurt. Six months later, he provided presentations across the United States' aviation community, describing his training and experience.

I attended one of Alex's first presentations. Though he could not speak English when he defected, just six months later, he gave a twenty-minute presentation to one of our Air Wings in English. An interpreter sat next to him and translated questions from the audience, but it was obvious Alex was a quick study.

As Alex's Contact Officer, I was charged with meeting him at the airport when he arrived in the San Diego area. I ensured he got to his hotel and met his scheduled events, and in the mornings, I picked him up at his hotel and drove him to his destinations.

On a separate visit, I picked Alex up at the airport and asked where he was staying. He indicated he was staying in a hotel in Mission Valley, which is a twenty-five-minute drive from my home. I had to get Alex to North Island the next morning by 0500 for a helicopter flight to the *USS Abraham Lincoln*, which was conducting workups off the coast of San Diego, so I suggested he stay at my place for the night. He agreed.

I called my wife from the airport, saying, "Anne, could you set another plate at the dinner table tonight? I am bringing a guest home to stay with us for the evening, and I think you are going to find him interesting!"

I will not discuss the details of Alex's life in the USSR and his decision to defect here. You can read about that in his book, *Fulcrum*, where you can also find pictures of his visit to the *USS Lincoln*, which occurred the day after he was a guest in my home.

The last time I saw Alex was a couple years later on the TV show *60 Minutes*, when he was being interviewed at an air show. I later discovered that on June 10, 2001, Alex died in a crash near Bellingham, Washington, along with another aviator. Their Yakovlev Yak-52 entered and failed to recover from an accelerated stall.

* * *

Normal tour rotations consist of a two-year sea tour and a three-year shore tour. I was beginning my third year at CNAP (shore tour) when I got a call from the Detailer indicating that there was an unplanned loss on the Amphibious Squadron Three (PHIBRON-3) staff and that I was standing on the ridge line. In other words, I was backlit by the morning light and had a big red bullseye on my chest.

Two weeks later, I transferred to the Amphibious Squadron staff. A week after that, the Commodore, his Marine counterpart, and their Operations and Intelligence Officers, including me, were on a plane to Washington, DC, followed by a trip to Central Command, Florida.

There, we received briefings on activities we might encounter during our deployment.

We were concerned about Somalia, as there were continued reports of local warlords stealing humanitarian aid meant for the hospitals and orphanages. We were told it would not be part of our mission statement. A mere two weeks later, I was on deployment, heading to the Indian Ocean and a rendezvous with destiny.

Pilots killing time between combat taskings, Balad Air Base, Iraq (2006). Pictured are Lt. Col. (Retired) Rick "Bunker" Shebib playing white, Major Daniel "Gump" Finnegan playing black, and Lt. Col. (Retired) Chris "Pooter" Caputo officiating. As those who have served in combat will tell you, the experience can sometimes be characterized as "hours of complete boredom, interrupted by moments of sheer terror."

Thirty Seconds

Lieutenant Colonel
Steve "Curly" Lambrecht

Chief of Standardization and Evaluation, 158th Operations Group

"No plan survives first contact with the enemy."

—Field Marshal Helmuth Karl Bernhard
Graf von Moltke

Aeronautical Notables:

Quick Reaction Force (QRF): Military formations varying in size and composition, coupled with vehicles and equipment, tailored to perform a specific mission.

Squirter: An individual who departs the objective, or target area, at a rapid pace. A squirter is likely a potential hostile.

It was 2006, and we were supporting an Army raid on a house in no-particular-location, Iraq. The plan was simple enough: establish airborne surveillance over the objective in advance of the **QRF**. Look for snipers on rooftops along the ingress route as the friendlies traveled toward the objective. Watch for activity at and around the objective. Provide top cover during the egress, when the friendlies left the target area and traveled to their home base. Search for potential ambushes, snipers, and IEDs (improvised explosive devices). It was a slightly more interesting mission than most nights, but these missions also tended to be fifty-fifty fruitful/ fruitless.

IEDs were a persistent problem in Iraq because they were simple to build, using materials more readily available than those used in traditionally manufactured mines and booby traps. The enemy made them in various "factories," then placed them in locations likely to be visited or passed through by friendly forces. Typically, they placed them at night, using darkness to conceal their activities.

It was incumbent on those of us who flew at night to search carefully for IED planters or for IEDs themselves. Searching for IEDs at night, with night vision goggles and a targeting pod, was meticulous work, reminiscent of finding a weed in a soybean field while speeding along the highway in a car. Without knowing it, I had been trained for this mission since childhood.

We were looking for a bad guy, reputed to be the builder of IEDs used against friendly forces in and around the local area. He was notorious and undoubtedly had friends.

The briefing specified that the QRF, an armored force arriving with Humvees and Stryker vehicles, were to position a ladder to access the roof of the objective and simultaneously ingress both the roof and the house. Meanwhile, a separate force was to ingress the end of the block from the opposite direction and serve as a barrier to anyone exiting the home and attempting to escape from the QRF by going down the street.

The plan seemed incomplete.

The objective was covered along the front of the house and the roof, but what about the back of the house? I figured they must intend to have forces cover the alley behind the house. I would be on the lookout for friendlies in the alley so that they wouldn't be confused with **squirters**.

We arrived about fifteen minutes before the QRF. Excessive noise might alert the enemy to our presence, so as the flight lead, I directed an orbital pattern far enough away and high enough in altitude to minimize our sound signature, thereby avoiding "burning" the target. I then set up a pattern optimizing our "sensor view" of the objective so that, between our targeting pods and night vision goggles (NVGs), we had near continuous coverage of the objective area, including all streets and alleys leading to it.

Initial reconnaissance revealed nothing unusual. It was just a typical neighborhood of homes built with shared walls, not unlike row houses or town houses in the US. These houses were usually one-story tall, with knee-walls on the roof along the ends of each home, which served as demarcation lines between properties. In summary, a typical block of homes was joined on each side and at the rear.

One particular disadvantage to our visibility was a tree about twenty to thirty feet in height, inconveniently located directly along the planned approach route of the raiding force. It was a nuisance, further accentuating the need for proper aircraft positioning and well-timed sensor/NVG coverage. Arriving overhead the objective prior to the raid, we had time to scope it out, develop our plan, and position appropriately.

As the QRF approached, I assigned my wingman to monitor the objective, while I scanned rooftops and streets for snipers and potential IEDs. With the QRF moving, scanning rooftops and streets was a full-time job. When the QRF turned the corner toward the objective, I moved my sensors onto the objective rooftop and adjusted my field of view to ensure I could see the front and back streets.

Sticking to the plan, the friendlies assaulted the objective, immediately placed a ladder from the street to the roof, and rapidly ascended. As they did so, I saw an individual rise from the roof and flee to the back knee-wall adjoining the neighbor's house. Two additional individuals rose from the same roof and fled to the back of their home's roof, which abutted the neighbor's roof and was also separated by a knee-wall. They remained there.

When I say, "rose from the roof," I mean that they appeared to have ascended through an attic or doorway. As analysis later showed, the individuals were sleeping on the roofs of their homes, due to the summer heat in Iraq being so incredibly oppressive. What appeared to be a doorway was, in fact, beds or mattresses. From our altitude and with the sensor resolution available at the time, it was impossible to distinguish between a small mattress and a door in the roof. These two individuals, it was later determined, were neither armed nor the objective of the raid.

One additional individual fled across the back knee-wall and onto his neighbor's roof. I was on him. I tracked him into the back alley, where he disappeared through a door into his neighbor's house.

I gave the friendly forces a "talk-on" and led them to the doorway using my infrared, NVG-compatible pointer, called a LASER Marker (LM). One of the most superb tools available, the LM is magical and fantastical—the LM emits a beam of energy from the targeting pod, visible only to NVGs. From the cockpit of the emitting aircraft, it looks like something straight out of *Star Wars*. A solid beam of energy originates from the aircraft at a selectable pulsating frequency, and the pilot is able to move the beam, illuminating any target of choice.

As viewed from a different aircraft, a sparkling light appears on the ground at the point designated. The term utilized while using this tool is "sparkle." Friendly forces also see the sparkle using their NVGs, guiding them toward a target.

The friendlies positioned outside the door and stormed in. At that point, I left sensor coverage of the door due to the limitations of my orbit and coverage. All I knew was that they had entered; I could not see what was happening.

Twenty-three seconds later, the ground force reported they had entered the objective. I promptly inquired about the results.

"One enemy KIA (killed in action)," the ground controller reported. "Your squirter. He was the one we were looking for." He continued, "Also, one friendly KIA. He took a round to the chest upon entry through the door."

It is impossible for me to articulate the feelings I experienced during the thirty seconds that followed. I knew in that moment that my attention to the task at hand had resulted in mission success, but also in the death of one of my own.

Every possible thought about mortality passed through my brain in the next thirty seconds. If I had been less attentive or had missed something, an American would still be alive. The bad guy would get his bullet sooner or later. I was absolutely devastated. Fighter pilots are trained to control our emotions in combat, but my cockpit was getting misty.

Then the radio operator provided an update. "The friendly took a round to the chest, but his body armor saved him. He is alive and well!"

I was overtaken by total relief. The report was completely unexpected. I went from absolute remorse for the loss of a comrade to exhilaration in knowing a soldier would live to fight another day.

I learned something that night: even your best work can lead to unexpected negative consequences. You still have to do it, however. If the bad news had been real, it would have been tragic, but getting the bad guy saved more than one life.

For me, combat mission number seventy-six made war real, changing me forever.

USS Tripoli underway. (Photo Credit: Wiki Commons open source)

Rapid Response Planning Process

Lieutenant Commander Ron "Warhead" Lambrecht

Amphibious Squadron Three

Intelligence Officer (Navy Staff Code (N2))

"Alright, they're on our left, they're on the right, they're in front of us, they're behind us...they can't get away this time."

— General Chesty Puller, USMC

Nautical Notables:

Military Staff: A group of Officers, as well as enlisted and civilian personnel, responsible for the administrative, operational, and logistical needs of its unit. This group provides bi-directional flow of information between a commanding Officer and subordinate military units. Staff positions are coded "N" for Navy and "S" for

Marine, beginning with N/S1 for Administration, N/S2 for Intelligence, N/S3 for Operations, N/S4 for Maintenance, and so on across all staff disciplines.

Amphibious Ready Group (ARG): An ARG consists of a naval element—a group of warships known as an Amphibious Task Force (ATF)—and a landing force (LF) of US Marines, in total about 5,000 people. Together, these elements and supporting units are trained, organized, and equipped to perform amphibious operations.

Commodore: A military rank used in many Navies that is superior to a Navy Captain but below a Rear Admiral.

Marine Expeditionary Unit (MEU): Pronounced "Mew." Each MEU is an expeditionary quick reaction force, deployed and ready for immediate response to any crisis, whether it be a natural disaster or combat mission.

H-Hour: Redundant acronym of hour since the "H" stands for hour (so it means "hour-hour"). The specific time at which an operation or exercise commences or is due to commence.

L-Hour: In amphibious operations, the time at which the first helicopter or tiltrotor aircraft of the airborne ship-to-shore movement wave touches down or is scheduled to touch down in the landing zone.

With 71 percent of the earth's surface covered by water and 372,000 miles of coastline, it only stands to reason that amphibious warfare plays an important role in any superpower's global strategy. The United States, for instance, has conducted amphibious assaults since the Revolutionary War, but the most notable are the D-Day landing at Normandy and the amphibious assault of Okinawa, both during WWII.

I confess, as a Navy Intelligence Officer, I never expected to participate in amphibious warfare, but boy, was I mistaken! I was about to experience a crash course in amphibious warfare.

Because I was assigned to the staff as the **N2** shortly before deployment, I did not have the benefit of participating in the workups designed to prepare an **Amphibious Ready Group (ARG)** for deployment. I soon learned that virtually every day while underway, the Amphibious Squadron and MEU staff engaged in the Rapid Response Planning Process (R2P2), an accelerated execution of crisis action planning. (The R2P2 presumes a six-hour timeline from the time of a warning and execute order, a process designed to respond to time-critical extreme situations.) Operations Officers (**N/S3**) of the PHIBRON and MEU staffs promulgated scenarios each morning, with the remainder of the day dedicated to mission planning and rehearsal. Every conceivable plot was fair game, from hostage taking by terrorists (who were then executing a hostage every sixty minutes) to pirates taking control of a ship (with the ship and passengers taken to a nearby port of an unfriendly country).

The process served multiple objectives: it prepared the ARG for potential missions, and it created a set of standardized responses developed from scenario-driven exercises. It also provided an opportunity to rehearse a potential mission prior to an actual warning and execute order.

The process started with an initial staff orientation, problem framing, and determination of information requirements. Next, the **Commodore** and **MEU Commander** promulgated guidance for Courses of Action (COA) development. This occurred within the first hour.

The Mission Commander, supported by select staff members, then developed COAs. These included phases, a timeline, a task organization, landing beaches and zones, if applicable, concept of fires, major end-items/equipment, a recommended **H-/L-hour,** and advantages and disadvantages for each.

At the two-hour mark, the Commodore and MEU Commander's staff convened for COA consideration and decision. They were briefed on operational or intelligence updates provided as required, while information requirements and rules of engagement were updated, staff estimates of supportability conducted, and a COA selected or modified. Once selected, the MEU and PHIBRON Commanders' guidance was issued for detailed planning.

In the following two hours, the Marine and Navy staffs, along with their subordinate elements, conducted concurrent, parallel, and detailed planning while unit leaders prepared for the mission. Simultaneously, all members of the staff who had any responsibility in the execution or conduct of the mission prepared the Confirmation Brief.

At the four-hour mark, the Reconnaissance and Surveillance (R&S) Confirmation Brief was presented. The intelligence folks worked frantically throughout the process, attempting to determine the situation at the crisis site. Both organic and nonorganic assets were leveraged to ascertain the situation as best as possible, and then patterns of movement, dispositions, and an assessment of strengths and weaknesses of the enemy were presented.

Following the R&S Confirmation Brief, the respective staffs and essential personnel gathered for the mission Confirmation Brief. The Confirmation Brief was to take no more than one hour, even though it was not unusual to have over twenty-five briefers and one hundred-plus slides of information. In order to keep the brief on schedule, known standard operating procedures were briefed by exception.

The final step was command and staff supervision. During this hour, all energy was focused on the ARG preparing to execute the mission. Final inspections and test firing of weapons commenced, aircraft spotted (positioned), vehicles prepared, Marines staged, manifests confirmed, and communications checks made. Mission planning and preparation requirements were conducted concurrently.

What I just described is nothing less than poetry in motion. The R2P2 was practiced until every team member perfectly executed their part of the mission and carried out that responsibility with precision and speed. By the time we entered the Indian Ocean, the entire ARG functioned as a perpetual crisis response machine.

Although my counterpart on the Marine staff and I were stellar Intelligence Officers (in our own minds), occasions occurred when an item or two went beyond our thought process. This intense mission planning regimen practiced across the Marine Corps resulted in the creation of databases that were used for the purpose of crisis planning. We contributed to, and benefited from, the same.

For example, in the case of pirates boarding and taking control of a ship, the database included a list of questions. Some of the more obvious included: Where is the Captain's quarters and communication room? Where are the antennas located? What is the composition of the crew? Are there females on board? What is on the cargo manifest? What is the most efficient way to disable the propulsion system? What is the maximum speed of the vessel? The databases were invaluable, as it was a summary of the efforts of countless mission planners around the globe.

These and a hundred other questions could be found in the database and used to support the planning process. Questions not in our resident databases were submitted to theater and national Intelligence Centers in the form of Request for Information (RFI) messages. Since RFI messages were templated to support specific types of missions, it was relatively easy to draft and send an RFI message within the first hour of planning.

As we transited through the Straits of Malacca off the coast of Singapore, we got the warning order: "Prepare for possible combat operations in Somalia."

A fully combat-loaded F-16 from the 134th Fighter Squadron (The Green Mountain Boys) over Iraq (2006). A typical combat load consisted of two AIM-120 air-to-air missiles, one GBU-12 LASER-guided bomb, one GBU-38 GPS-guided bomb, two external fuel tanks, a full load of 20mm rounds, and one LITENING II targeting pod. This aircraft, #83-1165, set the record for combat and training flight-time at just over 7,200 hours.

Steve was the last pilot to fly this aircraft before its retirement in 2008. It is on permanent display at the entrance to the Vermont Air National Guard Base and is seen here in the background of Steve's annual Logistics Readiness Squadron photo while he was in command of the squadron. Photos courtesy of the Vermont Air National Guard.

Wheelbarrow

Lieutenant Colonel Steve "Curly" Lambrecht

Chief of Standardization and Evaluation, 158th Operations Group

"Nothing good ever happens after midnight"

—THOSE WHO HAVE BEEN UP PAST MIDNIGHT

Aeronautical Notables:

Wheelbarrow: The earliest reference to a wheelbarrow is from the Han Dynasty, China, 118 AD, long before the birth of the first United States Navy SEAL. Wheelbarrows are used all over the world today for carrying heavy loads; the SEALs use them for carrying large, spherical objects made from copper zinc alloy. You'll see what I mean later.

High-Value Individual (HVI): There are many ways in life to increase your value; kill enough innocent people, and your value to the US military may reach the status of "high-value individual."

I have, from time to time, had the privilege of providing air support for various Special Operations Forces units. They are organized under a unified command called Special Operations Command, or SOCOM, which oversees the Special Operations Components of the Army, Marine Corps, Navy, and Air Force. I would tell you more about them, but then they would have to kill you.

They are unquestionably the most badass military organizations ever contrived. The sheer precision, professionalism, and lethality wielded by these people is eye watering. If someone knocks on your door at 2:00 a.m., and you have the choice between it being Satan or SOCOM, choose Satan.

Our F-16 unit developed a special relationship with SOCOM over the years and conducted many training exercises with them. In particular, we trained extensively with the renowned warriors of the Special Tactics Squadrons (STS). STS warriors are "jacks-of-all-trades": superb athletes, trained in all crafts of Special Warfare and uniquely capable of running entire air assault operations from the ground.

Because of their unique capabilities, once STS warriors are trained, they are often farmed out to other task forces for specific missions. (Their history and achievements are superbly described in the book *Alone at Dawn* by Dan Schilling and Lori Longfritz.) Our relationship was such that, once in theater, they requested support from our squadron by name.

The best of all SOCOM units are the United States Navy Sea, Air, and Land Teams, or SEALs. From front to back, left to right, and top to bottom, they are certified 100 percent USDA badass. More importantly, they are organized into Teams and call themselves Teams for a reason.

I always knew they were something special, but it wasn't until I saw them in action and, just as importantly, saw everyone *else* in action that I fully understood why they were so fabled and legendary. SEALs are utilized against only the most unsavory people in the world. They are the best we have, so we don't risk them unnecessarily. If you knew about some of the unsavory people they visited their crafts upon, you'd be glad we have the SEALs.

When supporting ground units from the air, without knowing the nature of the unit supported, it becomes apparent rather quickly if you are supporting regular ground forces or SOCOM units. The tactics, techniques, and procedures (TTPs) are different. The *tenacity* is different.

Further differentiation among SOCOM units also becomes apparent. The SEALs are a breed all their own. Suffice it to say that everything you've heard about them is "Chuck Norris legendary," only in their case, it's true. This story is about my first opportunity to see them in action.

When I deployed to combat theaters and chose to fly nights, I did so for many reasons. Those reasons ranged from making it easier to manage the time-zone change from home (eight hours, give or take) to using NVGs and the LASER Marker. Mostly, it was because I had the best chance of supporting SOCOM.

Two things happen in the very late hours in a combat zone: bad guys go out and do bad things, or bad guys sleep. Regardless, as the saying goes, "Nothing good ever happens after midnight." However, there is an exception: sometimes bad guys die in their sleep, or shortly thereafter.

As was the case before every flight, our Intelligence Officers/enlisted briefed us on all the preplanned missions for the evening. My flight was called to support a raid on an objective in search of a **high-value individual (HVI)**.

We arrived overhead very shortly before the friendly ground forces. Though we did not know who we were supporting, we did know it was a SOCOM unit of some sort, given the content of the brief and the nature of the objective. I had supported multiple SOCOM units prior to this night and was very comfortable and familiar with their TTPs.

Our tasking was fairly usual: we scanned around the friendlies while they infiltrated the target, and we also scanned outside the target building for squirters. The tasks were split between our two F-16s. One followed the friendly's infiltration route, ensuring there were no ambushes, IEDs, vehicles, or ground forces approaching them; the other scanned the objective, looking for activity, guards, or squirters.

Of the two, typically the more challenging job is following the friendlies, as it requires tracking them with the targeting pod and staring at a six-inch diagonal screen in the cockpit while searching for all the aforementioned threats. It also requires locating landmarks using the NVGs and LASER Marker, just in case you lose track of them in the targeting pod. It is very involved, technical, and difficult. All of this, of course, while flying a high-performance fighter aircraft at night and in formation.

Life or death applies here. Like I said: train, train, train, and then train some more.

Although less difficult, the most important job is to scan the objective, obtaining as many details as possible. Bad guys in their safe place use dogs, guards, and other defensive measures. All of this planning, training, and effort is for a singular purpose: to get the bad guy(s); if they leave, and nobody sees them leaving, all is for naught.

Typically, I covered the objective and assigned my wingman to cover the friendlies. Having already caught two squirters previous to this night, I had developed an acumen for it. This night was different—the SEALs were in charge.

As the friendlies approached the objective, I quickly slewed my targeting pod to their location to verify their proximity to the target. A wall defined the perimeter, and a small flash in my targeting pod let me know the friendlies had breached its gate. I quickly slewed my targeting pod back to the home, whose wall had failed its purpose, only to find a single individual sprinting from the house, heading in the opposite direction from the breached gate. It made perfect sense: the HVI hears a small explosion in one direction and runs out of the house in the other. I expanded my field of view slightly and saw the friendlies sprinting around all sides of the house, trailing the squirter by about seventy-five to one hundred feet.

I transmitted, "Squirter east side heading east."

Approximately one second later, *everyone* on the objective froze, including the squirter.

"Sparkle," came the response.

It was a command for me to sparkle the squirter with my LASER Marker. I did so. Immediately, everyone sprung back into motion, including the squirter.

"Friendly" was the subsequent radio response to me, meaning that the individual I saw, and subsequently sparkled, was a friendly.

The entire event (squirter call, everyone freezes, they call sparkle, I sparkle, everyone springs back into action) took no more than four seconds. Four seconds. To see it from the air was awe-inspiring.

The precision. The teamwork. It was a privilege to witness, except I had just gotten in their way. I cost them four seconds. Sure, there's a chance I could have been right, but not so that night. This was clearly a different SOCOM unit than the ones I'd previously supported; I later learned it was the SEALs.

I have often pondered how they moved so quickly, having to carry their enormous brass balls around in a **wheelbarrow**. In particular, I admire that guy who ran beyond the objective to cover the back door, dusting his teammates by seventy-five to one hundred feet in the process. His copper zinc accoutrements must have been exceptionally burdensome, although one would never know it by watching.

Oh yeah, remember when I said if you can choose between Satan and SEALs when the knock comes on your door at 2:00 a.m.? Let's just say the HVI chose poorly. But look at the bright side—he got to meet both.

Phase I consisted of our Marines landing and subsequently securing the Mogadishu airport and port facility, followed by the US Embassy compound. The Tripoli ARG was then directed to immediately begin Phase II: securing Kismayo to the south. As the operation unfolded, the Marines and other forces, now deployed in Somalia, moved to Phase III: expanding their presence to outlying towns, where orphanages and refugee camps were located.

A personalized flight jacket is the pride of every aviator on the planet, and Ron's flight jacket has plenty of history. Ron wore this jacket as an enlisted Aircrewman while flying in the S-3A, and it continued to be part of his attire through his Intelligence Officer years. This jacket sported several patches, but the most meaningful ones are seen here. They are a "Spy Navy" patch, and a "15th Marine Expeditionary Unit" patch worn during the Amphibious Squadron Three deployment to Somalia.

Operation Restore Hope

Lieutenant Commander Ron "Warhead" Lambrecht
Amphibious Squadron Three N2

"I am a Soldier. I fight where I am told, and I win where I fight."

—George S. Patton

Nautical Notable:

Commander, Amphibious Task Force/Commander, Landing Force (CATF/CLF): While afloat, the CLF (MEU Commander) is normally the supporting Commander to the CATF (PHIBRON Commodore). When ashore and engaged in operations, the CATF normally becomes the supporting Commander, and the CLF is the supported Commander.

By the fall of 1992, the situation in Somalia was out of control. Factions splintered into smaller factions, then splintered again. Agreements for food distribution with one party became worthless when the stores needed shipping through the territory of another. United Nations Operations in Somalia (UNOSOM) troops were shot at, aid ships attacked and prevented from docking, cargo aircraft were fired upon, and aid agencies, public and private, were subject to threats, looting, and extortion.[5]

General Mohamed Farrah Aidid controlled the northern half of Mogadishu and northern portion of Somalia. His rival, Ali Mahdi Muhammad, controlled the southern half of Mogadishu and the countryside. Ali Mahdi served as President of Somalia from January 26, 1991, to January 3, 1997, rising to power after a coalition of armed opposition groups deposed long-time President Siad Barre, but he was not able to exert his authority beyond the southern part of the capital. Aidid, meanwhile, had the stronger force of the two and had grown confident enough to defy the Security Council. He demanded the withdrawal of peacekeepers and also declared hostile intent against any further UN deployments.

The *USS Tripoli* Amphibious Ready Group's (ARG's) transit across the Indian Ocean to Somalia was nonstop R2P2 mission planning and rehearsals. The Marines practiced every aspect of the anticipated landing: they launched Landing Craft, Air Cushion (LCACs), Amphibious Assault Vehicles (AAVs), and helicopters. They practiced loading the vehicles with Marines, since every Marine had a designated means of transportation ashore. When not conducting flight operations, they practiced fast-rope insertions out of hovering helicopters and performed small-arms fire off the fantail of the *Tripoli*. At the same time, both the PHIBRON and MEU staffs, along with squadron and platoon leaders, conducted scenario-driven R2P2 exercises daily. Nothing, and I mean nothing, was left to chance.

---

5 "Somalia—UNOSOM I Background," United Nations Peacekeeping, accessed January 15, 2021, https://peacekeeping.un.org/mission/past/unosom1backgr2.html.

On December 3, 1992, the UN Security Council passed Resolution 794, unanimously authorizing the use of "all necessary means to establish as soon as possible a secure environment for humanitarian relief operations in Somalia."[6] A few days later, on December 6, our SEAL Team and Special Boat crewmen began conducting reconnaissance operations in the vicinity of the airport and harbor.

These operations lasted three days. In the early hours of December 8, elements of the MEU conducted leaflet drops over the capital city of Mogadishu. They read:

> United Nations Forces are here to assist in the international relief effort for the Somali people. We are prepared to use force to protect the relief operation and our soldiers. We will not allow interference with food distribution or with our activities. We are here to help you.[7]

I stood on the deck of the *USS Tripoli*, surveying the darkened skyline before me. We were anchored two miles from Mogadishu, the former capital of Somalia, and shadows shrouded the city, broken intermittently by distant campfires. One million people lived in this impoverished place, many of them refugees. There was no electricity anywhere in Mogadishu; locals stripped the only power plant and electrical grid of its copper wire and sold it for scrap long ago.

Over the past several hours, I had made multiple trips between the ship's Intelligence Center and the flag bridge, where my boss, "Swede" Peterson, was located. As the Commodore's Intelligence Officer, I was charged with separating fact from fiction in the battle space, and I had been sharing information in support of the impending amphibious landing.

---

6 "Somalia."

7 "US and Coalition Forces Arrive in Somalia," Psywarrior, accessed January 15, 2021. http://www.psywarrior.com/handshake.html.

Our entire inventory of helicopters marshaled overhead, waiting for the order to secure the Mogadishu airport, port facility, and the former US Embassy complex. AAVs and LCAC hovercraft assumed a marshaling pattern around the three ships of the Amphibious Task Force: *USS Tripoli, USS Rushmore,* and *USS Juneau.* Our SEAL team deployed earlier in the evening—as well as several nights prior—to survey the landing zones and provide "eyes on target" with reports back to the ship.

All the training, practice, more practice, and planning had come down to these final moments. It is the calm before the storm that gives people pause to consider everything in their history that influenced their destiny, and there, I contemplated the series of events and experiences that led to me standing on the flag bridge of a United States warship. I was about to partake in a mission that, before the action ended, would result in the loss of several American and many Somali lives.

At 0500 on December 9, Phase I began. Close to 1,800 Marines pushed ashore, first securing the airport and then the port facility. Small-arms fire was reported from the port facility back to the Commodore, but the show of overwhelming force intimidated the Somalis aligned with the warlord Aidid, and the gunfire subsided.

With the airport secured, aircraft launched from neighboring bases immediately landed, carrying additional Marines and military supplies. By 1000, a defensive perimeter was in place around both facilities, and the **Commander Landing Force (CLF)**, Colonel Newbold, notified the **Commodore (CATF)**, Commodore Peterson, that he was prepared to assume supported Commander authority. A verbal confirmation took place over the radio, and Commodore Peterson became supporting Commander. Colonel Newbold then gave the order to secure the former US Embassy complex. By noon, that objective was accomplished, with a security perimeter established around the hundred-acre complex.

The new US Embassy had just become operational six months prior to the collapse of the Barre government in early 1991. Although less than two years old, the embassy displayed only faint indications of its former glory: the locals had scraped the marble off of the floors, as well as removed all of the acoustic ceiling tiles, wall coverings, and electrical wire. The bulletproof glass was used for target practice, and although it survived, it was "spider webbed" from the gunshots. Everything of value removed, all that remained was a shell of a building.

The walls of the building were one-foot-thick reinforced concrete, with the rebar within the walls crisscrossing every four inches, but because of the ambient temperature, the building was uninhabitable. The locals used it as an outhouse. In fact, 90 percent of the population of the city lived in igloos constructed of tree branches, because the buildings were too hot to occupy. The "well-to-do" Somalis managed to find themselves tarps to drape over their igloo to keep out the elements.

President H.W. Bush had recently lost the election to Bill Clinton, and for his last official trip, he visited Mogadishu. We had four days to get the embassy complex into a "presentable" condition for his arrival, so we hired some of the locals, gave them shovels, and directed them to remove the human excrement. Other Somalis were provided hammers and chisels and directed to create holes through the exterior walls in all of the rooms to provide cross ventilation. It took an entire day of chiseling for a Somali to create an opening four-inches square that ran between the rebar. The Marines installed portable generators and began to blow air through the building. Still other Somalis were given paintbrushes and hired to whitewash the bare concrete walls. By the time President Bush arrived, he toured a fairly clean embassy.

Colonel Jess, a warlord aligned with Ali Mahdi, controlled the southern city of Kismayo. Mohammed Said Hersi (known as General Morgan) led a second faction located in the area, and he opposed Colonel Jess. Both factions had to be dealt with.

A day after our Mogadishu landing, Colonel Jess' troops summarily executed eighteen of the tribal elders in the city. We were then directed to immediately begin Phase II: securing the city of Kismayo.

Belgian forces' 1st Parachute Battalion arrived in Mogadishu on December 13. Led by Lieutenant Colonel Marc Jacqmin, the paratroopers, along with elements of the Army's 10th Mountain Division, were tasked with securing and controlling the Kismayo relief sector. Commodore Peterson was designated as the Commander of the Amphibious Task Force, and Belgian Lieutenant Colonel Jacqmin as the Commander of the Landing Force.

At one time, Somalia was a French protectorate, and the French still harbored a sense of responsibility for Somalia's welfare. Consequently, and in anticipation of our landing, they positioned a cruiser off of the coast of Mogadishu.

On the morning of the Mogadishu landing, the Commanding Officer of the French cruiser, *Dupleix*, arrived aboard the *USS Tripoli* via helicopter, requesting a meeting with the Commodore. During the meeting, the Commanding Officer advised that the French government had authorized him to turn tactical control of his ship over to the Commodore for further operations. The offer was accepted, and the help could not have come at a better time: our ARG consisted of three ships, and we needed to keep the *USS Tripoli* off the coast of Mogadishu to support operations. That left the *USS Juneau* and *USS Rushmore* for the Kismayo operation.

The Commodore decided to embark the SEAL Team aboard the *Dupleix* and have the ship sprint ahead of the *Juneau* and *Rushmore* to conduct a survey of the bay and port area. It was not known if the bay was mined or if vessels had been intentionally sunk to serve as obstacles in case of an amphibious landing. These questions needed answers before our forces approached. I stayed behind on the *Tripoli* and provided intelligence support to forces ashore. (Initially, the *USS Tripoli* was the only conduit to the outside world for high bandwidth products, such as imagery and other intelligence data.)

Commodore "Swede" Peterson was a former F/A-18 pilot with a wiry six-foot-one frame and commanding voice. The Pentagon directed him to meet with Colonel Jess and General Morgan and to secure Kismayo. The morning of the landing, Commodore Peterson got word to Colonel Jess and General Morgan that he wanted a meeting, and they agreed.

First impressions are critical in the game of military diplomacy, so the Commodore dressed in fatigues and combat gear and strapped on two side arms. He then directed the biggest guy on his staff (a lawyer who knew nothing about firing a weapon) to dress in full combat gear and serve as his personal bodyguard.

After the Marines and Belgians landed and took up positions on the outskirts of Kismayo, the Commodore, Lieutenant Colonel Marc Jacqmin, the bodyguard, and a small Marine contingent proceeded to Colonel Jess's headquarters. As the Commodore approached the headquarters, he noticed two technicals positioned in front of the building. "technical" was a name given to civilian pickups and jeeps fitted with heavy caliber guns. Some technicals were fitted with tubes, made to look like antitank weapons, but they served strictly as a show of authority to the civilian population.

As the Commodore entered the meeting room, he was escorted past Jess's armed Lieutenants, who were positioned around the perimeter of the room. A rag-tag group, Jess's bodyguards appeared to be still semi-hungover from the khat chewed the day before and had just recently awakened, as evidenced by the bits of straw embedded in their hair. (Khat is a flowering plant native to the Horn of Africa and contains a stimulant which is said to cause excitement, loss of appetite, and euphoria.)

Although cordial, the meeting consisted of a one-sided authoritarian conversation. The Commodore made it clear he represented the United States of America and the United Nations on a humanitarian mission, and his forces would secure the city of Kismayo.

As Somalia's second-largest port after Mogadishu, Kismayo served as an important base for the Somali Navy. An airfield appropriately sized for military cargo aircraft was located only a few miles outside the city. Commodore Peterson stated that Kismayo was to be an open city and its infrastructure would be employed by security forces and relief organizations. While Jess and his troops could remain in the city, Morgan and his followers needed to relocate twenty kilometers to the north. If Colonel Jess and General Morgan complied with the order, their forces would not be engaged.

In two separate meetings, both men blinked. Twenty-four hours later, Morgan's forces vacated the city and Colonel Jess' forces stood down.

The *Tripoli* Amphibious Task Force remained stationed off the coast of Mogadishu for two and a half months while the Marines maintained law and order. A farmers market was set up by the locals every Saturday morning, and Marines walked among the stands and exchanged flip-flops, candy, ink pens, and other basic essentials for AK-47s and various armaments being offered for sale (when you have nothing, everything has value). Our Explosive Ordnance Demolition team collected and disposed of all captured weapons.

The Marines also found entire warehouses filled with rows waist-deep in weapons and ammunition of every kind. All munitions and weapons were destroyed in huge holes dug at the edge of the city.

As the operation unfolded, the Marines and other forces now deployed in Somalia moved to Phase III. The Marines and allies expanded their presence to outlying towns, where orphanages and refugee camps were located. With roads leading from Mogadishu, Baledogle, and Baldoa now open, aid flowed to villages accessed through those towns. To the south, the ancient city of Merca was secured, providing a logistical link between Kismayo and Mogadishu. As a result of the presence of allied forces, non-government organizations stocked orphanages with food stuffs and medical supplies.

A semblance of calm occurred during the day, but at night? Not so much.

The warlords continued to control the drug trade. Khat is legal in Somalia, but it has to be chewed within twenty-four hours of being harvested or it loses its effect. We witnessed the Piper Cub Khat flights arrive every morning with the day's harvest, and by 1000, it was for sale on the streets.

To say "for sale" is somewhat of a misnomer. The only currency available was paper money, left over from the Barre government, and it was worthless. Still, the locals continued to use it as legal tender. Around 1700, the fireworks began. By then, most of the population was high on Khat, and "gunfights at the OK Corral" popped up all over the city.

The only way to describe the basic attitude of the population is that it seemed like life did not matter to them. At their peril, young men attempted to breach the gate at the embassy compound. It appeared as though people shot each other without requiring a specific reason.

Two and a half months after deploying 1,800 Marines on the shore of Mogadishu, Colonel Newbold put 1,800 Marines back on the ships and brought them home. The Marines were flawless.

Operation Restore Hope continued under the US-led Unified Task Force until May 4, 1993, when UNOSOM assumed responsibility for the humanitarian effort. The killing of twenty-four Pakistani peacekeepers in early June, followed by the Battle of Mogadishu in October (in which eighteen American soldiers were killed, as documented in the book *Black Hawk Down*), led to the eventual withdrawal of US forces. What began as a peacekeeping mission to provide relief to the starving people of Somalia essentially ended with a firefight during the Battle of Mogadishu.

After the withdrawal of all US troops in March of 1994, 20,000 UN troops remained in Somalia. By the late spring of 1994, all of the remaining UN troops were withdrawn, ending UNOSOM.

As a Lieutenant Commander, I served as the Assistant Intelligence Officer for two years on the *USS Constellation*, the Operations Intelligence Officer on the COMNAVAIRPAC staff and the Intelligence Officer (N2) on the Amphibious Squadron Three staff that had just conducted Operation Restore Hope. This included two tours afloat and one tour ashore on a three-star staff. With my Commander Promotion Board about to convene, I was reminded once again of the advice I had received: performance in billet mattered. They had me right where I wanted them!

Steve leads a four-ship of Vermont Air National Guard F-16s during a photo shoot. Steve is piloting the nearest aircraft, 2009. Photo Credit (Photo by Ted Carlson/Fotodynamics.com.)

Steve fires a live AIM-120C air-to-air missile at Weapons System Evaluation Program, Tyndall Air Force Base, Florida, circa 2009 (Personal photo).

Mission 92

Lieutenant Colonel
Steve "Curly" Lambrecht

Chief of Standardization and Evaluation,
158th Operations Group

"The power for everything resides within each of us."

—BILL CUMMING, THE BOOTHBY INSTITUTE

Aeronautical Notable:

Joint Terminal Attack Controller (JTAC): A qualified service member who directs the action of combat aircraft engaged in close air support and other offensive air operations from a forward position.

When it comes to exercising the fighter pilot craft, there's only one true way to know for sure if they are good enough to do the job: actually doing it. Imagine a surgeon who studies their surgical skills for years, practices performing surgery in a simulator, and even interacts with patients in need of surgery but never actually performs a surgery. How can they ever know *for sure* that they possess the skills, and the mental discipline, to be successful in their craft?

So, there I was. Sixteen years after finishing my fighter pilot "surgical residency," I had ninety-one combat missions on my professional résumé but had never "performed a surgery." All of that was about to change.

This was my second war, and it was very different from my first. In the eleven years since the war in Bosnia, technology had advanced dramatically. Targeting pods (TGPs) containing cameras capable of seeing the enemy, day or night, were attached to our aircraft. They could emit LASER energy to guide bombs on target and could emit a beam, visible only through night vision goggles, to mark the location of targets. They also searched for LASER energy emitted from any ground or airborne source.

Those capabilities, coupled with the ability to transmit targets via data link from one fighter to another, represent just a sampling of the enhanced capabilities available to the modern warfighter. As with any technological advancement, these capabilities can be negated by an enemy with the technology *and* a good plan. Both are required. On this particular night, the enemy had neither.

It was 2007. We were flying a standard night mission after being briefed by intelligence and assigned a preplanned area in which we would search for IEDs. More importantly, we were hunting for their planters, along with any other suspicious activity.

Part of our preflight preparations included an intelligence briefing of known missions that were being conducted by other military units, including Special Forces, functioning in the area of operations. A raid on a relatively small village near the border with Iran was planned that evening. Just prior to launch, we were reassigned to support it.

I happened to be the wingman that night. My flight lead was an old Marine running mate of mine named Patrick "Pig" Guinee. As the flight lead, Pig was responsible for multiple things, including talking to the **Joint Terminal Attack Controller (JTAC)**.

The JTAC coordinates air support, as well as support from other external agencies. They also grant clearance to deliver munitions as required during combat. The JTAC usually co-locates with the ground forces but can be airborne in any one of a number of types of aircraft. In fact, I was a qualified JTAC as well.

When we arrived on station, the Army had already begun taking the village. They pushed in from the southwest toward the northeast, in the direction of Iran, where the insurgents were rumored to have come from. Having been born and raised as a United States Marine, a service that prides itself on the ethos of "every Marine is a rifleman," I knew, on a level most Air Force Aviators didn't, what things were like on the ground. Watching it from tens of thousands of feet doesn't provide the observer with the same perspective as someone who's "Been there. Done that." I had the benefit of a Marine rifleman's training, accentuated with graduation from the Marine Infantry Officer Course, so I understood ground tactical warfare.

Almost immediately after our arrival, we were forced out of the area due to the assault force's helicopters receiving fire. The Army was running an artillery mission to suppress the enemy ground-fire, but because of the max altitude of the artillery rounds, our aircraft were in danger if we remained in the area. Pig and I were immediately surprised by the absence of a combined-arms game plan with deconfliction measures for aviation assets, something organic to every USMC operation.

Due to the proximity of the village to the border, the Army had limited capability to affect a blocking position. If you invade a village from one side, it is reasonable to expect the enemy to exit from the other; if all you want to do is push them out, then mission accomplished. If you want to kill them, you must first prevent their escape, and there were limited measures established to prevent the enemy from exiting out the "sides" of the village. It was there that we were able to offer assistance.

The JTAC we worked with informed us that a villager had spotted several enemy combatants exiting the village to the north along a complex system of canals. Using my targeting pod, I began my search along the canals. First, I began a "macro" search of the canal complex, looking for anything that was obvious and stood out as worthy of further investigation. No luck. I then returned to the point of origin of alleged travel and used a higher magnification setting on the TGP.

Searching along the edge of the village, I found possible exits that were passable by foot. I followed one such route of travel along a switchback of canals. There they were! I found a group of ten armed combatants following the irrigation canals out of the village, and I quickly reported my find.

Throughout the operation, we used secure communications, meaning utilized radios that automatically encrypt verbal transmissions and unencrypt them once received. A brilliant, if imperfect, system of secure communication, there was no chance the enemy could hear us.

One of the unperfected aspects of this particular technology is antenna placement. The antennae are directionally sensitive, so if the communicators aren't properly aligned geographically, not everyone can hear everyone. Imagine if you can, the scenario that follows.

I could hear the JTAC. The JTAC could hear me. I could *not* hear most of what Pig said to the JTAC. Pig could *not* hear most of what I said to the JTAC. We all needed to be on the same sheet of music. But hey, look at the bright side: at least it was at night, on night vision goggles, with the enemy fleeing and at risk of getting away!

As stated earlier, I reported my find. I did so first to Pig, who couldn't hear me, and because I knew he couldn't hear me, I reported it directly to the JTAC, which Pig *also* could not hear.

What came back immediately from the JTAC was, "Standby for nine-line."

I thought my heart would explode right out of my chest. *Be calm,* I told myself. *You've got this. This is what you do.*

It didn't matter. After ninety-one combat missions, sixteen years of training, TOPGUN, the Weapons and Tactics Instructor Course, the Air Combat Tactics Instructor Course, several night carrier landings, and years and years of instructing junior pilots in the art of war, this was it. I was about to be tested in combat.

Adrenaline coursed through my veins. My pulse raced. This wasn't going to be a test, as I had planned. This was going to be a slog through the thick fog of war.

Holy shit! This is it! A nine-line is the next, and second to last, step before the final clearance to deliver munitions, and it was going down!

The nine-line contains all of the pertinent data necessary to determine the position of friendlies, the enemy, and what munition(s) to deliver. Put it all together and you have the recipe for combat success. The "Cleared Hot" call from the JTAC is the icing on the cake; it provides authorization to release weapons.

I chuckle to myself when I think of being in Pig's shoes that night. We are orbiting above the fight, and he's getting instructions from the JTAC: "We have pushed into the village." "Look to the north." "Look along these roads." Then the next thing he hears is: "Standby for nine-line."

When conducting operations, the various services use procedures unique to their culture and mission in order to increase the probability of success. These procedures are known as "tactics, techniques, and procedures" or TTPs. There are lots of them. When a TTP is agreed upon by the various services, it becomes known as "Joint Tactics, Techniques, and Procedures" or JTTPs.

Sometimes, however, the warfighter has to make them up on the fly. When that happens, and it's me doing it, I refer to them as CTTPs ("Curly's Tactics, Techniques, and Procedures").

This is where the years of training and experience came in. I knew Pig didn't know what was going on. He knew he didn't know everything that was going on. We both knew there was no way in hell either one of us would know what was going on unless we cheated. Time for some of Curly's Tactics, Techniques, and Procedures.

We had a second radio that transmitted "in the clear" (not encrypted). It was perfectly audible, so I said, "Squirters north along the canals. Hook point."

That meant I had found enemy combatants fleeing the village and that if Pig "tagged" the data link target I was transmitting on the network (hook point), their precise position would be automatically loaded into his targeting system. He tagged the data link target but couldn't see the enemy. It mattered not.

The F-16 is equipped with Global Positioning System (GPS) capability, meaning any coordinates, if correctly entered into the aircraft, are extremely precise. As professional fighter pilots, we generally demand that we have at least two methods of correlation to ensure we have the correct target. The methods take several forms, including confirmation of coordinates via radio, data link, LASER, visually, and others.

When the JTAC read back the nine-line and got to the part about the target coordinates, he merely said "your coordinates." He was supposed to read *actual* coordinates. Technically, this wasn't good enough to be either legal or safe, and we both instantly knew this.

Pig, having hooked my point, had target coordinates available in his jet. Instead, understandably, he directed me to read the coordinates from my jet. I did, using our encryption radio, which was the only one with which we were talking to the JTAC. Of course, Pig couldn't hear me.

So, here's what we have. All three of us need to have the same coordinates in order to make this thing legal and safe. I have the right coordinates, since I found the bad guys and I'm looking at them in my targeting pod. I read them to the JTAC; the JTAC, therefore, has the right coordinates. So far so good, right? But since Pig couldn't hear me read the coordinates, he doesn't know that what the JTAC is reading back to me (us) on the radio is a correct read-back of the coordinates I provided to the JTAC. With me so far? No? Welcome to the fog of war.

No worries, though. The enemy is on the move. The coordinates are no longer valid anyway!

Helmuth von Moltke, a Prussian General from the nineteenth century said, "No plan survives first contact with the enemy." Stated another way, it means "nothing will go as planned." In the United States Armed Forces, we are trained to know this. Clausewitz referred to it as "the fog of war." Whether or not we can overcome it is a function of training and experience.

But wait! There's more. Via data link, we suddenly received a re-tasking order to support a priority-one mission elsewhere. We had the enemy in our sights. If we left now, they would almost certainly escape. We conferred and elected to remain on station to finish the job at hand, which we assessed would only take a few minutes longer.

On the clear radio, the discussion between Pig and I continued. "Match sparkle," I said.

I told him to match his sparkle to mine. Once his LASER Marker flashed on top of mine, we now had a second form of correlation to ensure we were both on the same target. We now had data link and LASER Marker. All we needed was an official read-back of coordinates from the JTAC. This time, Pig read the coordinates, and I heard him. I heard the JTAC read-back. I informed Pig on the clear radio that I had copied the coordinates. They matched, and we now had three correlated sources for location. It was game time.

"Shooter sparkle," Pig directed over the radio. This meant he would deliver the bomb, and I would LASER it in. This was the perfect call, since he could deliver on GPS precise coordinates while I guided the bomb in. Having tracked the enemy all along, I knew exactly where they were. An appropriate division of labor, increasing the odds for success.

Pig called, "In."

The JTAC replied, "Cleared Hot."

I awaited the "bombs away" call from Pig, which meant he had delivered the weapon, so I knew when to provide LASER guidance for the bomb to track. DID I MENTION MY HEART WAS ABOUT TO LEAP OUT OF MY CHEST?

"Bombs away, twenty-six seconds," Pig transmitted.

That meant there were twenty-six seconds remaining until the system-calculated bomb impact, during which it was all on me. I had to make sure to keep the LASER energy directed at the best point of impact for the bomb, while not blocking the LASER energy with part of my aircraft, at night, using night vision goggles, looking at a very small gray-scale screen in my aircraft, while traveling roughly 400 miles per hour. What could *possibly* go wrong?

Plenty. But nothing did. The bomb impacted near one end of the enemy combatants. It was difficult to know by looking at the screen how many of the enemy we serviced.

We were below tanker-bingo, meaning we had to be supremely efficient in getting to the tanker, refueling, then proceeding on to the
previously tasked priority-one mission. No room for error. If there
were any delays getting our gas, we would have to return to base and
would not be able to support. After successfully refueling, we arrived
overhead a river-raid egress in progress. Four Zodiac Special Operations boats were traveling high-speed down a river, having completed
a raid of some kind. We provided top cover until they reached their
final destination.

Later, in the debrief, upon reviewing our video recording, we made
a pessimistic approximation of three out of ten KIA. The Army later
reported eight confirmed KIA. The next day, our intelligence shop
reported the capture of multiple small arms, heavy machine guns,
AAA pieces, munitions, and dozens of enemy combatants. The raid
was a resounding success.

I'm not going to lie to you—it felt good. While I am genuinely truth-
ful when I say I long for a day when the world no longer needs my
services, I was happy to provide them that night. It took ninety-two
missions before this surgeon finally performed a genuine surgery, but
at that point I knew I had what it takes. After twenty-three years of
military service, sixteen years as a combat fighter pilot, and all of my
training and experience, I could say *for sure* that I could perform in
combat.

Lieutenant Colonel Steve Lambrecht completes the preflight of his F-16 on the occasion of his one-hundredth combat mission (2007). The mission was a night sortie, with Colonel (Retired) Patrick "Pig" Guinee. Steve was met upon his return by his Squadron Commander, Colonel (Retired) Dave "Smitty" Smith. The occasion was toasted by all present with a non-alcoholic beer, as alcohol was not permitted in Iraq.

My Finest Hour

Lieutenant Colonel Steve "Curly" Lambrecht

Chief of Standardization and Evaluation, 158th Operations Group

"Dude. You have big 'ole brass balls."

—LT. COL. CHRIS "POOTER" CAPUTO

Aeronautical Notable:

Forward Operating Base (FOB): A temporary base of operations, usually smaller in size and positioned strategically in locations forward from permanent bases. The purpose varies, but it is generally used to provide a place of relative safety and resupply for units operating in hostile territory.

During a sustained combat operation, such as the one in Iraq in the 2000s, we never knew where the tasking might take us. Sometimes we launched and flew the mission we preplanned with our Intel Officers and enlisted. Other times, we launched and were reassigned to an emergent mission.

It was a pretty usual night in Iraq: clear skies, with decent luminescence from the stars and city lights. Conditions were conducive to night craftsmanship, where NVGs and infrared-targeting pods reigned supreme.

Previously, I have described many of the technological assets available to us in the F-16: data link, the infrared targeting pod, LASER emitter and LASER tracker, and finally the LASER Marker (sparkle). The LASER emitter could also be used to derive precision coordinates to be programmed into a GPS bomb and were accurate enough to place said bombs within mere feet from the intended target, or less. That night, we used *all* of the aforementioned tools at our disposal, plus a few more that showed up on the scene, unbeknownst to us.

As was always the case, shortly after takeoff, we changed frequency and contacted "Warlord." Warlord orchestrated all tasking. If the pilots had not been notified of alternate tasking prior to takeoff, this was the next opportunity.

On most missions, Warlord passed the expected tasking for which we had briefed. When this happened, it was somewhat of a disappointment, as one always hoped there was something more than "routine" in their future. That night, Warlord did not disappoint.

We were directed via secure encrypted communication to proceed to an **FOB** in northern Iraq, about a twenty-minute flight. It was not what we were expecting. It was farther away than usual for a re-tasking, but Warlord was clearly waiting for us to check in so that he could pass the info. Someone was waiting for us.

We had time to think about it. Twenty minutes is a long drive when you are accustomed to normal operations and highly experienced with re-tasking, and Bunker and I were both. Lt. Col. Rick "Bunker" Shebib fought in Kosovo, and, like me, this was his second tour in Iraq.

We were both instructor pilots and good friends: we shared holidays and frequent family dinners together, and our wives and children were close. Though we saw the world and our country differently from a political standpoint, we shared a common bond of humor and patriotism that was more than enough to bridge any differences.

In combat, there are no differences to bridge among warriors. That night, I was the flight lead, and Bunker was my wingman.

We checked in again via secure encrypted communication with the Forward Air Controller (FAC) near Mosul, call sign "Slapper 11," and immediately heard the magic words: "Standby for nine-line."

While it was not common by any standard to hear those words on a given mission, when you heard them, you *knew* something was going down. Although this was no longer my first rodeo, my heart rate increased a few beats per minute, nonetheless.

The nine-line, if you recall, are the nine lines of instructions required for delivering weapons on non-preplanned targets. After reading us the nine-line, Slapper 11 said, "Say when ready for remarks."

Remarks include any information that aids understanding. The reason for this approach to information delivery was to allow the pilots time to digest the nine-lines of information, enter data into their navigation and targeting systems, and briefly build situational awareness. Then, the remarks were given in order to expand on the data, fill in any information not provided in the nine-line format, and diminish any gaps in understanding.

While receiving nine-lines, seasoned pilots can usually enter data into their aircraft, write information down on a kneeboard, and be mostly ready for remarks by the time the FAC says, "Say when ready for remarks." Ready enough, that is, for the FAC to start reading them and for the pilot to finish entering data into the aircraft while listening to and retaining the remarks. It's an art and a science. Accuracy matters, and where target locations are concerned, read-backs for confirmation are an absolute must.

When Slapper inquired about our readiness for remarks, Bunker and I had both entered the target coordinates into our systems. Normally, the target was within about ten miles, or one to one and a half minutes away from the FAC, often much less. In this case, the target was a ten-*minute* flight away from Slapper's location. This was a first for both of us.

In the remarks section, Slapper elaborated. The coordinates provided were accurate but not precise enough for weapons delivery; we needed to derive our own coordinates based on the target description he was about to give us. It was clear he was talking to someone else with better information and was relaying the information to us.

The target, we were told, consisted of two or three individuals next to a small structure in the desert. We were given no further information. We were to proceed to the area, derive our own coordinates, relay those coordinates (an absolute must), and receive clearance to attack the target.

The main concern was "burning" the target. At zero dark thirty, in a remote corner of Iraq, there isn't a lot of noise to be had. The sound of two 500 mile-per-hour F-16 "Death Vipers of Justice" going by while deriving the precise coordinates of your position could be perceived by some as suspicious activity, even from high altitude.

Time to develop new CTTPs, and I had about three minutes to do it. This is precisely why humans still occupy cockpits.

We knew the altitude, distance, and angle we needed to derive the coordinates, and we agreed to pass the target within those parameters. We also knew there was a potential for our LASER energy to conflict with each other's systems, so we planned for that as well, all while on the way to the target. We relayed our plans to Slapper, who relayed them to the other yet-to-be-identified party, and all parties articulated their satisfaction. Upon passing the target, we would egress to a safe distance, pass the coordinates for confirmation, make the final arrangements, then return to deliver the goods, hot and fresh, to another satisfied customer.

We proceeded inbound to the target. First pass.

En route to the objective, Slapper called with an "Oh, by the way..." There was another airborne asset in the area. Deconfliction measures would have to be established.

Neither Slapper, nor the other airborne asset, were qualified to establish those procedures, but he saw from the mission nomenclature used to identify our flight that one of us was a FAC(A). A FAC(A), or Forward Air Controller (Airborne), is qualified to control all airborne assets over a target area and provide final attack clearance for aircraft weapons delivery. I was the FAC(A) in our flight, so I established deconfliction procedures for all assets.

This scenario was a very simple one by FAC(A) standards: I had to ensure there could be no potential aircraft-to-aircraft or bomb-to-aircraft impacts. There was no need to worry about deconfliction from ground forces, as Slapper confirmed there were none in the area. Procedures were established, and everyone was satisfied.

Less than two minutes remained until we passed the target.

As we passed the objective area, we were struck by the absence of everything. There was nothing else in the area. Nothing. There was a small structure, no sign of human activity, and a small group of warm objects huddled together nearby.

It wasn't until we reached our closest point of approach to the target that we identified two people either sitting outside or leaning against the side of the structure. In conversation with Slapper, we confirmed the group of warm objects to be a small herd of sheep. The two people outside the structure were the target. We derived the coordinates for entry into our systems and subsequently to the GPS-guided bombs we planned to deliver. We had what we needed.

We proceeded outbound an appropriate distance from the target to conceal our presence, while hoping we had not burned the target. When we made final coordination and turned inbound toward the target, I passed a final confirmation of coordinates. An abbreviated nine-line followed, and clearance to deliver was given.

"Cleared Hot."

We released our weapons, then turned slightly away in order to observe the target with our targeting pods. What happened in the next sixty seconds was nothing less than astonishing.

As expected, the objective disappeared in a plume of infrared energy, as our two bombs impacted the target. For approximately thirty seconds after impact, as the energy that blinded our targeting pods dissipated, we could see little to nothing of consequence—but given the obvious accuracy of the bomb impacts, we were certain the job was done. We had "shacked" the target. Two direct hits. We heated them up, and they would eventually cool down. The bad guys were no longer bad.

"Squirters heading west. Stare 1234." The call was completely unexpected!

The other airborne asset, observing from a lower altitude and from outside the target area, was LASING survivors heading away from the objective! "Stare 1234" was a directive for us to enter frequency 1234 into our LASER trackers, allowing us to lock onto the squirters, which immediately revealed to us their location. We did. It did.

In our targeting pods, we saw two squirters that had somehow managed to escape the previous thousand pounds of blast-frag delivered to their location less than a minute prior. Time for plan B.

Next, we confirmed we were tracking the squirters by using our LASER Marker (sparkle), visible through our NVGs. We each "sparkled" the targets and confirmed that our sparkles were co-located. I requested final clearance authority from Slapper, which he granted, giving me the ability to clear weapons deliveries for the subsequent attacks.

I directed the next attack by transmitting "sparkle shooter."

As fighter pilots, we train, we train, and then we train some more. We plan, brief, execute, and debrief, over and over and over again so that when it comes time to execute at zero dark thirty in some remote corner of the world, we are ready. No need for long discussions.

Bunker knew exactly what I meant by "sparkle shooter." I would sparkle the target and guide the bomb to the target, thus the term "sparkle." He would deliver the weapon, thus the term "shooter."

While the previous two bombs delivered were GPS-guided, requiring no further support from the pilots after release, the next attack would be conducted using a LASER-guided bomb (LGB). This meant the bomb required guidance from LASER energy all the way until impact.

This is not a simple attack; timing and communication are everything. The geometry of both aircraft has to be right in order for success. The delivery parameters of the shooter have to be correct. The bomb must be released at the correct altitude and dive angle to allow sufficient time for the seeker head to acquire the LASER energy reflecting off the target. Release too high and the bomb may acquire the target too early, expending significant energy while making corrections, and fall short of the target. Release too low and the bomb may not have enough time to acquire the LASER energy and make corrections, or it may not have enough time to fuse prior to impact, causing a dud.

Adding to the complexity was the requirement for me, as the sparkler, to know when the shooter released the bomb. Prior to weapons release, the shooter needs to see the sparkle on the target and use it to visually aim the bomb sight. Once the bomb is released, the sparkle is no longer required, but LASER energy is required for guiding the bomb.

As the sparkler, upon hearing the shooter call "bombs away," I would switch from sparkle to LASER and guide the bomb to its destination. The "bombs away" call was paramount. If all went as planned, the bomb had twelve seconds' time of fall before impact—not much room for error. The plan was to attack one squirter, then swap roles and attack the other.

Less than two minutes after the first bombs had impacted and the squirters were on the run, we both called, "Ready."

Bunker called, "In," meaning he was rolling in.

I called, "Cleared Hot."

Bunker called, "Bombs away, twelve seconds." I switched from sparkle to LASER. We waited. Turns out twelve seconds can be an eternity.

The first squirter disappeared in a giant ball of infrared plume, once again blinding our sensors and denying us immediate gratification. We waited for another eternity: thirty seconds.

Then the other airborne platform reported, "Squirters down." We had apparently gotten both of them with one bomb. We confirmed the same with our targeting pods, although we found only one of the two targets, the one we were not directly targeting.

We remained in the area until sunrise, at which time we were relieved on station by two of our squadron mates. We returned to base to review our videos. In the cockpit, we use two-tone gray-scale displays, six inches on the diagonal; in the debrief room, the video review is on a full-size television display. Playback can be done in slow motion, frame by frame, in superb detail. What we discovered was impressive.

The first two weapons we delivered were GPS-guided 500-pound bombs with fuses set to function five milliseconds after impact. We had no control over the fuse function from the cockpit—the fuses were set manually on the ground, and while they could be set to function on impact or after impact at a variety of time intervals, five milliseconds was the standard.

A five-millisecond setting meant that the bomb would typically detonate four to five feet into the target, and it was considered a good compromise between attacking buildings and attacking ground combatants. Since it was seldom known in advance whether we'd be attacking bad guys in a building or bad guys in the open, five milliseconds was generally enough to penetrate and collapse a building or provide good results against hostiles in the open.

Get up right now and pace nine feet from where you are sitting/lying. Nine lengths of a human foot, from heel to toe. Go on. Do it. Now look back to where you started. Imagine two 500-pound bombs detonating four to five feet below the ground, where you began your short venture. That's what happened.

Two 500-pound bombs went off nine feet away from the bad guys and buried four to five feet in the ground. The video revealed there were three bad guys, and the first two bombs killed one, albeit not immediately. The other two survived and ran away. It turns out four to five feet of bomb burial makes a big difference.

When we reviewed the sparkle shooter attack, we could see the bomb in relation to the squirter. If the bomb didn't hit him directly, he could have hooked his thumb into his back pocket, pulled it open slightly, and let the bomb fly into it like it was his own wallet. Unlike the GPS-guided bombs, the LGBs were set to detonate on impact. The frag pattern was sufficient to get both squirters with one bomb, despite the second squirter being ten to twenty meters from the first.

After the debrief and video review, a squadron mate and friend of mine, Lt. Col. Chris "Pooter" Caputo, who I consider to be as fine a warfighter as I've ever known, said to me, "Dude. You have big 'ole brass balls." He was referring to a technique I employed during the final delivery, the details of which cannot be disclosed. It required an extra step I used to lessen the possibility of the HVI knowing he was being targeted, which would slightly increase the risk of failure.

The next day, we received photos and a report from the intel exploitation team. Three confirmed KIA. The only remaining whisper of the first squirter was a bloody grease spot on the side of a shallow crater, which is why we couldn't find the body in our targeting pods post-attack. DNA evidence confirmed his identity; he was the HVI we were looking for and, unbeknownst to us at the time, the one we targeted with our final bomb.

He masterminded multiple attacks against schools, killing hundreds of children and their teachers by using car bombs and suicide bombers. If ever there was a son of a bitch that needed killing, this was he. As he ran in fear from the scene, I sincerely hope he was in immense pain, held a brief hope for survival, then died, surrounded by the sound of freedom the children and teachers he killed would never know.

As a warrior in defense of our nation, and in defense of anything about humanity worth defending, I declare it to be my finest hour.

Captain Frank Kelly, Commanding Officer, Fleet Intelligence Training Center Pacific, and Ron's wife, Anne, do the honors of affixing Ron's Commander shoulder boards (September 1994).

Steve officiated the wedding of Ron's daughter in 2016. After dusting it off, Ron fit into the uniform he was issued in 1975 at the age twenty-six and wore until his retirement in 2002

Twilight

Commander
Ron "Warhead" Lambrecht

1994–2014

"There are no great men. There are only great challenges which ordinary men are forced by circumstances to meet."

—FADM William F. Halsey, US Navy

Nautical Notables:

Brow: The proper term for what is often called the "gangway," a temporary bridge from the ship to the jetty or, in some cases, to another ship.

Constant Bearing, Decreasing Range: When two boats are approaching each other from any angle and the angle remains the same over time (constant bearing), they are on a collision course. Because of the implication of collision, it has come to mean a problem or an approaching obstacle.

Above Board: Today, this phrase means someone who is honest and forthright. Its origin comes from the days when pirates masqueraded as honest merchantmen, hiding most of their crew behind the bulwark (side of the ship on the upper deck); they hid below the boards.

Knock Off Work: Aboard sailing ships, the galleys used to be rowed to the rhythm of a mallet striking a wooden block. When the knocking stopped, it was a signal to stop rowing.

Fair Winds and Following Seas: A blessing wishing the recipient a safe journey and good fortune.

Avast Ye, Matey: "Avast" means stop or desist. "Ye" means you. "Matey" means friend, person, or individual.

We enjoyed an uneventful return from Somalia and arrived back in San Diego early one morning to much fanfare from friends, family, and well-wishers. After spending six months on deployment, everyone was eager to be home.

My wife, Anne, met me at the base of the **brow**, put her arms around me and said, "Welcome home, Commander."

The board results came out that morning, and my former boss at CNAP called Anne to tell her the good news. She knew it before I did. It was a happy homecoming.

I had some significant career decisions to make at this point. Anne's father retired as a career Naval Surface Warfare Officer, having spent many years at sea and having endured countless duty stations; his family was never able to enjoy the continuity of connection with neighborhood and community. In contrast, except for my being away from home for extended periods of time, Anne and our daughter, Robin, lived close to a normal non-military life. They felt established in our San Diego home, having been able to maintain close and lasting friendships, which is difficult to do when orders require moving to new duty stations as often as every two to three years.

My next promotion opportunity was to Captain (O-6), with by no means any guarantee I was competitive, given my **constant bearing, decreasing range** focus on staying in San Diego. The Detailer was clear: I needed to move, and it appeared an overseas tour was in the cards.

Should I put my daughter, about to enter high school, through what my wife experienced? Should I stay in the game and compete for Captain, or should I prioritize quality of life? I chose quality of life. An Executive Officer (XO) position was available at the intelligence school where I had previously taught, FITCPAC, and I could take the job with the understanding of retirement after the tour. I accepted the position.

It turned out to be the *hardest* career decision of my life—and the *best* career decision of my life! I'd spent my entire career "in the hunt," and now I wasn't.

I had to swallow some pride, but I still had a job to do. At the end of my three-year tour as XO, I received a call from the Intelligence Detailer asking if I was about to submit my retirement papers. I answered in the affirmative, but I was also **above board** in my discussion. Proud of my career, I felt I had more I could contribute to the Navy, *if* another position was available in San Diego. There was.

Space and Naval Warfare Systems Command (SPAWAR) was in the process of moving from the East Coast to San Diego, and "non-career-enhancing positions" were available. Maybe the attitude in the intelligence community has changed since my retirement, but given the impact computer systems have on our line of work, it is interesting that the intelligence community felt at the time that Systems Command positions were low priority.

What happened next is why I consider my decision to not pursue Navy Captain (O-6) to be the best career decision of my life. Assigned to the Command and Control (C2) Division at SPAWAR, I managed a set of intelligence applications fielded as part of the C2 system deployed on Navy ships and operational commands, world-wide. It was a successful tour, and when I retired in 2002, I was immediately hired back as a federal employee.

Three years later, my promotion to GS-15 (O-6 Captain equivalent) came through, and I went on to manage approximately 120 personnel at the Space and Naval Warfare Systems Center (SPAWARSYSCEN) located at Point Loma in San Diego. Engineers, developers, testers, installers, and trainers of the Navy's C2 system were under my charge. From there, I became the Deputy for Business Development for the largest division at SPAWARSYSCEN.

After twenty-six and a half years of military service (185 in dog years) and twelve years of federal service, countless random drug tests and three polygraphs, I was debriefed and, therefore, no longer held a security clearance. It was time to **knock off work**. **Fair winds and following seas.** I finally entered full retirement on January 31, 2014.

And with that, **avast ye, matey**!

Steve straps into an F-16 for the last time as he prepares for his final "fini-flight" (2012). On his wing was a two-seat F-16 flown by Lieutenant Colonel and Fighter Squadron Commander Chris "Pooter" Caputo, with Colonel Mike "Diggler" Ricci (Flight Surgeon) in the back seat (pictured next).

As is the custom, upon returning from the flight, squadron mates physically inspire the pilot (Steve) to remain still while receiving a dowsing of champagne and water. After a prolonged struggle and admirable resistance, Steve was taped to an ejection seat and thoroughly moistened by Pooter, Diggler, daughter Leah, and son Logan.

Steve receives the guidon, symbolizing his assumption of command as the 158th Logistics Readiness Squadron Commander, Vermont Air National Guard (2012).

Steve and Colonel (Retired) Mike "Twistin'" Shoup are reunited on the occasion of Steve's promotion to Brigadier General (2019).

Sunset

Brigadier General (Ret)
Steve "Curly" Lambrecht

2007–2023

"The best time to start thinking about your retirement is before the boss does."

—Unknown

Aeronautical Notable:

Fini-Flight: An Air Force pilot's final flight. The celebration traditionally includes the pilot returning from the flight, being wrestled to the ground, and then being doused with champaign by their fellow squadron mates. It sometimes includes being duct taped to a bomb rack and/or other celebratory shenanigans.

In the years that followed my combat tours in Iraq, I went on to hold VTANG positions as the 158th Operations Group Advanced Programs Office Manager, then the 134th Fighter Squadron Director of Operations. After eleven years as an Air Force Officer, though, something seemed to be missing.

Having been "raised" in the Navy and Marine Corps beginning at an early age, I grew accustomed to being in charge of other people. During my delays while awaiting training during flight school, I was placed in charge of enlisted Marines. As a senior First Lieutenant and junior Captain in the USMC, and while going through ACTI/TOPGUN/WTI, I was simultaneously in charge of as many as thirty-six enlisted Marines.

In the USAF, however, I found the priorities to be different, with no charge greater than four Officers or two enlisted personnel at any one time. It was not a good fit for me. I had been eager to command for years, and when an opportunity arose, I threw my hat in the ring.

On June 3, 2012, I flew my **fini-flight** in the F-16. After twenty-two years as a fighter pilot, with 3,473 hours of military flight time and one hundred combat missions, I hung up my flying spurs. The next day, I took command of the 158th Logistics Readiness Squadron (LRS). I couldn't wait. As a warfighter at heart, I spent my entire life wanting nothing to do with logistics, but as with too many things in life, I once again found myself to be wrong.

Logistics proved to be dynamic and challenging. General Omar Bradley is credited with saying, "Amateurs study strategy; professionals study logistics," but I find both to be indispensable.

As I came to understand, logistics is among the least appreciated professions on Earth. The thought of rolling up to a McDonald's drive-thru and ordering a Big Mac, then hearing the server say, "Sorry, we are out of Big Macs," never occurs to anyone, nor should it. Nobody thinks about logistics until it's not there.

I reminded my Airmen of the Twelfth Law of the Navy:

> *If ye win through an African jungle,*
>
> *Unmentioned at home in the press,*
>
> *Heed it not. No man seeth the piston,*
>
> *But it driveth the ship none the less*

During my command tour, my Airmen served all over the planet in support of the War on Terror, the Status of Forces Agreement in Korea, and to locations both disclosed and undisclosed. They made me proud beyond words, expertly fulfilling our mission statement, "Team LRS: Delivering Combat Air Power and Full-Spectrum Logistical Support, at Home and Around the World." I signed my correspondence, "Your Proud Commander," which I was, supremely.

My tour as LRS Commander proved to be everything I could have dreamed of: I was finally able to shape people and an organization. It fed my soul in ways being a fighter pilot never could have. The privilege of command remains the most challenging and rewarding experience of my military career, worthy of another book.

***

After four years of Squadron Command, I was selected to Command the 158th Maintenance Group and promoted to the rank of Colonel. As any experienced military Commander will tell you, there is a notable difference between commanding at the ranks of O-5 (Lieutenant Colonel) and O-6 (Colonel). O-5 command is tactical; O-6 command is strategic.

As an O-6, one's ability to influence individuals across all ranks is diluted, due to an increase of responsibilities and purview. Nonetheless, I found it to be just as rewarding, only in different ways. I became engaged in strategic issues at the national level, briefing relevant topics and peddling innovative ideas to Generals, something this graduate of Ivanhoe High School never imagined possible.

Upon completion of three years of O-6 Command, I was humbled to be promoted to the position of Chief of Staff and Air Component Commander, Vermont Air National Guard, and to the rank of Brigadier General—and my TOPGUN WSO, Colonel (Retired) Mike "Twistin'" Shoup, attended the ceremony. After not seeing him for twenty years, we were reunited the year prior at the twenty-fifth reunion of the Moonlighters. It was deeply touching that he made the journey.

My new position required engagement in many endeavors and, as you can imagine, came with many responsibilities. I became qualified to lead large organizations in support of civilian authorities during times of natural disasters, and our skills were heavily leveraged during the response to the COVID-19 pandemic of 2020–2022.

The Vermont National Guard collected nearly 35,000 samples and shipped over 2 million test kits. Our team received and shipped over 6.5 million Strategic National Stockpile products, handled and administered over 500,000 doses of vaccine, and delivered over 3 million meals to the food insecure. Perhaps most impressively, our uniformed servants erected a 400-bed Alternate Healthcare Facility in just four days, for less than $300,000. It became the model for other states and territories to follow.

Approaching four years as a General, I reached a decision point. Pursuit of further rank entailed the prospect of relocating my family, which necessitated geo-dislocating from my children and taking yet another military leave of absence from my job at United Airlines. Alternatively, in addition to being gone 50 percent of each month for work with United Airlines, I might have commuted back and forth from my home to my new military responsibilities, located elsewhere in the US, or beyond. Either route meant more separation from my family.

It was time to make a choice, and I made the right one. After more than thirty-nine years of service, which began at the "ripe old age" of seventeen years and thirty days, I hung up my military spurs. As many years had transpired between the end of WWII and the day I enlisted in the Navy as had transpired between the day I enlisted and the day of my retirement. It was time.

This midwestern country boy was, for one final time, a dot.

Epilogue

Commander (Ret)
Ron "Warhead" Lambrecht

"My career has been full of remarkable coincidences that have nothing to do with me."

—JACK LEMMON

On June 3, 2012, I attended my brother's change of command ceremony. After completing Navy boot camp between his junior and senior years in high school, graduating from the Naval Academy, earning a commission in the US Marine Corps, earning his wings, transferring to the Air National Guard, and accumulating a career high of 3,473 hours in fighter aircraft, he was about to assume command of his own squadron.

I always felt Steve lived in my shadow, largely due to our eighteen-year age difference and my career experiences happening ahead of his own, as we both rose through the ranks. On that day, however, it became clear to me that the next generation of Lambrecht men was stepping into the breach.

It reminded me of a fullback and halfback running down the field, the fullback blocking the oncoming defenders and the halfback bobbing and weaving behind, until the end zone was in sight. Our team scored that day. It happened so fast I never saw him pass me.

* * *

Brigadier General (Ret) Steven S. Lambrecht

"Everyone has a plan until they get punched in the mouth."

—MIKE TYSON

I'm not certain what would have happened to me had it not been for the Tiger Cruise and for Mr. Roy Colman introducing me to the Naval Academy. There's no way to know for sure, but I think it's fair to say I wouldn't have ended up on the path I did and instead might have taken a lower road in life.

I owe much gratitude to my high school science teacher, Mr. Dennis Bernaciak, who made learning fun and interesting. Because of him, I sailed through the first six weeks of Plebe chemistry while those around me were dropping like heavy anchors off a tall ship. Mr. Greg Gile, my high school principal and guidance counselor, ushered me through the many missteps I made along the way and never stopped believing in me. My teachers, coaches, music teachers, and others helped round me out into someone capable of serving alongside the best America has to offer.

The lesson has never been lost on me what a heavy impact certain events, people, and even simple comments can have on the life of a child. My life was changed forever as a result of these people and events, and I can never adequately express my gratitude for it.

Ivanhoe, Minnesota, had a population of 765 in 1985, and I attended its one-and-only public school from grades K–12, graduating with a class of thirty. Still, Ivanhoe produced five service academy graduates, one from Annapolis and four from West Point. I'm grateful to have called it home.

I am humbled that my fellow Naval Aviators, Marines, and comrades expended the effort to train me, as well as steady me when I tripped along the way. They saw potential in me, and I owe them for it. I've given my best every step of the way since.

It takes a team for success. Though I had plenty of blockers along the way, the one who created the biggest hole—the hole I ran through, the hole that led to all of my successes—was my brother, Ron.

Acknowledgments

Thank you to all those who helped create these stories.

We would like to extend our gratitude to the many family members and friends who provided editorial guidance and input during the creation of this book. In particular, we'd like to thank Frank and Alina Marston, Pat and Bruce Ueland, Pam Mazzarella, Laura McClure, Anne Lambrecht, Randy Zoller, Leah Lambrecht (graphic arts), and those whose names appear in this book.

We would also like to thank our blue-collar parents for instilling in us a solid work ethic. We both began our lives and careers in the trades wearing civilian and military blue-collar uniforms. The farmers in bib overalls, apron-wearing waiters and waitresses, construction workers and miners in hard hats, and all the other blue-collar trade workers that make America strong have and deserve our enduring gratitude.

Finally, we want to express our appreciation to the countless heroes serving at home and abroad in defense of our freedom. To those standing watch in or under a corner of a remote sea, to those turning a wrench during the night shift in a hangar far from home, to those guarding the perimeter at a forward operating base in hostile territory, and to all the warriors past and present who served our country: every last one of you is an indispensable link in the chain of freedom. We thank you for your service.

About the Authors

Ron graduated high school with forty-seven other students from Ivanhoe Public School in Ivanhoe, Minnesota, in 1967. He went on to graduate from Southern Illinois University with a bachelor of science in occupational education. In 1979, he was accepted into Aviation Officer Candidate School (AOCS) in Pensacola, Florida, and obtained a commission as a Navy Ensign. He served as a Navy Intelligence Officer for twenty-two years with nearly 1,300 days at sea on Western

Pacific/Indian Ocean deployments. He retired from active duty as a Commander in 2002.

Ron continued his service as a federal employee assigned to Space and Naval Warfare Systems Command, San Diego (SPAWAR) (now Naval Information Warfare Systems Command [NAVWAR]). There, he achieved certification as a Level-III Acquisition Program Manager, accredited to lead contract awarding and procurement management. He later assumed a position as the Project Director for the Navy's Command and Control System and subsequently as the Deputy for Business Development for the Systems Center's Command and Control Division. He retired in 2014 at the highest General Schedule rank level, GS-15.

Ron lives with his wife, Anne, in the San Diego area.

Steve graduated high school with twenty-nine other students from Ivanhoe Public School in Ivanhoe, Minnesota, in 1985. He attended the Naval Academy in Annapolis, Maryland, where he graduated with a degree in aerospace engineering in 1989. From there, he became a Marine F/A-18 fighter pilot, graduate of TOPGUN, and went on to amass 3,473 hours of flight time in fighters, including the F-16. He received a master's in business administration with an emphasis in military leadership, as well as completed one hundred combat missions in Bosnia and Iraq.

Steve has run two small businesses, including a training and consulting firm (focused on medical safety in the operating room) and a small preschool. He earned a green belt in Lean Six Sigma (Dartmouth College, Hanover, New Hampshire), as well as graduated from the Leadership and Strategic Impact Course (Tuck School of Business, Dartmouth College) and the Senior Manager Course in National Security Leadership (Elliott School of International

Affairs, George Washington University). Finally, Steve trained and qualified as a Joint Task Force Commander and a Dual Status Commander for Domestic Operations.

Steve lives with his wife, Laura, and their four children in Vermont, where Steve served as a Brigadier General in the Vermont Air National Guard and currently works as a pilot for a major US airline.

Glossary

AAA: anti-aircraft artillery

AAVs: Amphibious Assault Vehicles

ACM: air combat maneuvering

ACTI: Air Combat Tactics Instructor

AGL: above ground level

AI: Aviation Indoctrination

AOCS: Aviation Officer Candidate School

ARG: Amphibious Ready Group

ASW: anti-submarine warfare

AW: Anti-Submarine Warfare Operator

AW2: Anti-Submarine Warfare Operator Second Class

BFM: Basic Fighter Maneuvers

C2: Command and Control

CAG: Carrier Air Group Commander, a Navy Captain

CAS: close air support

CASREP: inoperative, casualty reported

CATF: Commander, Amphibious Task Force

CAX: Combined Arms Exercise

CDO: Command Duty Officer

Clara: clarification

CLF: Commander, Landing Force

CNAP: Commander, Naval Air Force, Pacific or COMNAVAIRPAC

CO: Commanding Officer

COA: Course of Action

COMNAVAIRPAC: Commander, Naval Air Force, Pacific

CV: Aircraft Carrier

CVIC: Carrier Intelligence Center

DIs: Drill Instructors

DOPSR: Defense Office of Prepublication and Security Review

DOR: dropping on request

EE: Electrical Engineering

FAA: Federal Aviation Administration

FAC: Forward Air Controller

FAC(A): Forward Air Controller (Airborne)

FAM: Familiarization

FCF: functional check flight

FITCPAC: Fleet Intelligence Training Center Pacific

FITREP: Fitness Report

FMF: Fleet Marine Force

FOB: forward operating base

FOD: foreign object debris

FRS: Fleet Replacement Squadron (formerly known as Replacement Air Groups [RAGs])

GONZO Station: Gulf of Oman Naval Zone of Operations

GPS: Global Positioning System

HARM: High-Speed Anti-Radiation Missile

HUD: heads-up display

HVAA: high-value airborne asset

HVI: high-value individual

IEDs: improvised explosive devices

IFOR: Implementation Force

IOC: Infantry Officer Course

JO: Junior Officer

JTAC: Joint Terminal Attack Controller

JTTPs: Joint Tactics, Techniques, and Procedures

KIA: killed in action

LCAC: Landing Craft, Air Cushion

LGB: LASER-guided bomb

LM: LASER Marker

LRS: Logistics Readiness Squadron

LSO: Landing Signal Officer

MEU: Marine Expeditionary Unit

Mids: Midshipmen, or Naval Academy students

MOS: Military Occupational Specialties

N2: Intelligence Section

NAS: Naval Air Station

NAVWAR: Naval Information Warfare Systems Command

NFO: Naval Flight Officer

NJP: non-judicial punishment

NRTC: Naval Recruit Training Center

NSAWC: Naval Strike and Air Warfare Center

NSS: Navy Standard Score

NVGs: night-vision goggles

O-6: Navy Captain or Air Force Colonel

OOC: out of commission

OOW: Officer of the Watch

PGS: Naval Postgraduate School

PROTRAMID: Professional Training of Midshipmen

PT: physical training

QRF: quick reaction force

R&R: rest and relaxation

R&S: Reconnaissance and Surveillance

R2P2: Rapid Response Planning Process

RFI: Request for Information

ROTC: Reserve Officer Training Corps

RTC: Recruit Training Command

RWR: RADAR warning receiver

SA: situational awareness

SAM: surface-to-air missile

SD: standard deviation

SENSOs: sensor operators

Skipper: Squadron Commanding Officer, a Navy Commander

SOCOM: Special Operations Command

SOD: Signal of Difficulty

SOPA: Senior Officer Present Ashore

SPAWAR: Space and Naval Warfare Systems Command

SPIE: Special Insertion/Extraction

STS: Special Tactics Squadrons

SWOs: Surface Warfare Officers or "Shoes"

SYSCEN: Space and Naval Warfare Systems Center

T-Court: Tecumseh Court

TACCO: Tactical Coordinator

TBS: The Basic School

TGPs: targeting pods

TOPGUN: United States Navy Fighter Weapons School

TTPs: tactics, techniques, and procedures

UA: unauthorized absence

UCMJ: Uniform Code of Military Justice

UNOSOM: United Nations Operations in Somalia

UNREP: underway replenishment

USAFA: Air Force Academy

USMA: Military Academy at West Point

USNA: The United States Naval Academy

VTANG: Vermont Air National Guard

WSO: Weapons and Sensors Operator

WTI: United States Marine Corps Weapons and Tactics Instructor Course

XO: Executive Officer, second in command

YGB(F)SM: You've gotta be (effing) shitting me

CPSIA information can be obtained
at www.ICGtesting.com
Printed in the USA
BVHW051649300323
661465BV00010B/119/J